Volume 1: A Century of Transitions

In April, 1889 a piece of Denmark settled into place on the west bank of the Lower Yellowstone River - near its confluence with the Muddy Missouri - at a stagestop designated by the U.S. Goverment as Sidney, Dawson County, Montana Territory. It turned out to be HOME to the Peter-Bertha Anderson family, with its recurring pioneering patterns, community involvements and "doing good", under the aegis of its P Diamond brand security blanket.

CAMILLA

Montana Prairie Pioneer

Volume 1

A Century of Transitions

Camilla M. Anderson, M.D.

P Diamond Enterprises
Joplin Missouri

I wish to express special appreciation to those who have given assistance to me in the gestation and birthing process of this four volume autobiography. These special people are Mary Micheletto Jensen of Sidney, my niece, who started the ball rolling in 1986; Mary Anderson Davis, of Joplin, Missouri, also my niece, who labored during the years 1987 to 1993 to assure an accurate transcription of my illegible handwriting and endless changes; Dr. John Gronli, erstwhile pastor of Pella Lutheran Church in Sidney, who read the first computerized version and did not nix it, and made numerous helpful suggestions; Georgia Petersen, retired elementary teacher in Sidney, who read proof pages to me over many months, when I could no longer see to do the job; and to Jan Friendly, my daugher, who though deeply resenting the time it took to complete the book still wants to continue to live with me. And I would like to thank several local people who attempted to assist me but succeeded primarily in stalling me long enough to allow more time for gestation and development of a more creative focus. To Mary Davis, I entrust the task of editing and publishing the book. She is the only born-Anderson and the daugher of Carl, our P Diamond cowboy. The book is in good hands.

 Published by P Diamond Enterprises, 1520 Kentucky Avenue, Joplin Missouri 64804. This book is the first of four volumes of the autobiography written by Camilla M. Anderson, M.D.

To purchase additional copies of this book, contact P Diamond Enterprises, 1520 Kentucky Avenue, Joplin Missouri 64804. (417) 782-6885.

ISBN 1-888875-00-3
LIBRARY OF CONGRESS CATALOG CARD NUMBER: 96-83562

Table of Contents

VOLUME 1 - A CENTURY OF TRANSITIONS

I, Camilla, attended Sidney Public Schools, and am a graduate of Sidney High-school, Class of 1921; A.B. 1925 and M.D. 1929 courtesy University of Oregon and University of Oregon Medical School, now Oregon Health Sciences University; DIPLOMATE of the National Board of Medical Examiners; LICENSED to practice Medicine in New York, Pennsylvania, Washington D.C., Utah, California and Montana; PRACTITIONER of Psychiatry for over forty years in private practice and in hospitals, clinics, and a prison (California Institution for Women); LIFE FELLOW of the American Psychiatric Association; LIFE MEMBER of the American Medical Women's Association and frequent contributor to their professional Journal. PIONEER in Early Brain Damage - now Developmental Disabilities, and in development of a new Theory of Psychodynamics.

FACULTY MEMBER at six Colleges and Universities: Duquesne University, University of Pennsylvania, University of Utah, University of Portland, Willamette University, Chaffey College, and at two medical schools: Temple University Medical School and University of Utah Medical School. LECTURER in extenso. AUTHOR of five books: *Emotional Hygiene* and *Saints, Sinners and Psychiatry* (Lippincott Co.); *Beyond Freud* (Harper and Bros); *Jan, My Brain Damaged Daughter* (Durham Press); *Society Pays; The High Cost of Minimal Brain Damage in America* (Walker Co.). A chapter in each of two published books: *Handbook of Learning Disabilities* (Prentice Hall) and *Direct Psychotherapy/28 American Originals* (University of Miami Press); approximately twenty-five papers on Behavior, published in leading Journals; weekly COLUMNIST to the *SIDNEY HERALD* for seven years: My Day, My Say.

Listed in *Who's Who in America* - 1940; *Who's Who in the East - 1942; Who's Who Among American Women - 1975;* was chosen OREGON Woman of Achievement - 1964 and MONTANA Woman of Achievement - 1973. HONORARY MEMBER of Theta Chapter, Delta Kappa Gamma Society (of Women Educators) International.

Formidable, you say? Possibly. Boring? To some. But no matter! Because this book is about the flesh and blood daughter born in Montana near the confluence of the Yellowstone River with the Missouri known as the MonDak, to immigrant pioneers who had left Denmark in search of a better life. They landed on the west bank of the Yellowstone River at a stage stop called Sidney, in Montana Territory, on April 22, 1889, six months prior to Montana becoming a state.

During my journey from the MonDak to the present, in which one thing led to another, I became a professional woman, and wife of a professional musician, Leonard Friendly, He was a member of the American Guild of Organists; long time theater pipe organist in the Philadelphia area, staff organist at Radio Station WWDC, Washington DC, at Salt Lake City's 50,000 watt clear channel radio station KSL, and KWJJ in Portland, OR. I became a mother, and a retiree, and also an octogenarian who had survived many transitions. I sauntered, stumbled, and strode from the MonDak to the Pacific, and then to the Atlantic and back to the Pacific via Utah, and finally came back to Sidney for retirement. There, without warning, while on an unplanned side trip to Eden, I had an eye-opening experience which I shall share with you.

Because as a result of this trip everything was finally wrapped up and made complete sense. A fusion took place, uniting my psychodynamic theory with Judeo-Christian dogma, and out came a clear blueprint for the better life my parents - as well as others - have sought.

Coming Home

Since this is to be a story about me, it is important to get me placed in my setting, surrounded by the things and the people who helped shape me, and pressured by the attitudes and beliefs which prevailed

Here I am, in my own home at 405 West Main Street, in Sidney, Montana, sitting in my high-backed green Naugahyde swivel rocker, on September 30, 1987. I am a retired psychiatrist, born in Sidney, and after being away from here for fifty years, I returned home to Sidney, together with my daughter, Janet Carol Friendly, who is 45. The sun is shining beautifully, the air is mild and pleasant, there has been no frost yet, and I am told this has been Sidney's longest frost-free spell on record. As one might say with Pippa, "God's in His heaven; all`s right with the world."

This special occasion of my writing my story all started way back in 1971, shortly after I returned to Sidney. Prior to my return I lived in San Diego, California, a few years, where I had been Chief Psychiatrist at C.I.W., The California Institution for Women, the largest correctional institution for women in the United States. On my retirement in 1969 I had been busy writing a book titled *SOCIETY PAYS: The High Cost of Minimal Brain Damage in America*, published by Walker Co. of New York. Shortly after arriving in Sidney I received my first copies.

Sidney, an up-and-coming eastern Montana metropolis of some 5 - 7,000 citizens, located practically in the back yard of the Yellowstone River in the heart of the MonDak, and just a couple miles from the North Dakota line, was only a hop, skip and a jump from the confluence of the Yellowstone River with the muddy Missouri. Towns the size of Sidney are not a dime a dozen in Montana, and it doesn't happen every day that one of it's native daughters succeeds in having a book published. To celebrate the occasion, and probably also to welcome me back home, someone in Sidney sponsored a gathering - a tea - for me and my new book. It was held in our Library basement, which is a common and very good meeting place for the community. Lots of people came, and it was a warm and friendly occasion.

Mary Micheletto Jensen, my Italian niece by marriage to my nephew, Walter Jensen, was selected to introduce me to the assembled multitude. I felt honored and pleased that I had this opportunity to let people know about my book. Like most authors, I felt sure my book was worth reading, and I knew there was no other one like it in existence. But what I didn't know was that Mary Micheletto Jensen was so uncomfortable in her role that she nearly panicked, not because she was ashamed of presenting me, but because when she arose to introduce me, she had the horrible awareness that she really did not know anything about me. She didn't know what I had done, where I had lived or worked, or whether I had written other books or what their names were. She wished the floor would swallow her. I was aware the introduction was brief, but I certainly had no awareness of her agony. Probably she said all that needed to be said, but she hadn't forgotten her misery.

We never had an opportunity to get acquainted because I had left Sidney in 1921, long before Mary became a part of our family. Even after I came back here in 1971, it did not occur to me to talk about my life or fill in details. Then came a few years which I have dubbed "my fallow years" - perhaps from 1978 to 1986 - when I sort of lived in a fog and stopped participating in living. Then came 1986, and I was getting signals from myself that I was better. And those around me knew it too. Mary Micheletto Jensen also knew it. During those fallow years she had done so many kind things for me it was natural that she would have been aware that I was now better.

So what did she do about it? She began putting some pressure on me to get busy writing "an account of my professional meaderings and travels. Nobody knows what you have done or where you have been or worked." Then she told me of her stressful introduction of me at the Library tea party now so many years ago. I would have been happy to accommodate, but that was impossible, because I couldn't remember these things myself. But I tried. Sometimes I'd get hold of some fragment or some detail, but the sequences and the durations and the progressions eluded me.

I remembered early times better than more recent ones, but I was aware that I was able to recall more and more things as the months slipped by. Then I thought that if I just began writing, maybe this would help me to remember, and in turn would help me to know what I really wanted to write. I'd written so much - so many books and so many papers - but this was to be different; it was to be about ME. I knew Mary wasn't expecting me to publish another book, so there was no need for her to plan on another introduction of me. I think there was some genuine curiosity on her part, because as we got better acquainted, she really was interested in what my life had been like.

I also think she genuinely wanted to help me, and she thought this route might work. Then there was still another motive that occurred to me, and whereas it is not the whole answer, it just could have a sizeable grain of truth in it. That I had gotten better rather than worse was a surprise to everyone, including myself, and she had a sneaking suspicion that should I get worse again, and go to the Great Beyond, it would more than likely fall to her lot to prepare the obituary for the *Billings Gazette* and the *Sidney Herald*. In such an event she wouldn't know any more about me than she had at the Library party, and she wanted to be able to do a better job of it than the first time around. Whatever her motive, she got the seed planted in my head - and kept it watered. And here I am, many months after she started picking on me, ready to set it all down in black and white. Hopefully, before I stop writing, I will have been able to pull it all together.

From Denmark to America

My parents had come to Sidney, a locality where the U.S. Postal Service and the Stage had been stopping regularly since October 28, 1888, to pick up and drop off mail. It was then in Dawson County, Montana Territory, one of the largest counties in the entire United States. It's area was about 30,000 square miles and had a population of about 3700 people, as Dad recalled from the 1890 census. Perhaps 1500 of this number lived in Glendive, which was its County Seat.

My parents came from Denmark to this new world April 22, 1889, which was a very special year, but I never heard them mention this fact. It was special because that was the year Montana ceased to be a territory and became a state. I doubt they were aware of this event or I surely would have heard them mention it. Their arrival actually antedated statehood of Montana, since they came here April 22, 1889 and Montana wasn't admitted to statehood until November 8, 1889. They had come full of hope that they might find a better life for themselves and their growing family. They had heard from Mother's brother Carl - or Charlie - Josephsen that here was good land FOR FREE to prospective settlers. Uncle Charlie had written them in Denmark giving them the latitude and longitude of the area. When they looked it up on the map they figured the climate must be comparable to that of Paris, France.

Uncle Charlie had come south from Canada, where he first landed in the New World, and then headed westward over the newly established Northern Pacific Railroad, out of St. Paul. Because prospects looked bleak to them if they remained in their homeland of Denmark, with no chance to get ahead no matter which way they turned, Uncle Charlie's suggestion - or should we call it invitation? - grew on them until their thoughts were permeated with the possibility of making that vast move to SIDNEY, MONTANA TERRITORY, U.S.A.. Or as the Danes would have said: Forenede Stadter - United States.

They didn't realize that Sidney as a locus didn't even exist; a postal service stop of the weekly stage had come into being only recently, and even that was a moveable feast. But those two words, SIDNEY, MONTANA, became a symbol of promise of a new and better kind of life. They weighed and considered; they talked with relatives. Dad got the promise of financial help from his father, Anders Christoffersen, through releasing his inheritance money early for transportation costs for Mother, himself and three children.

Because they could see no point in delaying further, they made ready to sail. They decided which ship they would sail on, and Dad went to the big city to buy the tickets. They were to go steerage class because that was the best their money would provide. However, when Dad reached for his billfold to pay for the tickets, his billfold was gone! He had no idea what had happened to it, and the shock was terrible. Everything - their plans, their hopes and dreams, the money, nothing left - even his inheritance gone!

He returned home where Mother was waiting for him, and told her the terrible news. They wondered and wondered what could have happened. Then Dad recalled that he had gone to feed their animals in the barn prior to leaving for the city to buy the tickets. He went out to check if by any possibility he could have dropped the billfold there. Praise the Lord, there it was! Both he and Mother were full of gratitude to God that everything was safe. Now it was just a matter of going back to the city to make arrangements again for steamship tickets. To his dismay, when he was able to make the second trip a few days later, the steamship was completely booked and it would be necessary to select another one.

This he did, and he and Mother guarded the tickets carefully as they made their final preparations for leaving their homeland and their relatives. They had three children, Marie, almost 5, Niels 3 ½, and Dagmar, 10 months old. They didn't have to buy tickets for the children, and in steerage class, which was the lowest class provided, they would be provided with a single bunk for the five of them, with other families in bunks above and below them. But no matter what kind of accommodations they had, they would be able to travel from Denmark to America, and would land at Ellis Island in New York, and then by train to Montana.

Their baggage consisted of a couple handbags and a wooden chest or kiest in which they had packed all their homespun clothing for themselves and the children. It contained a homespun and home woven covered featherbed - tan with a border of light red stripes - which should help to keep them warm, no matter what the weather; a big thick Danish Bible given them by Dad's father; a Danish-English work book, and a few odds and ends. Dad had the balance of his inheritance securely sewn into his undershirt, and this amounted to nearly $300.00.

When they were in mid-ocean they learned that the ship they had expected to travel on had been lost at sea. They were sure God had His hand in Dad losing and finding his billfold. There was renewed thanksgiving, and they became increasingly sure it was God's will that they make this tremendous trip, and that they were actually in the palm of God's hand. Mother and Dad were in complete agreement on this. They could bemoan the accommodations on shipboard, where prevailing seasickness made nausea and vomiting over the side of the bunks - including theirs - the only noteworthy passenger pastime. But they were agreed that they were very lucky people who could look forward to better times.

This was a most natural conclusion because they had both been strongly influenced by their experience in the religious organization called The Inner Mission with which they had become affiliated. The official or state church in Denmark was the Danish Lutheran Church, but they had found it to be a cold, lifeless body that seemed to offer them nothing. This other group, The Inner Mission Church, was something else. It was warm and meaningful, and both of them accepted happily and gratefully everything it had to offer. They became actively practicing Christians, trying to live as they understood God wanted them to, and blossoming in the fellowship they had found. This agreed with the text the preacher had used when he performed their marriage ceremony on August 17, 1883: Everything works together for good to them that love God. (Romans 8,28) They now had renewed assurance of God's care, and they rededicated themselves to His loving concern. This was what they lived by. It was such a present tense influence in my own life that in 1971, when I happened upon a tiny wall plaque in a Williston, North Dakota store, with this inscription on it, I bought it and hung it on the wall beside my dressing table. It still hangs there. I have always thought it helped me keep close to my roots.

The one in the family who was most severely punished by the conditions of the trip was the baby, Dagmar. Mother, with all her seasickness, stopped secreting milk, and the poor baby got nothing to eat. It was a wretched time. But finally they landed in New York. The family was glad that the worst of the journey was over, and they were still alive - and together.

At Ellis Isle they were used to foreigners from many lands, so they had no particular difficulties there by reason of language.

From New York, they had tickets on one of the Immigrant Trains to St. Paul and then to Glendive, Montana Territory, which was the closest point on the railroad to Sidney. Uncle Charlie was supposed to meet them in Glendive, but he didn't show up. The railway stationmaster in Glendive let them know they couldn't stay there all night, but they couldn't really communicate, because of the language barrier. The station master thought they were probably Scandinavians, so he went looking for a Swede he knew to come and act as interpreter. This man took them to a place where they spent the night, and the next day Hymie Otis, a man Uncle Charlie had engaged to take them from Glendive to Sidney showed up with his horse-drawn triple-box wagon, and they set off for their new home. It was about a 60 mile drive, so they had to spend a night on the road. To while away the time, Mother, holding the baby on her lap on the only seat in the wagon, with her feet dangling because there was nothing to rest them on, started singing some of her familiar Danish hymns. To her delight, Hymie Otis chimed in, singing the same tunes in English.

The long hours riding in the lumber wagon passed and it was Easter Sunday, April 22, 1889 when they arrived at their prospective home. There hadn't been any towns they had passed through after leaving the train at Glendive. In fact, there was nothing to be seen anywhere other than rolling hills and prairie. There weren't even any trees for miles and miles. The only place trees grew was down close to the river. Dad, who was a gardener from the old country, did not recognize the cottonwood trees, which constituted practically the only sizeable trees to be seen anywhere. He, together with the two older children, sat on the floor in the back of the wagon, scarcely able to peer over its high triple-boxes, but eager to see all he could of this new land which was to be their home.

Uncle Charlie was there waiting for them when they arrived at their new home on Easter Sunday. It was a two room log house with a flat sod roof that stood on the west bank of the Yellowstone River. The logs in its walls were 6 to 7 inches in diameter and grey in color from weathering. It had no furniture other than a stove, a table of sorts, a couple chairs and a bed. Anything else was contrived from empty boxes. It had a wood and log floor. They were glad they had brought the dishes assigned to them by the steamship. They rather promptly decided they would use only one room because there was no furniture to outfit another one.

Problems crowded in on them from the very beginning. There was no store closer than Glendive where they could buy even the smallest item they needed. There were no roads - only a trail here and there; no methods of transportation. There was, literally, nothing, other than prairie, the sky and the river - FREE LAND! - and bands of roving longhorn Texas cattle that roamed the prairie. People on horseback stopped by occasionally, but they could not understand one another.

Of course the biggest problem was language. Almost before they had settled into their strange surroundings Dad was conducting daily English language classes for the family out of their Danish-English book. By good fortune they had acquired a discarded Montgomery Ward catalog that served them handsomely because it not only had words, but pictures, of EVERYTHING! They were really in luck.

Dad tells of the time, shortly after their arrival, that a woman on horseback came riding by and said something to him. He had no idea what she was telling or asking him, but he said in response "I don't know." The woman rode off without further adieu, and he wondered for a long time what he could have said to her that had upset her so much she had to ride right off. Such neighbors as there were, were miles away.

English gradually became their natural tongue, and it became the exclusive language of the family. Many years later both Mother and Dad wrote their life stories - in English. The facility with which they handled the new language was amazing. In 136 pages of Dad's fine script I found innumerable misspelled words, but only one word that he had written the Danish rather than the English word: he wrote og instead of and.

Becoming Americans

Great as the language problem was, there was an even more pressing one: MONEY. The three hundred dollars they had safeguarded in Dad's undershirt would soon be gone, and they had to find some source of income. There was nobody to hire them or pay them wages. They had no skills to sell, and they were worried. Dad had learned the gardener trade in Denmark, but nobody in this part of the world needed a gardener. There was no possibility of trying to farm because they had no implements, and there were no fences, so the longhorns would soon trample down anything they might grow. They talked it over with Uncle Charlie, and between them they decided to try selling something to the soldiers at Fort Buford, which was approximately 30 miles away, right at the confluence of the Yellowstone with the Missouri.

They racked their brains as to what they ought to try to sell. The only logical answer was butter. But they had no cows and no money to buy cows. Butter was the logical solution because Mother had been trained as a dairy maid at the same establishment Dad had learned gardening. Mother was entirely willing to do whatever she could. Uncle Charlie urged them to buy cows on time the way they do in America, and pay for them out of the money they would make from selling the butter. They visited the Fort and Uncle Charlie talked for Dad to the officers in charge. They came away thinking their idea just might work.

This meant they would have to locate and buy the cows on time; it meant they would have to find some means of transportation to haul the butter to the Fort; it meant finding some way to acquire all the utensils necessary to implement their undertaking; and it also meant making some sort of corral where the cows could be held while Mother did the milking. Believe it or not, they did all that. They purchased 20 cows with their calves, at $35 a pair. They scrounged for castoffs or spare utensils such as pails and pans. They bought a churn that could churn 8 lbs. of butter at a time, so if they churned twice a day they could plan on taking about a hundred lbs. of butter to the Fort each week. Without stores, it was very hard to outfit any type of project. Glendive, the nearest trading point, 60 miles away, was out of the question.

In the weeks that followed, they had acquired a buggy, a couple of ponies, an old blind mule named John to do the heavy work, and a small boat from a man who wanted to trade it for a good meal. They had shored up the ailing corral, and Dad had discovered a spring close by the corral as it flowed into the Yellowstone River. They dug out and enlarged this spring, making the space big enough to hold the butter Mother churned and made into one lb. molds. The cold spring water flowed through the box they installed to hold the butter, kept it fresh and firm for the entire week until the next trip to the Fort.

Sometimes the weekly trip to Ft. Buford with the butter was made in the buggy - or buckboard, as it was called. Sometimes it was made by boat, with Dad floating the many miles downstream to Fort Buford. Then Mother would make the trip in the buggy later in the day to meet him and bring him and the boat home for the next trip. There was good demand for their product because there were about a thousand soldiers stationed there against any Indian uprising. They soon learned there was constant change in the personnel at the Fort. Men would finish their tour of duty, or new ones would be assigned. This always made their business and income precarious. The men would buy - on credit - promising to pay next week, and then be shifted elsewhere, and Dad and Mother would be left holding the bag.

During their second year there was a big shift in personnel in that the men were now black instead of white, and these new men were not very interested in butter but wanted chicken. This was an unexpected problem, but they did their best to accommodate, and sold chickens as well as butter. It was never quite possible for Dad to know whether he was being snookered, or it was a matter of language inadequacy, or something that neither he nor the soldier could help. But they didn't get rich fast. The income from the Fort was neither great nor dependable, but it sufficed to keep things going for a couple of years. Something is always better than nothing. In addition to supplying some income, the Fort had been helpful on a couple occasions through its medical services, but they had no sense of dependency on such help, so they were not devastated when they learned such help would no longer be available because it would be dismantled.

They found other ways of making a little money. Mother would wash clothes for stray bachelors, rubbing them clean on a washboard. It seems to me she charged a dollar a month. Mother and Dad, together, would cross the Yellowstone on the ice and cut down cedar trees and haul them back for posts for corrals - or houses - or whatever, and sell these to other homesteaders. While they were gone from their home they would leave Marie, now 5, in charge of the younger two, always leaving all three of them in God's care too. They could trust their little Marie to carry what amounted to grown-up responsibility.

A couple of random thoughts cross my mind as I remember Marie - or Mame, as we all called her. As she was establishing her own home in Sidney years later, frequently turning from an interesting telephone chat with a friend, and of course speaking English, she would reprimand one of her disobedient kids with a Fy skam dig, Danish for "shame on you," and promptly returning to her telephone conversation. She would resume her conversation in English, with no awareness of the shift. Obviously, scolding was to be done in Danish. This was much like my own pattern of assuming religion was something one carried out in Danish.

The other memory-story flitting through my head concerned old John, the big, blind mule. He had to be tied to something, or one of the ponies would wear a bell, and John would follow close by, so they would stick close to home and John would be reasonably safe. He did lots of hauling of one thing or another, such as heavy logs they had felled and had to bring back from across the river on the ice.

One time, however, their precautions didn't suffice and John got too near the riverbank and toppled into the water. They became aware of his plight quite promptly because of his loud complaints. They didn't know quite how to help him, and they knew they would have to hurry or John would be lost to the river. As they ran to the river shouting his name, "John! John!" and followed as the stream carried him downward, he heard them and they managed to get him swimming toward them and the shore. Through their mutual cooperation, shortly old John was back on terra firma, and they were delighted, for old John was an important segment of their family.

Each one of them had particular job assignments, and everyone depended on the others to do their part in their cooperative venture. Both Mother and Dad rounded up the cows on the plains and brought them home for milking. Mother rode side saddle and came home with the first batch of cows while Dad completed the roundup. Mother came home first so she could get at the milking job as soon as possible, for there were at least 20 cows to be milked. Sometimes neighbors who wanted to be gone a few days on vacation would turn over their cows to us while they'd be away. My family was allowed to keep the milk for the service they performed in milking and thus preventing the cows going dry.

Dad's job was to carry the pails of milk Mother had produced to the nearby spring house and poured it into the cooling pans. They helped each other with the churning twice a day, and Mother was in charge of molding the 100 lbs. of butter into one lb. molds every week. Then early in the morning of the day for the trip to the Fort, Dad would get up very early - to beat the heat of the day - and head for Fort Buford with the butter. It was a perpetual-motion sort of life, but they took it in stride, and mostly with good humor.

I had always thought that Uncle Charlie had tired of his role of interpreter, helper and advisor to Mother and Dad, and had walked out on them, leaving them high and dry. But in reading Dad's story quite recently I got a totally new slant on things. It seems that Dad had become increasingly annoyed with Uncle Charlie's patronizing attitude toward him - making him feel like some incompetent no-good, so he asked Uncle Charlie to leave. Obviously this caused problems of all sorts - both emotional and reality-wise - but Dad's story, which, incidentally, was never finished, never indicated that he was sorry for what he had done. Uncle Charlie left and never again returned to visit them or set a foot in Montana, but he did on rare occasions write them letters.

But life took it's toll, and Dad reports in his story that Niels, who was now 4, was sick a lot and had a hard time getting over whatever ailed him. Dad speculated that it was probably malnutrition. That first year was especially difficult in part as a result of their failure to comprehend the magnitude and duration of Montana winters. They had believed they were going to a place with a climate similar to that of Paris, so they had made no adequate preparations for what they ran into. The logs of the house had cracks between them so that the cold came sailing into the house, and ice would form on any water left standing in their one room. The stove worked well, but not well enough to keep them warm. They had failed to lay in an adequate supply of foodstuffs, and their supply fell farther and farther down.

Dad was neither a hunter nor a fisher, so he never attempted to snag fish from the Yellowstone, which was so muddy no one could ever see anything below the surface of the water. I can recall my amazement and disbelief when I later moved to Eugene, Oregon, and learned that all rivers weren't that way. There, one could see clearly through the water, way to the bottom! Besides, everyone knew how treacherous the Yellowstone was, and nobody would think of venturing out on it for any reason if it was not absolutely necessary.

The time came their first winter when everything possible to eat was gone, and they did not know what to do next. Then a young neighbor woman from the Fairview area, Carrie Chestnut, later married into the Hjalmer Davidson family in Fairview, came riding up to the door as she had done several times before, and sensed that things were pretty desperate. She rode away and came back in a few hours with sufficient supplies to make sure there would be food for quite a while. Another rancher brought part of a deer, but Dad figured it had been shot when it was in a fight, because every time they tried to eat its meat they got sick, so they had to discard it. I can recall Dad telling us that only once in his life had he held a gun in his hands and shot a deer. The deer had turned it's head and looked directly at him - and that was the first and last time he ever shot anything.

Aside from fishing tackle, there were a few other things we never had at our house: we never had any alcoholic beverages, and we never had any guns. Oh, yes, there was another taboo: playing cards. These things were of the devil, and they intended to have no truck with him. There was not the slightest disagreement between Mother and Dad about these prohibitions. In my youth we had hops growing on the latticed summerhouse which stood on the southeast portion of the front yard. Most people would have made beer or ale from the hops; but not our family! Alcohol was not a no-no; it as a NO-NO. We never had anything to do with either Bert Betty, brother of Jane Kemmis, or with Andy Mercer, both of whom owned saloons in Sidney in the early years of its existence. To Mother and Dad those who sold liquor to people were stumbling blocks to the weak, and therefore worse than those who drank. Doing anything that might hurt another person was as strictly prohibited as was vanity or puffing up oneself.

By their second year in their home on the river bank they knew that they would have to move because they had learned the limitations of their property. In order to qualify for free land they had to file on a claim, or homestead, 160 contiguous acres, live on it, make improvements on it, and after three years it would be theirs, for free. There was no spot near where they were living that they could find that many contiguous acres. Furthermore, the isolation they experienced was partly due to their distance from the only real trail or road the area had: the stage road on which they had come from Glendive. So they made plans to find an acceptable place to claim. This turned out to be a spot a couple miles to the west and farther away from the river, right adjacent to the stage road. They not only got their claim filed on, but they bought additional acres along both the east and the west sides of the stage road, and they had at least a section - 1 mile square - 640 acres - of land that they could claim as their own. It was a wonderful feeling for both of them.

Their little milk industry had gone well, and by reason of their cows having calves, their herd of cattle increased and supplied both food and something to sell and bring in money. Mother knew how to keep everything sweet and healthy in her milk business. She was not like the man I once read about, who had attended a lecture on how to keep milk separators from spreading bad germs. The answer was to keep the separator scrupulously clean - sterile. So he began sterilizing - boiling - all the parts of the separator every day, only to find he lost his treasured market for unique cheese, because his milk no longer hosted the bacteria that gave it it's special flavor. One must not run a good thing into the ground. They tried planting a garden that first summer and the next but the cattle - their own and the longhorns from Texas that roamed freely in this land without fences - never gave the garden a chance to grow.

When they first came to Sidney they had set a goal of working hard and accumulating enough money in 5 years so that they could return to Denmark. It was always home in Denmark that they spoke of. But the 5 years came and went and they still did well just to keep their heads above water. They had accumulated and paid for only a few acres of land

and a few cattle. Then they set a ten year goal for return to Denmark. But as the years passed by they became more and more attached to Sidney, Montana, to their life here, to the people who became their friends. They became full fledged American citizens, speaking English, taking part in community activities and projects, voting, dreaming new dreams for their new homeland, and certainly never any longer pining for Denmark. The deactivation of Ft. Buford fit into their changes but not as a major factor in bringing them about.

Making the move to their new location by the stage road necessitated lots of careful planning and preparation. They would have to use the logs in their present home by the river to build a new one. But they also had to have a place to live while construction was going on. To this end they built the chicken house first, and they made it big enough to hold both the people and the chickens during this move. This was to be their home for many months. They dismantled the house, log by log, and marked each one with the numbers that would tell them where it was to go in the new construction. They added more logs and finally had a house with several more rooms than the original one did, and sod from the prairie was placed on top for the roof. It was a magnificent accomplishment and was completed in 1893, less than five years after they had arrived. The logs were covered - inside - with white 100 lb. flour sacks sewn together to cover the entire wall and ceiling in each room - to make it look like plaster. The logs of the floor, laid as tightly to one another as possible, and cut with a flat side to resemble boards, were covered with braided rugs which Mother had made from pieces of cloth she had gathered from here and there. They felt almost as if they were living in some kind of palace.

Log House after move from the river

There is no doubt that Mother had long been discouraged with her perpetual job of cleaning up the log house after every rain. It leaked muddy water all over everything every time it rained. They would put out pails to catch the water, and hold umbrellas over the children so they wouldn't get wet as they slept. It was inevitable it would rain several times a year, and it washed right through the sod roof. Every time it rained the leak seemed to get bigger and bigger. The muddy water would accumulate in the muslin or flour sack ceiling lining, and then run down on to her big braided rag carpets, and the whole place was a muddy mess again! It always seemed to rain in the spring, on the 4th of July and at threshing time in August or September. These were the 3 or 4 day rains. Then it also rained in between times too, and every time it rained the whole ceiling and wall and floor covering had to be taken down, washed, dried and put up again. It was enough work to discourage anybody.

There was another problem that was more than an annoyance to Mother, namely bedbugs. She had never met such critters in all her years in Denmark. These vermin lived in wood and seemed to thrive on human blood. They came out of the logs and bit us while we slept, and settled down happily in the crevices of our wooden frame beds, waiting for us to show up again the next night. She tried ridding us of them day after day, but it was a losing battle. She washed the beds with kerosene and went over every inch of each mattress day after day but would always discover some in the crevices that had eluded her. She would be glad not to live in a log house any more.

This "scourge" was not too different from our bringing head lice home from school, and we did this from time to time. Mother washed our heads in Kerosene until she learned about oil of larkspur, and whatever she did was sufficient to rid us once again. As she often said, "It's no disgrace to have lice. It's only a disgrace if you keep them."

There were lots of Indians here, and Mother, who had never heard of them before she arrived, was fearful of them. They came, walking on the ice of the river, quietly and without knocking, went directly to the stove, lifted the lid and warmed their hands in the flames. They said nothing for a while, and then began trying to communicate by uttering a few words such as "guns", "papoose", and "pony", obviously trying to determine how each one was stacked up against the other in such important assets. They held their fingers up to indicate how many they had, and Mother responded in a like language.

She had no guns, and she had only a couple ponies, but she could always top them when it came to papooses.

Only very recently I read in the Billings Gazette of a new study to be undertaken by the federal government to determine the cause of the high incidence of deaths among Indian children under the age of two, I believe it was. I couldn't help thinking of that wet, chilly Fall day when I was perhaps 7 or 8, when some Indians came by our home by the stage road, in a 3 seated buggy with 2 sick children on its floor in cold, soggy blankets. After Mother had invited them in and fed the adults and provided warm dry coats for the children, the squaws appropriated the coats for themselves, putting the kids back in the cold wet blankets. The children had died before they reached the reservation.

I also recall an Indian woman I knew when I worked at the California Institution for Women. She was in prison because she had assisted in the killing of a couple of her young children. It seems she and her boyfriend had been drinking, and in their exuberance and playfulness each of them had grabbed one of her kids by the ankles and swung them around and around in the smallish room. The game went on until both children had had their heads banged against the walls, and died as a result. There was, in my experience at the prison, a great deal of difference between the Indian women's attitudes toward cruelty to children, as compared with the attitudes of Blacks, Whites, and Mexicans. While this was my impression, I would be happy to see a competent study undertaken, such as the Billings Gazette reported.

In the Fall of 1890, Dad writes in his "story", there came word through the officers at Fort Buford, that an Indian uprising was imminent and that the settlers were to take proper and adequate precautions to protect themselves. Before sundown everyone was to come to a stipulated home, and stay there until morning, with some of them on watch through the night. When it was light, they could return to their own homes to do their work until evening, and then repeat the pattern as long as necessary. They did this for 2-3 days, and then decided the emergency was not sufficient to disrupt their lives any longer, and that was the end of their efforts to gather together for protection. One evening Dad and Mother were out on the road in the wagon when they heard a loud noise of what sounded like horses hooves coming closer and closer. Finally they could see it WAS horses - and no riders. The horses overtook and surrounded them, and then passed on. No harm was done to anyone.

The Indians have come into our lives in a different way since that time. My nephew, Pete Jensen, my sister Lil's oldest son, married Marcella Trenk, an Indian related to the Ekalaka Indian Tribes, soon 50 years ago, and the marriage still endures. They had two children, boys, one of whom married a white nurse. They have two daughters - one black haired like her father, my great nephew, and the other a decided blond, like her white mother, as well as like our family. Another relative, my great nephew, LeRoy Anderson, sister Mame's grandson, married an Indian who was an R.N., and they had a son and a daughter. The daughter, Lisa, has a blond son. Lisa's brother LeRoy is a registered pharmacist. All are blonds. The world turns, and it would seem that the Anderson genes and chromosomes are inseparably mingled with those of the Indians, from here on out. My best to everyone!

Dad said the buffalo were plentiful in our area until a couple of years before they came here in 1889, but were completely "cleaned out" so that he never saw any on the plains. He notes in his story how difficult it must have been for the Indians to adjust to white foreigners in their lands, making the decisions and shoving them off their ancestral territory, and taking advantage of them in large or in subtle ways. Nor does it seem strange to me that Indians should resist being "Americanized", even if what we had to offer them seemed, in our eyes, far superior to what they had. One can count on resistance and hostility in response to down-grading. This often masquerades as 'being helpful." I have talked with some of the younger generation Indians, who have told me how difficult it is for the younger ones being forced to choose between many good and desirable things, and losing their identity, through rejecting their Indian ways, by the simple fact of affirming the value of the white man's ways. Security is lost as the price for "Progress." It is bought at a price. There is no free lunch - for anyone.

As soon as Mother and Dad began to have a few words they could use in communication they began replacing their meaningful friends of the Inner Mission in Denmark with new friends here. They gravitated toward people who were involved in some religious activity. Although there was no formal or organized church, there were meeting places and others who also believed in and worshiped God. The Methodists were the most prominent group, and the Catholics came next. We, the first Danes in the MonDak, were friends of everyone, but our sense of at-homeness was with the Methodists. The Kemmises, and the Dawes were members of this group.

Other Pioneers and Homesteaders

The Kemmises were solidly entwined in the pioneer population years before my family arrived here. They came in 1884, and we arrived in 1889. Old man Kemmis, Thompson Kemmis Sr., was a Civil War Veteran and always walked with the aid of one crutch. His wife, Jane, seemed like a very old white-haired lady even when I first knew her, probably about 1905-6. I don't know where they lived originally but by the time I knew them, they were living in a 2-story frame house just east of where our new post office is located on the west side of the stageroad. I don't recall that we ever ate a meal at their house or they at ours. That was such an uncommon thing to do I can't recall it ever happening with any of our friends. We always ate at home, at least for regular meals.

The Kemmises had a big family of several boys and only one girl, but they were all grown by the time I knew them. They were John and Walter, Thompson Jr., and Phoebe, Orra and Willie. John had a farm down by the river, and his two daughters, Lydia and Floy, were my classmates in high school. Eventually they moved to Oregon, and I saw them while I was attending the University of Oregon. Walter was probably the best known of the Kemmis family and through most of his life he was in the public eye. He was a lay preacher, and perhaps even an ordained Methodist minister, but he would often pinch hit for a minister who was unable to meet his congregation, and everyone agreed he was always able to keep his congregation awake and interested. Then he went into politics and served Dawson or Richland Counties as Representative or Senator in Helena for at least 20 years.

Once he was invited to speak to my Civics class at the Sidney public school, and he kept us interested with a series of human interest stories about events in Helena, e.g., his name among the legislators was "Mr. Can't Miss." The Walter Kemmis family had lots of sons and no daughters, so they adopted two sisters, Clara and Lucy, from another part of the state. I suspect the girls themselves spread the gossip at our school that the Kemmises wanted them only for the work they could do, and they wanted out of the arrangement. After a few years, the adoption arrangement was actually terminated. It was my first encounter with adoption. Members of the Kemmis family still live in Sidney. Walter's great grandson Eldon owns and operates

The Toggery, a men's store, on East Main St. This was the store Cap LaRue built in Sidney's earliest days; the LaRues were our close neighbors during our first move into Sidney, and Aileen LaRue was my high-school classmate. Eldon Kemmis has also been on the Board of Directors of our Community Memorial Hospital for many years.

Phoebe, the only daughter in old man Kemmis's family, taught school and was regularly away from Sidney, so I did not know her well. Orra was a local merchant for several years, and then purchased an interest in a threshing machine and did custom threshing. The youngest of the Thompson Kemmis family was Willie, who was different from other people, but nobody ever told me why. I believe that today he would be considered a developmentally disabled person.

The Kemmises were ever solid, dependable people - a family that made not only an enormous but long - continuing, constructive contribution to our area. Their social orientation was beyond question.

Mrs. Kemmis - Jane - had a brother, Bert Betty, and a sister Annette Meadors. Bert opened and operated one of the two saloons in Sidney that no doubt gave pleasure to some and worry and trouble to many more. I haven't heard any other information about him. Annette Meadors was much younger than Jane but they still seemed close and affectionate. I always thought her husband was John Meadors, but *Courage Enough* tells me it was William Meadors who was her husband, and he was drowned in the Yellowstone in 1905. This was too early for me to have remembered him personally, but he might be the Meadors who always meant "ferryboat across the river" to me. John Meadors is listed in our local history book as Annette's son.

My sister Lil, the first white child born in this area, was named for Mrs. Meadors, Lillian Annette, and Lil's grand daughter Mary Annette Jensen Siegfried, who helps me keep my health correspondence as a senior citizen straight, got her name right out of the olden days and from the Kemmis family.

Annette Meadors was mixed up again and again in the early days with health care. It was in her home that the first in-patient service or hospital was set up, and Dr. Beagle's patients were cared for by her. I remember when she was caring for typhoid fever patients in her home, and when they were no longer considered contagious, she would get Mother to give them continuing care for a brief period in our home. Her home-hospital is still occupied and in use in Sidney, but hasn't for years had any health significance.

Just as in other people-situations, the settlers were people with a wide spectrum of values, and so there was an absence of uniformity among them. It also made it likely that when my parents found others with values similar to their own they regarded them especially highly. Or, also possibly, their needs had seemed to them so great that when someone satisfied these needs, they were especially cherished and valued.

Old Bill Cheney was someone who was here "before the beginning", but whom I never met. I didn't know what he had done or why he was important, but it seemed to me everybody knew who he was. I thought he couldn't have been one of the real old timers because he didn't live in a log house, but a smallish frame house a couple miles north of our place, and some distance west of the stage road. Everyone seemed to know Old Bill drank too much, but nobody talked about it. When I became aware of him he didn't work at anything and he was taken care of by his niece, Susie Harrison, a woman of 40 or more, who always accompanied him wherever he went and did the driving of the beautiful team of horses for him.

Eventually I learned he had long been an Indian scout, and his occupation was supplying wood to the riverboats that plied the Yellowstone. The only place I ever saw him was driving past our farm, he sitting stiffly and alone in the back seat and Susie driving the spirited horses he was famous for, sitting - also stiffly - in the front seat, and managing the horses like a pro. I never saw either of them on the street, and as far as I know he never invited people to his house, and he certainly never stopped to chat with people along the way. Maybe he knew we - as well as others - were tee-totalers and would look with disfavor on his daily practices. In fact, I never knew anybody who talked to him. He never asked anything from anybody. He minded his business and we minded ours. We were not friends. How regularly or how often the two of them went to town I have no idea, but it probably had some relation to how often he needed his supply of liquor replenished. I never saw or knew where they went when they came to town, and I don't recall ever seeing them headed for home. As far as I was concerned, the only place they went was "to town."

Late on a very cold winter night there was a knock at our door and a couple of men were carrying Old Bill and wanted to know if they could bring him in. Apparently he had set off for town alone - in the bobsled rather than the surrey - and Susie had not accompanied him. Apparently Susie was not at home and he had imbibed so much while he was in town that he was incapable of handling the horses, and they had run away, tipping the sleigh and dumping Old Bill onto the snow-covered road. In the process he had been badly cut about his face and head by the barbed wire fence on both sides of the road. The men who came asking for help apparently knew Old Bill was alone and Susie was not available.

I had long since gone to bed, so I knew nothing of what transpired until morning, when Mother told me. I peeked into his room occasionally, but I was not permitted to go in or really take a look. A doctor had come to sew up his lacerations. Mother gave him creature care for 2-3 days, and then he was able to be taken home. I do not recall hearing that he ever returned to thank Mother for her care. It is entirely likely that he had some memory lapses for the entire incident - as is characteristic of alcoholics - and that the omission represented no moral lapse but a factual amnesia.

The Lossie Dawe family that lived to the north of the ditch marking Sidney's north boundary line, had a variety of reasons for being included in my list of important people, in addition to the fact that my parents considered them their friends. They lived in a house made of stone like the Old Stone Church was. They had four attractive children, Enid, Eva, Glen and Mary, three of whom I considered quite a bit more worldly wise than I was, as well as very good looking, so that I admired them from afar. Mary, being younger than I was, thereby was too young to pay any attention to. Enid gave her name to a prairie town west of Sidney, and Mary was the only one to cast her lot permanently with Sidney. She married, had a family and still lives here. I'm told she has Alzheimer's disease. I finally lost my awe of Glen, whom I decided was more like other boys than different, in that he also would play pranks on unsuspecting girls. Once in Sunday School, when I had to get up from my chair and go someplace, he emptied a package of tacks on my chair seat; but I saw what he had done in time to avoid being stuck when I sat down.

This seems to me much like the time Frankie Seal came from MonDak with his parents, the John Seals, to visit us. The two of us played in the closet under the stairs until he left for some reason, slamming the door shut as he left, thus latching the door and making it impossible for me to get out. I felt trapped and was sure I would suffocate, since there was no window or other opening present in the closet, but I found all I had to do was to yell loud and everyone came running to find out what was the matter. The Seals were etched into my memory as a result of Mr. Seals' high regard for my mother's frugality, so that he made it known he had determined he was going to marry a Dane. He actually did go to Denmark with the express purpose of finding a wife. He brought her back to MonDak, and they occasionally visited us.

The Owen Loverings were another pioneer family that seemed important to me. It is difficult for me to be sure just why they achieved this status, but I suspect it was partly because Owen Lovering had only one arm and he still drove a team of horses. Also, a picnic ground we often used, because there was a clump of trees to shade us, was called Lovering's Grove. It was closer to where we lived than was another picnic area known as Natural Corral, which was short on trees. It was at Lovering's Grove we had our big family picnic celebrating our parents' Golden Wedding Anniversary, August 17, 1933.

On one winter occasion, Mr. Lovering was the driver on a sleigh ride party, and as usual, the reins were looped and tied around his neck and body, and he had control until one horse got skittish and upset the triple box sleigh, tipping all of us out on the snow-covered ground. Mrs. Lovering kept calling "Owen, where are you?" until he was located, not much worse for wear than the rest of us. I can't remember whether he drove us home or gave the reins to someone else.

The Mike Kelly family was always important to me. Both Mike and his wife Bridget had come from Ireland - Bridget from County Cork - but they first met in Glendive, Montana, where Bridget was visiting her sister, a Daugherty. After a brief courtship they married and shortly thereafter moved to Fort Buford, where Mike had been hired to be tailor to the military establishment. They lived and worked there for perhaps ten years. He was even retained for a year beyond the deactivation of the Fort in the 1890's, and then they, with their several children, moved to Sidney where they built a log house on

Mother and Bridget Kelly

their claim just below the brow of the western foot hills and were still living in it when I left Sidney in 1921.

Their children were Pat, Mary, Joe, Agnes, Ilene, Jim, and Julia, and all of them were important to Sidney because they were much beloved by all. Pat and Mary married into the well established ranching family of the Obergfells; Joe became Sidney's semiofficial cowboy and yarn spinner, who remained unmarried and lived with his mother, to care for her. The sister Ilene died as a result of the scarlet fever epidemic I set off when I was about 4 years old, and Jim died of pneumonia later. Agnes married Ben Weibler, who had moved to Sidney and was our village blacksmith. Eventually they moved to the state of Washington. Julia married Joe Niehenke who also was a blacksmith, and she lived her life out in Sidney.

Bridget - Grandma Kelly never lost her Irish brogue, or the twinkle in her eyes, and when she was in her 80's she was "elected" by the citizens of Sidney to the position of "Sweetheart of Sidney." I often heard Mother comment on the differences in Bridget's and her own beliefs, namely, Bridget freely expressed her feelings that her children could never repay her for the fact of having given them life and birth, while Mother said she never had a feeling of need to be repaid by her children for whatever she had done for them. The Kelly's were ever the very heart of the Sidney Catholic community. Many of the descendants of this couple still remain here, and are very important. I have in my china closet a tiny little 3-legged blue bowl from my playhouse days that Mrs. Kelly gave me.

One of the things that impressed me greatly was how beautiful were the clothes the Kelly girls wore to school. I had good grades; they wore beautiful clothes. It was hard to figure out which was the more desirable goal. I didn't know until after Mike Kelly died that he was an expert tailor and that their clothes were his creation.

In 1899, 10 years after my parents' arrival in Sidney, all of Mother's remaining relatives, 13 of them, came from Denmark to Sidney at one time to set up permanent homes here. They were met in Glendive with horses and wagons and then headed for Sidney. It was spring breakup time and the river ice was breaking into vast chunks. The creeks were full to overflowing, and there was a near disaster on their way home. Nobody was drowned, but there surely was no paucity of drama: horses swimming in strong currents, water washing over the people in the wagons, baggage and supplies washed downstream, and anchoring a wagon to a tree lest it be swept away. Delays were inevitable, and nobody could be apprised of what was happening because there were no speedy means of communication, such as we now take for granted. When the angry floodwaters had subsided and they could move on again, items of clothing and pieces of cloth as a part of the many supplies purchased in Glendive before starting home for Sidney, were hanging high in trees that had been partially submerged by the flood.

It was quite an introduction to Sidney for all of them. There was Grandmother, Mother's mother, Maren Willumsdatter Josephsen; and there was Mother's only sister, Josephine Olsen, and her husband Ole Olsen, and their 4 children, Laurence, Niels, Marie and John. There was my Mother's brother, Uncle Louie and his bride, Aunt Tina (Teenah). Uncle Louie Josephsen had already established himself in Sidney and had a farm close by ours, but he had returned to Denmark to marry and bring his bride, Katrina Andersen, back with him. There was also Mother's brother, Uncle Walter Josephsen, and his wife, Aunt Lizzy (Tante Elisa) together with their two children, Marie and Christian Josephsen, who were Uncle Walter's stepchildren - Aunt Lizzy's children by a former marriage.

I don't know how long they stayed with us in the log house by the stage road before they went to their own newly built homes, but it surely must have been a busy time. They had to find acceptable land and file on their claims, and then build some sort of shelter on that land that would tide them over until they could replace it with something better. Building a log house might take several months. Mother and Dad were both surprised and shocked to find out how Denmark had slipped away from them in those ten years since they landed in Sidney, because their kids, now 7 of them instead of the three they had brought with them from Denmark, couldn't speak or understand Danish at all. They came asking how they should invite the relatives' children to come and play with them. Eventually all the necessary things took place, and we were a very large family, all living in their own homes within a radius of 5-6 miles north of our log house.

All of Mother's family was now living in America, and 4 of her 8 siblings were in Sidney: Uncle Louie Josephsen, Uncle Walter Josephsen, Aunt Josie (Mrs. Ole Olsen) and Mother. Uncle John Josephsen and Uncle William Josephsen lived in Spokane, Washington; Uncle Charlie Josephsen and Uncle Emil Josephsen had also lived in Spokane, but Charlie eventually moved to Seattle and then to Los Angeles, and Emil lived out his life in Oregon. Mother's father, Niels Josephsen, had died of stomach trouble the year before their mass exodus from Denmark, so that not a single member of Mother's family remained behind.

During the years before Sidney had stores, one could buy whatever was needed from Glendive, where we went twice a year for supplies, or one could order from the Sears Roebuck or Montgomery Ward catalog. The order would be shipped by rail and unloaded at MonDak some twenty miles away, and we would drive there with a team and wagon to pick it up. Then came the establishment of the Ridgelawn Store and Stage Stop, only about 6 miles from our home, half way between what were to become Sidney and Fairview, right on the stage road.

It was only a single building, but it was big and had two floors, and it was run and perhaps owned by Guy L. Rood. On the ground floor was the Post Office and general store, where they sold everything. The second floor had it's own entrance and was adaptable to whatever was called for. If necessary it could provide cots or it could accommodate all manner of community activities, large and small. It was a place for church services as well as for dances. It had parties and meetings of all kinds. Our family never danced, but I distinctly recall the big Christmas parties. I particularly remember the extensive precautions that were always taken to guard against fire from the lighted candles on the tree.

Pella Danish Evangelical Church had it's earliest church services there and I can remember being quite smitten with a little boy in my Sunday school class. Einer Holl, the son of a Danish homesteader, Jens Holl, who lived with his family "out in the hills," in a sod block house with dirt floors, rather than in the customary log house of most families. I always tried to save a seat beside me in Sunday school for Einar. His older sister Carrie remained my good friend for many years.

On one of the Sunday church visits to the Ridgelawn Hall I spied a big barrel-like container in the side yard. It was obviously the trash barrel, but this time it contained a whole bunch of overripe bananas. It didn't take me long to make up my mind what to do; I reached down and lifted out a lot of bananas that still had some yellow on them, and began eating happily. I thought it was a shame Mr. Rood had done this, because I knew it was wrong to waste anything, so I had a certain smug sense of virtue as I ate and ate. I couldn't remember ever before having access to so many bananas. They never before had come so easily. Then someone came along and ordered me to cease and desist. It was not easy to comply, but he obviously meant business. I did not try to save Mr. Rood's bananas again, but I continued to feel I had done the right thing.

I recall not only the fascinating Store and Hall but I recall most of the Rood family. Mrs. Rood and Mother were friends. They had three children, Carroll, older than I was, Erma and Glen. Years later Erma attended high-school in Sidney along with me and became a teacher. Carroll seemed to be a neighborhood problem. He had had some kind of operation on his head, so that he told people he had a metal plate in his skull. At least he had a large scar on his scalp, but I never knew what had gone wrong. I recall one Sunday after attending church services in the Hall over the Store, we all had been invited to have lunch at Uncle Walter's place, which was only a couple miles southeast of the store. When we arrived, there was Carroll ahead of us and he was brandishing a long buggy whip, frightening the daylights out of all of us kids, and we didn't dare scatter and play.

The store was eventually closed and moved to Sidney, along with the Rood family and they remained many years in Sidney, doing a variety of public service jobs. Guy was the long time Clerk of Richland County Court, and Erma taught school. Eventually they moved to Washington State.

About the turn of the century the Methodists decided to build a church, and it soon became the project of the entire community. Fort Buford had been deactivated and dismantled and it gave its chapel - furniture, fixtures and even its lumber - to this new church. It had to be hauled away from the Fort to

Sidney, and Dad made many trips to accomplish the transportation. The stone for building the church came from a place a number of miles west of Sidney where the sandstone was there to be quarried, and everyone pitched in to help quarry and haul it to the building site. It didn't make any difference whether the volunteer for service was part of the Methodist group, or the Catholic group, or no group, everybody pitched in and helped. The church building - the Old Stone Church - was ready for use by 1901, and it was a cause for widespread rejoicing. It was the first building located on what eventually became Sidney. I liked the name I gave it: The Prairie Methodist Church.

The Old Stone Church

While this was primarily a do-it-yourself land, there were certain tasks that were regarded as beyond the capacity of ordinary people. Preachers were such specialists. Both the Catholics and the Protestants were served by clergymen who came from elsewhere from time to time, in the tradition of "circuit riders", and eventually there were preachers who were here full time.

The first resident preacher I knew was Pearl Blake. He and his family lived in the parsonage right by The Old Stone Church. He was tall and skinny, while his wife, May Blake, was unusually fat. I remember all their children very well. There were Stella and Louella, the oldest, who were identical twins that no one could tell apart. It seems to me they must have been close to twenty. The next was Eula in her teens, and all were very good looking. Their next child was Forrest, who, as I recall, was just like any other boy, i.e. - not noteworthy - and the youngest was Vivian, who never got old enough to merit my attention while they lived here.

There were several details about the Blake family that seemed really important to me: e.g. Mrs. Blake served as midwife at my delivery and I was named for her (Camilla May) and Pearl Blake's signature is on my baptismal certificate, which was framed and hung on my bedroom wall for many years. I have often wondered if the basis for the close relationships that existed, especially among the women of the community, might have been due to the intimate "birthing service" the neighbor women gave to one another over the years.

The second memorable detail was that I once had the opportunity to watch the Blakes open a "missionary barrel," full of everything imaginable. Such barrels occasionally came into the possession of Methodist ministers, because they never were paid enough salary to recompense them for their services. It was a truly exciting experience for me. Rev. Pearl Blake also had a brother, Burt, a carpenter, who contributed his know-how to meet Sidney's needs as long as he lived here.

I have few actual memories of being a part of that Prairie Methodist Old Stone Church, but those I have are vivid. I remember the night my brother Niels came home and asked me if I'd like to go with him to Epworth League. Anything he asked me to do would have been more than acceptable, so the fact that it was a very cold winter night and it meant we would be walking the almost 2 miles each way was no deterrent. This must have been about 1909 or 1910. We bundled up warmly and started out on a brisk walk through the crunchy snow on the stage road.

We listened and we sang and we greeted the other people who had come for the meeting, and then it was time to head for home. I had a vague awareness that I ought to go to the outhouse and empty my bladder before we started out, because there would be no opportunity to do it later, or indeed until I reached home. But this was not something I could mention to Niels, because he was a male, and one never spoke of anything like this to any male. So I trudged on hopefully. But the pressure in my bladder finally became uncontrollable and I knew there was nothing I could do about it. I still couldn't tell Niels. The only possible thing for me to do was wet my pants as I walked, trying to keep in step with Niels. It was so cold my pants froze stiff, and in the morning I had a bad cold that made me so hoarse I could hardly whisper. The fact that Niels had wanted me to accompany him outweighed everything else.

Still another memory relating to the church was of some new lights having been installed. They made a steady hissing sound that one had to get used to and learn to disregard if one was to understand what the preacher said. I think they told me the new lights were called acetylene, and they were much brighter than anything we had had in the past. I knew most of the interior of the church had been given by people in charge of the deactivation of Fort Buford, and these lights might have been another belated gift, but I never found out for sure.

Associated in my mind with those lights I have another memory of an evening service and being aware that people here and there in the room were beginning to nod or openly drop off to sleep. Then would come the man whose job it was to prevent such unacceptable behavior. He always carried a long wooden stick which he would tap gently on the head of the sleeper, startling him awake, and then he would move on to the next one who needed help to keep his eyes open. I battled manfully to keep away from ever being one whose head had to be tapped.

During the summer of 1989, my nephew, Oscar Anderson, invited me to meet a guest who was stopping in Sidney briefly and had asked to see me. Oscar said he didn't expect me to know her even though she had once lived in Sidney and her father had been the Methodist minister here. Her name was Vivian Blake. How could he have known that the Blakes were indelibly intertwined with my life! To Oscar's surprise, we had a thoroughly enjoyable hour of good conversation, and the Blakes came alive and once again were the meaningful family I had known as a little child. Vivian Blake was as charming as my memory pictured her. I'm indebted to Oscar.

The Old Stone Church was in use for many years and gradually sank (literally) into disrepute. The heavy stone walls kept sinking farther and farther into the ground while the floor maintained its crown: High in the middle and low around the edges. After a couple of decades, they finally had to discontinue using it for services and then a new church was built across the street from the schoolhouse. The old church was sold and Gurney Electric Co. bought it and used it as a warehouse. It's beautiful gray-brown sandstone exterior was covered with a layer of ugly speckled stucco, and a gas pump was installed in front of the entrance. No one could ever guess by looking at it that it once was a noble building and housed tremendous pieces of history. I still hope it doesn't get razed to make room for progress. It is too important a facet of our history to come to such an ignominious end. I visited it only once since returning to Sidney in 1971. I hadn't seen it since 1921, but there are still some remnants visible of its noble heritage.

What caused the sinking of the Old Stone Church? That constitutes another segment of our history.

There were big important changes, or almost imperceptible little changes that had been taking place. Our family had changed from essentially foreign intruders to part and parcel of the fabric of the pioneer group of people who have been called "the last frontier." They had never intended to be pioneers anywhere, but that was their happy fate as they managed to survive one year after another in that time of change. Fort Union, the largest of the Astor fur trading posts on the Missouri river, had become a thing of the past even prior to 1889 when the Anderson's had arrived in the MonDak. The buffalo roaming the prairie were part of history, and stage stops, with mail drops, were almost regular fare not only in Sidney but in nearby settlements: Tokna, Savage, Ridgelawn and the O'Brien stop at Newlon.

Schools grew along with the size of the families and the relative safety of transportation. At first school was in somebody's home; then a place was designated at some specific locus. Children walked to school or they rode horseback, or they rode in buggies or buckboards. As fenced areas began to emerge, the days of roaming long-horned Texas cattle ceased, as had the buffalo, and trails and even rudimentary roads began to emerge. Names of people began to appear in relation to the business of education of children. In fact, education was an important business from the beginning of my memory. I even heard tell of such things as colleges, but they were merely words and had no specific or concrete connotation. Finishing the eighth grade was the customary goal of every family for its sons and daughters. Few families had encompassed the idea of "going to high-school," because there were no such places extant.

The Olsen kids, my cousins from Denmark who had come in 1899, had a bad time with school because of language hurdles. There were so many kids in the Ridgelawn school - for all attended in one room and under a single eagle-eyed and often forbidding-in-appearance teacher, Professor E. C. Hicks - that they got a bad start and some of them developed considerable resistance to going to school at all. Prior to the erection of this Ridgelawn log school, by the stage road, my siblings had gone by horseback or in the buggy to some designated place, perhaps a home, and had to brave the miles of roadless prairie, dotted with bands of Texas longhorns. Mother feared they might be trampled to death. It was a relief to have the school built so close to home, and where there was a road and not just a trail, or even less.

Although one could buy some items at the Ridgelawn store, our family drove the 50-some miles to Glendive twice a year and stocked up with anything and everything we thought we might need to carry us through the next six months. Mr. Hollecker, who owned and operated the store in Glendive, acted as banker to the homesteaders, and thus permitted buying "on time," as Uncle Charlie had taught us was the American way, so the business of life could proceed. It helped change hope into reality. We recognized it as a trust.

The railroad, running through Williston ND - but not through Sidney - had become a fact of life. It made a stop at MonDak - which was a town of only a few buildings on the Montana-Dakota border twenty miles away - and was a tremendous boon to commerce and general community development. The mail brought every family the Sears Roebuck and the Montgomery Ward catalogs twice a year, and these were what really made life interesting as well as possible. They took the place of towns and stores because they carried everything one could imagine; they weren't wish books - they also delivered. Make out one's order on a proper blank, put it in the mail drop at the post office, and shortly, there came back exactly what one had ordered. So, in addition to being a teaching book for foreigners such as my family, it was also the necessary informer as well as the vehicle for obtaining whatever one thought he needed. I don't remember what we used for money before we had banks and checks, but there had to be something, and there no doubt was. During the early - and some of the later - days, it was possible to order goods of any size from the catalogs - to be delivered to MonDak. It might be a cream separator, or forty rolls of wallpaper, or a half dozen boxes of apples for winter eating. Someone would drive a team and wagon to MonDak, and fetch them home. It was always easier in the winter, when the ice would be thick enough on the river so crossing over to the railroad yards on the other side was easier than depending on being ferried. But difficult or easy, shopping was never a simple matter.

Thank goodness for telephones. They can be an annoyance, particularly if they are used by cranks of one kind or another, but they are one of the most important "utilities" we have - perhaps even more important then roads, though that is doubtful. In Sidney's very early days - when there was actually no Sidney, as a locus, we had telephones - big boxes on our walls, which were connected by wires which settlers had strung along fences, and we did our own ringing with a crank on the side of the big box. We had certain agreed-upon rings which meant one thing or another: an emergency - fire - danger, be alert - general news item, and listen to this music. Everyone would pick up his receiver and get the details, and follow the instructions if they seemed applicable to him.

For our music in the very early times we relied on Hans Larsen, a bachelor directly from Denmark who lived a few rods south of our house. He had a phonograph, which used the old-time cylindrical records that were heavy and took up a lot of space.

When he got a new record, or if he had a request for an oldie, he let everyone know by means of a certain ring on the telephone that he was about to play music. Everyone would gather around the big box telephone on the wall in his own home, take the receiver off the hook, and listen in rapt attention to the sounds coming over the wires from Hans's phonograph. This was the way we learned about the latest hits. Some of the ones I can still remember Hans playing for us were "Any little girl is a nice little girl, is the right little girl for me; she don't have to wear rats in her hair, or a straight-front XYZ", or "Rastus take me back; I won't drink no more; I'll sleep on the floor", or other equally delectable items. Hans would signal with a long ring on his hand cranked phone, and everyone knew the concert was beginning, so we had better hurry and listen. I can still hear the melodies.

Hans Larsen went back to Denmark to get married, and returned with his wife to Sidney. After a few years, Hans, his wife Marie and their two children, Lawrence and Carrie, returned to Denmark permanently. Only Carrie is left there now, but I still hear from her regularly at Christmas time, and she has been back here to Sidney at least once since 1971 when I returned here. Long retired, she still maintains a fairly good command of the English language both in writing and speaking, even though she couldn't have been more than 3 or 4 when she left Sidney for Denmark. In 1990 she suffered a stroke and had to relinquish her family home and move into a nursing home, but she is cooperating with rehabilitation plans and her spirits are good, so I hope good things may still be in store for her.

My parents were happy to be part of this new life that was filled not only with bright blue skies and with the lilting song of the meadowlark, but with hope for the future. They wished for nothing beyond what they had. They liked living beside the stage road that was always bearing some new person or element into view. Returning "home to Denmark" no longer was a goal, because they were so busy living in the present moment. Their family was growing, their friendships were warm and meaningful, and they were forever involved with the business and the problems of living today. They felt lucky to be exactly where they were. Love of our nation, of our little strip of the MonDak, and believing fully that this implied an even better future, almost gave them the feeling that we were all eating pie in the sky - day by day. And gratitude to God was a part of their daily verbalized life.

Dad's Dream

I am always a firm believer in the importance of timing as a major factor in progress, not that one can determine the appropriate time for this or that particular step, but nothing can happen if the right things have not come together already. It takes the past to make the present possible. I see our family's coming here as one of those essential details which made change and progress possible for this particular part of the world. Dad was trained as a gardener in the old country. He had learned to assess soil's suitability for growing plants, and there was the promise of free land. He was dropped down on the west bank of the Yellowstone river where he got intimately acquainted with the land lying to the west - toward the encircling foothills, and he rated that land extending 50-60 miles to the north and south along the west bank of the Yellowstone River as far superior to anything he had previously seen.

Dad hadn't been here more than a few years when he became aware of the extremes of our climate: too cold, too hot, too dry, too much wind, too little rain, too much snow. Nothing seemed to follow a reliable pattern other than one should always be ready for some extreme behavior in the weather. The lack of dependable moisture really troubled him because he saw the land as being of very high quality for farming. Repeated dry years discouraged settlers from becoming farmers. Stockmen, yes; farmers, no. And daily he saw that immense Yellowstone river winding its way through the area - the MonDak - and all that water going to waste year after year, when it was so badly needed, and it troubled him. Added to all this information he was entering into his "computer" was the fact that the wide, flat, fertile valley lay right next to the river, for miles and miles. The river water could surely be diverted and redirected in such a way as would provide water for this lovely, fertile valley. He not only wondered about it; he talked about it - to anybody and everybody who lent him an ear.

The soil was superb for growing, but almost nothing grew in it because one could never count on the rain. There were big rains, but one could never count on them to come at the right time, so trying to farm was a hazard and a heartache. As he looked at the situation day after day he began to speculate as to what might happen could some of that huge body of water in the Yellowstone river be diverted from its channel and enabled to flow over the fertile acres to the west of the river. The longer he thought about it, the more feasible the idea became, so that he eventually had a sort of blueprint in his mind that he felt sure could work if it were possible to implement it. He talked to other settlers, but they didn't seem too impressed, because the cost would be prohibitive. But his dream would not leave him alone, and he finally thought maybe he had come up with the answer he was looking for.

He knew it was a huge project and no local effort would suffice. He knew it would take the Federal government to do the job. Then the times seemed right - at least to him - because Teddy Roosevelt was elected President of the U.S., and Dad believed that if only he could get the ear of that man, whom he adored, and he could relay to him what was the substance of his dream, then Teddy Roosevelt would surely grasp its importance and make the dream a reality. So he had to devise a way of getting to Washington D.C., so he could tell him about it. Money did not grow on trees, but somehow he bought his ticket from Glendive to Washington D.C. and set off on his mission. He sat up in his coach seat all the several days of his trip, and he ate only the box of food Mother had packed for him. In Washington, he found his way to the appropriate offices with high hopes in his heart. He was definitely not a verbal person, but he felt so sure of the rightness of his cause.

But Teddy Roosevelt did not come out to greet him or to give him encouragement. In fact, he never got to see Teddy Roosevelt. But he saw many other people in those offices and he gave them his dream - the product of his speculation - some in the Department of Agriculture, to others in the Department of the Interior, and he had the feeling he had been well received even though he had not talked to the man he most wanted to reach. I don't know how many days he spent in Washington, but he had the feeling he had been heard and that there were those who had really listened to him. I suspect that as he headed for home he prayed a bit, because God had to be included in such important matters. But HE DID WHAT HE COULD, at his own expense and bidding, and as far as I know, he was the only one who did anything at all.

I cannot say that Dad accomplished his mission, or that had he not done what he did nothing would have happened. But I can say that he spared no effort; he sincerely tried to transmit his dream to people who had power, and that it was less than a couple years later that surveying for the irrigation project that he envisioned and presented, not only was begun, but was completed, and his dream was made into reality, and has continued for soon a century to spread its benefits far and wide. I doubt if the logs of the offices he visited would say that Peter Anderson of Sidney, Montana had been there such and such a day, but I can tell you that never a day goes by but what I feel grateful for what I feel very sure he has meant to this area, and indeed, to the entire state of Montana. To me, he accomplished his self-appointed mission in a magnificent fashion.

In 1903 the surveying for the ditch - the canal - was accomplished. Diversion of the water from the Yellowstone river was carried out a few miles northeast of Glendive - at what is now known as Intake. The big ditch was routed for 50 or 55 miles down the valley (northward) along the western boundary of the flat terrain. Smaller ditches led periodically from the big diversionary canal eastward, back toward the river, and still smaller ditches networked the entire area. It was built to do the job by gravity flow. It was a massive undertaking and was not fully completed until 1912.

The Federal government bore the original cost, but every farmer making use of the water pays in fees and taxes an amount related to the size of his acreage, which determines the quantity of water he receives. It was geared to pay off the original cost in a certain number of years.

Almost all of our farm was under irrigation, and the entire valley produced lush crops year after year. At first the crops were wheat, oats, barley and alfalfa. A flour mill - Russell Miller Milling Co. - was built in Sidney and made flour which was exported everywhere. It so happens that we can raise here - probably because of climate factors - a very hard type of wheat that is extremely high grade and in high demand. Shortly before I left Sidney in 1921 sugar beet raising began to dominate the picture. Sometime during the 50 years I was away the flour mill closed down and we no longer have such a mill. This no doubt relates to the change of crops to sugar beets. Now we have a sugar factory, and our product is sold under the name of Holly Sugar. Holly Sugar is the third largest employer in the valley, and its product is as good as comes from anywhere.

In 1988, we had the huge and horrible drought - with only one snowstorm all of the winter of 1987-88, and only 1 ½ inches of precipitation from winter to September. Our erstwhile beautiful hills never sprouted a blade of green grass, and the prairies looked gray-brown and desolate. But the valley under irrigation went right on producing beets and making a livelihood for the farmers in the valley. They in turn supported the nonfarm population in the area, and paid vast sums in income taxes to help support the state and the nation. Dad would have shed tears of joy had he been here to see it: that his dream had been realized and had brought such a difference to the people who were lucky enough to have land under irrigation in our valley. I'm quite sure most people living here take the trees and the fertility for granted and have little or no awareness of its history. Current (1991) headlines talk of the pressure in the Montana legislature by western interests to make our water serve the recreation interests of the western region at the expense of the agriculture interests of this eastern end of the state. I hope Dad doesn't turn over in his grave.

I distinctly remember the big crews of men working on the construction of the main ditch, or canal, in our 50 mile long valley, - the MonDak - and on the smaller ditches along its path. Every bit of the dirt was moved with one-horse drawn molded "scrapers" about a yard square, made of heavy shiny steel, with two straight wooden handles at the rear corners and the front edge sharpened so when guided by the man handling the scraper handles it could cut into the soil and move it into the scraper. When the scraper was full, the dirt was dumped on either side of the trench being made, thus making the walls of the canal higher and higher. Then the scraper was loaded again and again and dumped until the job was done. One man drove the horse that was hitched to the scraper, and another man manipulated the scraper. It was all done by teams of two men. Scores of such teams were employed, extending the canal inch by inch. It was hard, hard work.

Finally, after several years of such hard work the job was finished: the big canal, with water diverted from the Yellowstone River at Intake, only on command, flowing into hundreds of secondary laterals, or ditches, from the canal to the farmland eastward toward the river, and tertiary laterals to the farms to be irrigated. In the secondary laterals, the descent might be sufficient so that devices for retarding the speed of the water had to be built, so erosion would not occur. At those points the water would run over wooden "falls", and these became bathing centers for people who had no bathing facilities at home. Since there was no possibility of privacy, our hired men went there at night so as not to be public spectacles. There were several drownings in the main canal in the early years, because it seemed to take a long time for people to learn that the "ditch" was a dangerous place and not meant to play or swim in.

Mother was probably one of the few people who felt troubled at the successful outcome of Dad's irrigation dream. When the project was completed - and she had never once interfered in any manner with it - she cried bitter tears, "because now a lot of people (farmers) will be moving to Sidney on account of the water, and all those people coming in will spoil all the good times we have had these many years." Losing those close-knit ties was inevitable, and that was a great sadness, but life - and change - and "progress" - marched on.

Irrigation changed the whole appearance of the valley. Formerly there were literally no trees. Our one sizeable creek was Lone Tree Creek. Now trees are everywhere. Many kinds of trees grow here now, whereas only a few would grow prior to irrigation, even with pampering. Water, no doubt, has seeped through the walls of the big ditch, as well as all the little ditches, and from the irrigated fields, infusing the entire valley with moisture year after year, so the roots of the trees can get plenty to drink. The valley, the MonDak, is no longer an arid land. It is a gem, an oasis in the desert, that even the people of western Montana are scarcely aware of.

Why aren't they aware of it? Partly because western Montana, which has plenty of trees of it's own, has never had the habit of being interested in eastern Montana, and partly because we are not easily accessible by any means of transportation. It is only in the past very few years we have had good roads. Before that we were, in effect, stepchildren and not heirs to funds for road building. We are not on any mainline or "thru" roads. We are not even near main line railway passenger service. The southern railroad route through Billings no longer carries passengers, and it is inconvenient to get to the northern main line running through Williston, North Dakota. We have no bus service. Airline service is difficult to come by, and too expensive. It is entirely understandable that it would never occur to people living their entire lives in western Montana, to visit our area because it would be too great an undertaking. Why should they be interested in visiting Sidney? We're just "too fur off." It's too much trouble getting here.

And now we are back to where I think you can understand what happened to the Old Stone Church. The seepage from the ditch and saturation of the entire valley from irrigating the land year after year, caused the soil to be soft enough to be unable to withstand the weight of the stone walls of the church, so they just sank and sank - a millimeter at a time, year after year. And that's the way it is.

Our Farm

Mother's yammerings took their toll on Dad. In 1902 they decided to take the long-postponed trip to Denmark, including in their plans Christine, their youngest child, who was 4. While much of the trip was a disappointment, it served the purpose of freeing them from their emotional bondage to Denmark, their homeland, which had become far "too small" to be effective competition to the MonDak, which grew in importance to them as they looked at it from a distance.

It may have been the necessary factor in prodding Dad to build us a new home only a few rods north of the log house which had been home - whether by the river or by the stage road since 1889. He engaged the services of a contractor and builder by the name of Mavity, and planning and blue prints began to become a wonderful reality in 1907 and 1908. This fit in with the developments in and on the small piece of land which Eddie Kenoyer had bought in 1904, platted, and laid out as the town of Sidney, with lots for sale. Everything was booming, and dreams were coming true. We were all on our way to better times and amounting to something.

Our new house - 1908

Our new house, designed and built by Mr. Mavity and his men from some nearby community was ready for occupancy in 1907-08, and without exception we were delighted with it. I was sure it was not only the biggest but the best and finest house anywhere around. In 1989 I was invited to attend the 40th wedding anniversary celebration of my friends Georgie and Oscar Petersen at their beautiful "earth home" built a few years ago in the Andes community hills west of Sidney. Among their other guests were several Mavity's, relatives of the man who built our house so many years ago, and I was meeting them for the first time in my life. They had not known that that "landmark" house in the valley had been built by a Mavity. It was of frame construction, painted on the outside, usually creme with brown trim. Though it has undergone many changes, both on the inside and the out, since 1921 when I left Sidney, it still stands there for all to see.

Nothing about the house now is quite as attractive as it used to be. Essential parts have been deleted, and it has a stucco exterior - but it is still in use now 80 years after it was built. I recall vividly not only its individual parts but its totality. The large rambling 2 story house, with its changing colors of paint and trim, its many big outbuildings, all red in color, the long white picket fence separating the barnyard from the house yard, and also surrounding the house on three sides; the long lilac hedge Dad planted separating the front house-yard from the more utilitarian back yard. The row of wild plum trees along the south side of the front yard; Mother's flower beds at the north end of the front yard, and the latticed wood-slat "summerhouse" in its southeast corner. The 2 tall swings for me and whatever company I might have, stood between the south side of the house and the row of wild plum trees that grew to be 6-7 feet tall.

Our new house - the entire complex of buildings - was big but also beautiful to me. The red barn was even bigger than the house, in order to hold the 20 cows we habitually milked, the long row of work and saddle horses, the hay in the loft, and all the horse equipment such as saddles, bridles, bits, reins, harnesses, collars and whips that were used. Each saddle and harness had its own place on which to hang it, and each was properly adjusted so it could be easily put on the specific horse it was meant for. The horse barn was in the east side, and the cow barn was in the west side of the barn, and ventilation, lighting and temperature - without benefit of electricity - were entirely comfortable.

In 1922, the year after we left Sidney, there was a terrible cyclone that struck our area, demolishing scores of buildings. It killed Mother's sister, Josephine Olsen and injured her two youngest children, Emma Dorothy and Ann, and generally devastated the region for miles. It demolished both our barn and the schoolhouse that stood about 1/8 of a mile to the north of us. Both were rebuilt, but they never looked the same again as I caught a glimpse of them from the stage road as I drove by. The barn was rebuilt smaller, and the school was rebuilt bigger.

A fence separated the area where the house stood from the area of the farm buildings, which were north and west of the house. A big swinging wooden gate at the east end of the barnyard opened on to the stage road, and was wide enough for any vehicle to go through it. On the house side of the yard a white picket fence stretched from the corner of the outhouse eastward to the northeast corner of the front lawn - even with the big east gate. The woodpile was on the barn side of the yard. The vegetable garden lay beyond the woodpile to the north and east, out toward the stage road. We went out through the picket gate to get an armload of wood for the kitchen stove, or for an armload of vegetables for the next meal.

The icehouse, where the ice blocks harvested from the Yellowstone River were stored, was between the woodpile and the granary, by the north fence of the barnyard. It really wasn't a house at all; only a hole in the ground where the ice was stored and covered with straw, making a mound. The picket fence became an ordinary wire fence west of the outhouse and on to the shop building. That fence was equipped with a big gate through which one could drive a team and buggy. I used to have fun swinging on this gate, and the hired men went from the house to the barns through it.

I knew my place. It was inside the fence - on the house side, and definitely not outside, where the hired men came and went. Of course I could gather eggs, or bring someone a message, or carry out some specific errand, but I was not to lally-gag. The granary, a huge red building to the north, was divided into very large bins or rooms for storage of the various types of grain we grew, until it could be sold, or fed to the stock, or planted, using the big seeder.

In 1912, the railroad came to Sidney with the tall grain storage elevators built up close to the tracks, and home storage of grain for shipment elsewhere was no longer as necessary as it was before the advent of the railroad and elevators. The prairies are dotted with these tall, uniformly shaped buildings up against railroad tracks where farmers brought their harvests to be sold and transported by rail to distant places. Sidney even got a flour mill and shipped our flour to the world, but even though we raised the wheat and made the flour right in

Sidney, and neither the finished product nor the grain had ever left the lot, our flour cost more than it cost anywhere else. The Company charged for the flour as though the grain had had to be shipped to Minneapolis, and then the flour shipped from there back to Sidney. I asked for an explanation and was told "Somebody had to pick up the cost of shipping", and that was the one who bought the flour. It was hard to understand, but that was the way it was. It may still be that way. Freight costs here have always seemed exorbitant.

Our farms in this area had no silos, seen elsewhere so commonly. These are not only storage places for a variety of farm products, but a place for a sort of digestive fermenting activity to take place before it is fed to the farm animals. Our farm raised a lot of hay, both alfalfa and range grass, and this was left outside to dry and then stored in the high part of the barn, on the upper level, or in big hay stacks. Outside, it was hoisted into the barn loft by pulleys, ropes, hay forks, lifts, and horse power. In the hayloft, hay was kept dry and free from mold, and was accessible as needed for feeding the various animals tied in their stalls or held by stanchions while milking went on.

The granary not only had the many large storage bins holding hundreds - or maybe even thousands of bushels of wheat, oats, rye, and barley, but also had a place for storing farm machinery such as plows, seeders, discs, and even binders when not in actual use, so they were protected from the elements. When cars arrived on the scene, the granary was where we stored them when they were not in use on the roads. In the early days the car wheels were "jacked up" with wooden blocks inserted under the axles so the weight of the car would not damage the tires when the car was not in use.

We had two wells right beside one another in the barn yard perhaps 50 feet from the barn. One gave us gray water out of the windmill pump that emptied into the big cement tank for the animals to drink, and the other one didn't really serve any purpose because we knew it was contaminated, probably from animal droppings in the yard, and the water was brownish. Then we had another well immediately under our kitchen, with a pump in the kitchen, which gave good drinking water through the years, although I never heard of a sanitarian ever testing it. It seemed remarkable to me that wells drilled so close together could be so very different. Nature seemed to be a strange and unintelligible thing. Nobody told me that the depth of the well probably had a lot to do with what came out of it - more than its specific location.

The gray clay in the big cement tank had to be emptied every few months. I loved playing in the slippery clay, squishing the slick gray muck between my toes. I also used the clay for making mud pies in my doll dishes and pots and pans, sometimes garnishing them with peas and carrots from the garden. I recall that it was while I was busily making these pies out by the cement tank clay when Montana was having such big forest fires in the western end of the state that the sky was quite dark and we had to burn lamps all day. Not even with the big Yellowstone Park fires in 1988 did we have much daytime darkness here.

The chicken coop was adjacent - attached - to the barn, at the northeast corner. It's roof had only a single slant - northward, and with a very gentle slope - just enough to help it shed the rain or melting snow. It was a little below the level of the barn roof, which ran north and south. The combination of roofs served me wonderfully as a place to play. I could climb up on the chicken coop roof and then on to the lower pitch of the barn roof, up to where it took a sudden upward turn, and I could go no farther. Then I would squat on my heels, hold on tight to my ankles, and sail down the lower segment of barn roof and jump off as I came to the chicken coop roof. I'd do this again and again, never misjudging distances, never getting hurt, and having lots of fun, either playing by myself or with other kids. My coordination must have been pretty fair or there would have been more than casual mishaps.

The hog pens were between the chicken coop and the granary to the east. A part of these pens was protected by a roof, and part was open to the sun and rain. There were pens for the various size pigs, and each pen held troughs for water or whatever was to be discarded from the kitchen, including milk. Pigs never had any manners, and were very noisy and demanding, but they were also fun to watch and to try to understand. They did a lot of talking. I recall Mother telling me that way back in the early days something went wrong between a little piglet and it's mother, and the mother pig rejected and would not let her baby feed from her breast. This meant the piglet would likely die, so mother, who still had milk in her breast from feeding her own baby, took on the job of nursing the baby piglet. Everything went fine; the piglet lived and grew strong enough to eat from a spoon or a dish, and took its place in the world of pigs. It was the only time she nursed a pig.

The big straw stack, resulting from threshing, was northeast of the barn, back of the chicken coop and pigpen. No longer does one see straw stacks standing nearby almost every home, because grain is no longer threshed and therefore there is no straw blown out of the big long pipe, which was part of the threshing machine. The straw is left in the field through the use of modern combines. The straw-pile size was silent testimony of the size of the farmer's operation, but it also served many practical purposes. In the barns and pens, every animal's stall was well supplied with this bedding, and more importantly, the straw stack served to keep the barnyard animals warm and dry when it was cold or stormy. They burrowed themselves into it and were sheltered and protected from the elements. Rarely does a farmer have enough barn space to keep his entire flock indoors, and the straw stack shields those left outside, from the rigors of harsh winters, such as we experience.

There was still another out building in the house - part of the back yard, and it opened through a wide double door on the north side, into the barn yard. This building housed the shop, on the west side, where all implements for fixing things were kept and used as needed. The northeast corner of the building was our smoke house, a small space about 5x6 ft. and kept tightly sealed from the world around it. We smoked our meat there, usually sausage Mother had made or hams or other cuts that the hired men had slaughtered. The walls were dark reddish brown from previous smokings, and the floor was dirt - the ground. The southeast portion of the building - south of the smokehouse, was my playhouse, and this room and the smokehouse opened only to the house side of the yard.

My playhouse, a single room, was perhaps 6x10 ft. and it contained all sorts of delectable items, such as a doll house about 18x40 in., open all across the front side so as to give ready access to its contents. It had 2 stories, with several partitions and rooms on each floor. Most dolls were too big to be played with there, but it was ideal for playing with paper dolls - which really were my favorites. The two windows of the doll house were curtained with lace curtains, and it had carpeting on the floor.

My playhouse had many pieces of furniture: a miniature chest of drawers about 15 inches high of natural wood grain and varnished; a tiny dresser painted white and decorated with teeny tiny painted flowers of different colors; a doll bed; a little rocking chair big enough to hold me; two little straight chairs; a baby sized ironing board, a small table, a couple of wall cupboards, and a miniature kitchen range. I remember being unhappy because it was not connected with a chimney so I could cook on it. The dresser had a mirror that would swing back and forth, just like a real dresser, and the drawers would hold lots of doll clothes. I also had a tiny iron, a doll buggy, a couple sets of doll dishes, pots and pans, a blackboard, and about anything my little heart could want. My sister Christine was 6 ½ years older than I was, so she rarely attempted to play with me there, but this meant that everything belonged to me and to nobody else. The playhouse gave me great pleasure for several years.

Our house, it seemed to me, had everything we could possibly want - ever. One thing it didn't have was electricity, but it never occurred to me to miss it. There was a cellar under the entire house - dirt floor and unfinished, but who ever heard of a finished basement? It had 2 full floors and an attic over the whole of it. The cellar had numerous rooms separated by partitions. It had an outside entrance to the west with stairs rising outside the walls of the basement, leading to our back yard, and covered by two board flaps that closed toward the middle and covered the stairs below. Then there were the indoor stairs a little north of the middle of the cellar which led upstairs into the kitchen. These were comfortable to climb, with low rises, and had a wood backing. The walls of the stairwell to the kitchen had places to hang all the pots and pans used in everyday cooking. There was also a dumbwaiter which carried anything and everything up and down from the cellar to the pantry, which was directly off both the kitchen and the dining room - so as to "save steps."

Niels had his photographic developing and printing rooms in one compartment of the cellar, and I used to spend hours with him there. There was the room where milk was kept in big, shallow pans, and the coal storage room to feed the furnace, which stood in the middle of the cellar, and had big shiny metal pipes carrying hot air which led to every room in the house. This provided us with central heating. There was the room with lots of shelves right beside the dumb waiter, where we kept newly baked pies and other baked goods and some other food that didn't need to be kept in the ice chest. Then there was also the compartment which was the "root cellar" where we stored our potatoes and some other vegetables that kept well and needed a cool dry home through the winter, such as carrots, hubbard squash and onions, as well as boxes of apples.

The first story of the house had four entrances: the back door to the north, the side door, also to the north, but leading to a small porch off the conservatory where Mother had all her potted plants and flowers that bloomed the year around. The porch also provided access to a room about 12x15 ft., Niels's bedroom, and to a stairway to a large room above the back entrance of the house which we called the "bunkhouse," where the hired men slept and lived when they were not working. There were two additional entrances - or exits - on the east side of the house, one from the dining room and one from the parlor, both of which opened on to a big screened porch overlooking the front lawn. The conservatory at the northwest corner of the main floor opened through a big archway to the dining room. When the family table was fully extended it would seat up to 14 people, but we were more typically only 9 or 10 at the table, with Dad always at the head of the table - at the north end - and Mother next to him at his right and closest to the kitchen with its swinging door, and to the pantry.

Evening in the sitting room - Mother, Dad, Jim Hendrickson, Me. Dalma, Ira, Lil, Christine, Jo, one of our hired men

Between the dining room and the parlor to the south of it, were double sliding doors. The construction of the house had determined that the air movement outside made a whistling or whining noise at these doors, and always gave me an eerie feeling. The parlor had lots of windows and was perhaps 15x18 ft. and was in the southeast corner of the house. Directly west of the parlor was the "sitting room", which one entered by way of double sliding doors, that also moaned or whistled. It was a little smaller than the parlor and everybody tended to gather there winter evenings for reading and talking, playing flinch or dominoes, eating the delicious apples we had ordered from Sears Catalog and had hauled home from MonDak where the railroad had unloaded them, or munching popcorn made in the nearby kitchen. Sometimes the group would include a special hired man, whom we admitted to family status, like Jim Hendrickson, who was sweet on sister Jo, and they eventually married. Later the sitting room became a spare bedroom rather than a family room.

The sitting room opened on its north wall into the hallway which led to the stairway going up to the second floor, as well as to the dining room and to the kitchen. The kitchen had a large Monarch range, dropleaf oak table and a few chairs, movable cabinets to hold everyday dishes, silverware, cutlery, towels, dishrags, pot holders, etc., and another cabinet for spices, flour, sugar, salt and whatever belonged in such a place. The coffee grinder was screwed to the wall. There were no built-in cabinets in the house as we have now. There was a pump at the sink in the northwest corner of the kitchen, which fed from a well in the cellar. A big granite wash basin stood in the sink and a cabinet fastened to the wall above it held supplies such as soap and towels. Everybody used this sink many times a day. It was the only place in the entire house where one didn't have to carry water, either before or after using it. When we were finished washing or getting a drink, the water left over ran out the sink drain and into the back yard, where our rhubarb, horseradish, and bushes such as currents and gooseberries grew, and prospered.

The sewing machine, a trusty old treadle type machine - probably a Minnesota Model A - was a most important part of our family's equipment. My sister Dalma was the chief seamstress, but everybody sewed. Ordinarily the machine in its cabinet was kept upstairs in the southeast bedroom, which was used for a sewing room. I used to say I wish I had a nickel for every yard of tucking, and lace insertions that Dalma made. In these days it wouldn't buy very much.

I remember one Christmas everyone was busy getting ready for the holiday and this seemed to involve congregating in the southeast bedroom upstairs. Dalma, as usual, was busy running the sewing machine, making everything from clothes, to doll clothes to rag dolls. The kerosine lamp was on the sewing machine's open and extended top. Suddenly, as a result of the vibration of the machine, the lighted lamp tumbled off on to the floor, and pandemonium ensued. Everyone rushed in to help by grabbing this or that, and I tried to do my part by trying to stomp out the fire which was involving scraps of cloth and paper resulting from our many activities. They were afraid the kerosine in the lamp would be ignited and we'd have a real conflagration on our hands. The moment I jumped into the scene to stomp out the fire, I was dragged out and ordered away from the room. Luckily, no one got hurt and nothing of value was destroyed.

Quilting was done on wooden frames held together with special clamps, making quilting easier by adjusting the size of the quilting area to be worked on. The frames, in turn were balanced on the top of four chairs at the four corners of the quilt. Quilting, commonly a social affair, was usually done in the parlor, the biggest room, so numbers of women could work at the same time without getting in one another's way. In between quilting times the frames were kept in the stairway to the attic. Under the stairs, in the main floor hallway, was a fairly large but low closet where we kept all manner of things no one wanted to see cluttering up the house, such as old magazines, and the door had a latch rather than a hook or a knob, so if someone slammed the door shut, not knowing any one was inside, he or she had to have help to get out.

The back door of the kitchen led to several small rooms on each side of the central walkway, each of which had its individual purpose and function. One room led into the next until we came to the last two, which were quite large. The room on the east side was the milk room where the separator stood, ready to separate the milk from the cream. Milking 20 cows twice a day, morning and evening, remained about standard throughout all our years on the farm. The hired men milked some of them, but Mother was the champion milker. There were tables, pails, pans, 5 and 10 gallon containers. But the water for cleaning everything still had to be carried from the kitchen, or the things to be washed had to be carried to the kitchen. Everything one did meant lots of work. The ice chest was near the door in the milk room, so that if the water from the melting ice overflowed the top of the container at the bottom, it wasn't a major catastrophe because the floor had linoleum on it and the back door, where one could empty the full container into the conduit from the kitchen sink, was real handy.

The other sizeable room, the back entrance, to the west of the milk room, had the main back door from the house to the outside. It also had linoleum on the floor, because there was a great deal of traffic through that room. The men coming in from work shed their wet wraps there, including their boots, overshoes and rubbers before coming into the kitchen and dining room. They could hang their things on hooks or nails in the entrance, and pick them up again as they went out, and they were in nobody's way. Everybody ate at the same table at the same time, and Dad always said grace and terminated the meal with a "Vel bekom Dig" - a Danish formality meaning "May it agree with you."

Every room from the kitchen to the back door was covered with linoleum. The washing machine stood in the large entrance, waiting to be used. There was no electricity, and we had no gasoline motor; we moved the handle of the machine back and forth with elbow grease. This caused the wood agitator in the washing machine to swish the clothes around. Everything that was likely to be sloppy was done back there. A couple of the little rooms on the way to the kitchen contained cupboards where we put freshly ironed clothes and supplies. The other had additional storage space for fixing things that went wrong in the house - including the kerosene lamps, which were always in need of kerosene or having their wicks trimmed, or their chimneys cleaned and made spotless. For a couple years we had gas lamps in addition to kerosene lamps, because their light was brighter and whiter, and these lamps frequently needed new mantles and filling with gas. I tended to keep my distance from these because it was very easy to break the mantles and I was not for doing damage to anything. A narrow board walk led from the back door to the backhouse, or outhouse, a 2-holer, which was well supplied with Sears Roebuck catalogs, because we hadn't yet heard of toilet tissue. It seemed to me everyone tried to look nonchalant when he used that walk. But it remained chilly in winter and dark at night.

On the second floor of the house were four bedrooms, three of them real large, and one small one, perhaps 10x10 ft. There was also a bathroom right at the head of the stars that was never used except as an emergency bedroom, because the room had no window and no bathroom fixtures or running water, and it was too much trouble to carry water up the stairs from the kitchen, where it would have to be heated on the stove, and then carried down stairs again when one had finished his bath. We did have a folding bathtub made of some black nonporous rubberized material, which we could have used, but it was almost impossible to empty it. The water had to be dipped out, which was a next to impossible task. So we took sponge baths at the wash basins on our wash stands in our bedrooms, or if we insisted on having a real bath, we got into a wash tub of water in the kitchen, and emptied the tub into the sink when we were finished. Bathing everyday would never have occurred to us. There was neither privacy nor facilities for that. And we weren't trying to conserve water, as people in California are urged to do.

The attic was a place that held perpetual fascination for me, and for the kids who came to visit me. There were trunks full of old clothes, pictures, broken parts of furniture, boxes of who knew what, and even a package of Dad's love letters to Mother that she treasured and had tied a ribbon around. I still have these in a trunk somewhere. At the time I could not read them because they were written in Danish and in Dad's very fine script, but I have read some of them since, and whereas they were full of true love, they were not terribly shocking. The attic was reached by a stairway out of a small closet belonging to the southwest bedroom. Everything had its place, from the quilt frames, to the boxes and trunks full of clothes we could put on and play grown-up. It was a part of the history of our past.

Although I have not really seen our place since 1917 when I left it to live in town, it is obvious my memories of it are still vivid. Here were my roots. It was home from 1907-08 to 1917 when Dad sold it to Holger Petersen and moved to town so I could go to high-school. Besides that, moving to town meant we were not only going to have electricity but indoor plumbing with all the advantages these services imply!

On a morning very recently when I awakened too early and had time to let my mind wander, I made a discovery concerning this old home of mine. I had known ever since returning home in 1971 that the whole place looked different from the road, and I felt critical of the people we sold it to who had taken away its charm and even covered it with stucco! I just could not understand why they had done this to my erstwhile home. Then it occurred to me the changes were no doubt due to the 1922 cyclone which had not only demolished the big barn, but eliminated the granary and tool house together with my play house, and no doubt wiped off the porches as well as part of the north entrance and bunk house and the rooms leading to the kitchen! The stucco probably wasn't a choice but the only functional material that would cover the wounds of the storm. It's interesting how moralistic judgment enters the picture when one doesn't understand the whole story! As I began to understand, my critical stance disappeared. It was probably the best way out of a very bad situation. The Petersens hadn't ruined it. It was an "act of God" that had!

The pastel bluish hills, the "badlands", running north and south beyond the east bank of the Yellowstone River, always look the same. They are beautiful, especially looking eastward across the river, but they are minimally arable and few people in the early times attempted to live among them. To me it always represented the Great Unknown, but they were there to look at from a distance from our side of the river - not to be explored.

Nobody we knew filed on claims on "the other side" - east - of the river because the river - the Yellowstone - was definitely the dividing line between our world and the world beyond the river, which was nothing but "badlands" and nobody went there. To be sure, there were horse ranches there, but no farms. There eventually came to be an exception to this finality in my mind. Lena Larson was from "across the river," with her mailing address at Gossett. She was a school marm who had been my second grade teacher, and had roomed and boarded at our house, and with whom my sister Jo had become fast friends. She was about to be married to Johnny Larson, and Jo was to be her bridesmaid.

So, on that cold, blustery autumn day perhaps in 1911, we set off in the 2-seated buggy, with no top, for Gossett, across the river, and Lena's wedding. There were scarcely any roads or even trails, and definitely no road signs. (We still have a dearth of them.) We got hopelessly lost, and there was nobody available anywhere to give us any directions; no farms, no houses, no buggies on the road, or horseback riders, just bitter cold and the feeling I had that we would never find our way out again. I was totally ready to believe all the stories I had heard about "the badlands" - with rattlesnakes, and everything - and I vowed never to go there again - which vow I have pretty well kept.

We didn't quite freeze to death, and we finally arrived at our destination, but we were two or three hours late, and the wedding party had almost given us up for no-shows and gone on with the ceremony sans bridesmaid. They didn't even have any good idea as to where they should start looking for us. They were relieved that even though late, we had, indeed, showed up. It took a long time to warm up sufficiently so that Jo could change her clothes to her fancy bridesmaid dress with its yards and yards of teeny tiny tucking and lace, that sister Dalma had made for her, and got her long white gloves on both her cold numb hands. But she made it. After the wedding ceremony and after we had eaten a sumptuous meal and talked to all the guests, we started for home. We had to make it to the river before dark to catch the last ferryboat that would bring people across before the next morning's light. Johnny Meadors probably owned the ferry.

Many years later I met Lena and her husband, Johnny Larson, in Portland. They had come there to help their only child, a daughter, Viola, matriculate at the University of Oregon Medical School, the same one I had left only recently. Viola completed her 4 years there, too, and received her M. D. degree.

Both Lena and her husband Johnny later died of cancer of the lung and ironically, neither of them had ever smoked a cigarette. I have no idea as to the cause of their almost simultaneously developing cancer. They had always lived in rural settings and were not in any hazardous occupations.

Until recreating that trip I had completely forgotten that I had had still another encounter with "no man's land" across the river. Perhaps I was in the second or third grade, and I think it was my teacher who invited me to spend a night at the McGlynn ranch across the river. I don't recall how I got there, and I don't recall who was there other than a girl a little older than I was. I don't even remember having a meal there. What I do vividly recall was the night itself. The other girl and I left the ranch house, when bedtime came, and went some distance, - perhaps as much as a couple or three blocks - on a trail that led to a small house or shack with one room, and there we were to spend the night. The whole thing seemed a bit scary. The 2 of us were alone. There were no grown folks around, and no way to call for help should we need it. But it didn't seem to bother her, so I guessed it was OK.

We had no sooner gotten into bed than I heard the coyotes start to howl. It is always an eerie noise they make, and I had heard them in the distance since before I can remember; (we always locked the chicken coop door every evening lest the "kyutes" get in and eat our chickens.) I had never seen one of them up close. But that night I heard them - sounded like lots of them - up close. I wasn't entirely sure they couldn't scratch open the door to our room, and I didn't know what would happen then. I didn't actually cry, but I must have sounded frightened, because the girl reassured me and held my hand - like my sister Christine did when the lightning was real bad - and eventually I fell into a fitful sleep. Those beasties sounded as though they were right outside the door - howling and howling. I was glad to get home the next day.

Our day in the badlands was never replicated. Once was enough. But then time had moved along and cars replaced horses and buggies, and Niels had established himself on his claim on Figure Eight Creek 100 miles west of Sidney, which had Prairie Elk as its postal station. Then Carl and Christine joined him and made his little 12X14 tarpaper shack their home until W.W.I disrupted things. Their "spread" was more primitive, and the terrain just as difficult to access as the Lena Larson wedding had been, but we never tried making the trip in winter, so it did not seem so formidable. Also, the terrain was flattish, not rugged.

The roads actually were worse going to Prairie Elk; there were no road signs, and the 100 mile trip which we made perhaps 3 or 4 times in several years was fraught with greater hazards than we had encountered in the badlands, and it took a full day to complete the trip one way. In some spots there were no roads at all, and often we had to get out of the car and push in order to make it through another gully. I recall one trip we made in a lumber wagon in which we killed two rattlesnakes on the roadway when we stopped to open gates blocking our passage. We took the wooden brake-handle from its proper position "up front" and clubbed the rattlers to death and then drove on.

Looking at current maps of Montana I don't find any of the landmarks we were heading for: Paxton, Weldon, Prairie Elk, which were the "towns" which had names and post offices. They were one or two-building towns - post offices contained within a store which sold a few staples. They were in the Fort Peck Dam drainage country, and I have wondered if they were swallowed up while I was away, by the dam-building process and formation of Fort Peck Lake, which happened in Franklin Roosevelt's presidency. I have inquired at the court house, but they have no records of any such places.

Times were a-changing not only for Sidney but for the Andersons. We had abandoned the old log house and moved to the new home a block or so farther north but still on the old stage road, in 1908. Our new home was even a better place for having company than was the log house, and that house had served very well. By and large, we had an open house. I recall an incident occurring in Eugene, Oregon a couple of years after we had left Sidney in 1921 so I could attend the University of Oregon, and my brother Carl was visiting us for the winter. There was a knock at the door, and I got up from the table to see who it was and what they wanted. Carl became very irritated with me and wanted to know why I didn't just shout "Come in!" rather than having to inspect them before letting them in. Even products of the same family don't necessarily have assumptions in common.

We had not been in our big new house long, before it was August 17, 1908, and that was a very important date in our family. It was Mother and Dad's Silver Wedding Anniversary. People began dropping by to congratulate them and wish them well even before they were out of bed that morning, and this unplanned and informal drop-in continued throughout the day. Their wedding anniversary had always been very important to all of us. They never failed to mark the event every year. Whereas it was never an occasion for gift giving, it was a time for remembering and cherishing. I still celebrate it, often all by myself, every year.

The next really big occasion in our new house was the double wedding, on June 1, 1910, when my sister Dalma was married to Ira Albin, and sister Lil married Thorvald Jensen, in our parlor, with Rev. Niels Damskov officiating. Literally everybody came from miles and miles around. The service, I am sure, was in the Danish language, and I wonder now how

Ira felt about that - for he was a proud Hoosier, and this may have been just one more offense against him that made him so hostile to my parents through the years. As I can now see, but did not at the time, my sister Dalma didn't have any great love for Mother either, so no doubt their feelings reinforced each other's.

If I were to specify the individual whom I thought had made the greatest contribution to Sidney's growth and development, I would say it was Charles Earl Varco, owner and manager of the Yellowstone Mercantile Company, a general and department store which opened for business in the very center of Sidney in 1906. It was enlarged twice and still stands here, big, proud, dependable, and uniquely stocked with first class merchandise. This store has set the tone for Sidney's sense of identity - which equates with "several cuts above" its competitors, not only in Sidney but in any small town anywhere.

Mr. Varco came here when he was a very young man, newly married, handsome, blond, intelligent, personable and before there was tangible evidence that Sidney, the town, would indeed, materialize. He came from Minnesota, and the idea of coming here had been given him by none other than Dr. J.S. Beagle, who also came here a couple years later. I did not know until quite recently that Mr. Varco's father before him had owned a store in Minnesota, and that Earl had been well trained by his father to deal with the endless minutiae involved in running a store. He had a very attractive wife, Antoinette, and 3 attractive children, Catherine, Charles and Winifred, who were born in Sidney. Mr. Varco contracted the flu in the 1918 epidemic and as a result he developed Parkinson's Disease and died of it in 1952. His daughters are still living and maintain control as well as ownership of the store, but they live elsewhere.

The store offered many excellent features, in addition to quality merchandise, right from the start. In the early days it stocked some groceries in addition to drygoods, and it had one of the early self service groceterias. Mr. Varco served as banker to many settlers who needed credit and no bank was here. For many years it offered a 2% cash refund to customers who paid cash, as evidenced by their cash-register receipts.

What sets the store apart is that it's merchandise has always been top quality - as well as the latest - and its prices are commensurate with the times. Many times through the 50 years I was away, when I have returned for a visit to Sidney from some eastern or western metropolis, I would find the very thing I had looked for in much larger stores, and could not find. Here it was, in Sidney's Yellowstone Mercantile. Considering the quality of the goods it carries, its prices are truly fair. In early times, it stocked items that would have had to be ordered from catalogs, and it's brands were top quality, thereby setting the tone of our image. It was and is ever like a cool breeze in the desert.

The store now has the same system for handling payments that was installed decades ago: carriers, or containers, extend by cables from stations at each part of the store to the centrally located cashier seated above on the mezzanine level. The money travels through the air to the cashier, and change and receipt are returned via the container on its wire rails to the main floor station from which it originated. It is a most ingenious device - and furthermore, it works. Currently the store has 6 departments; Women's Wear, Mens Wear, Infant's and Children's Wear; Shoes, Basement Variety; and Hallmark Shop. Changes are made whenever needed. Everyone is a winner. I still miss Clyde Kendall in his shoe department of long ago. I believed it was impossible for him to make a poor fit. He just knew feet.

Dad, who had already left his mark through his efforts in behalf of irrigation and the rural settlers, made still another contribution both to the agricultural sector and to the urban and merchandising sector of our area. Mother's lament regarding the influx of new people to the area by reason of a dependable water supply, was certainly prophetic. People from all over flocked here, some still looking for free land, some for dependable water supply, and others merely for a place to live. A sizeable percentage of those who came were Danes. Some came directly from Denmark, but most were from other states, chiefly Nebraska, Iowa, Wisconsin, North Dakota and Minnesota. Many of them spoke little or no English.

Dad was happy to see them coming here, but he became increasingly aware that they needed something that we did not have to offer: a church home. Of course, they could have done as our family had done: worked hard at learning the English language and seeking integration with the people already here. But as he began speculating he chose another route.

He had had no contact with Danes in America, but he knew they were here somewhere, and he set about locating them and seeking their help in ministering to this area's spiritual and factual needs. He wrote a letter to The Danish Lutheran Church in America and because he had no address for them, he mailed the letter without any address, and trusted to God and Uncle Sam to deliver it to the proper people. He set forth the local situation as best he could and asked for help in solving the church-need problem. In a matter of weeks he received an answer to his letter from the Danish Evangelical Lutheran Church in America, headquartered in Blair, Nebraska, and shortly plans were made for meetings and development of further plans. The result was that Sidney became the hub of a Danish-speaking community that would prove to be exactly as Dad had visualized, namely hard working, stable, law abiding, frugal and an asset to any community.

He had not visualized what this move would do to our family, but for good or ill the dye was cast and whether he liked it or not, he moved away from the pioneer Methodist group and toward the Danish Lutheran group. Up to that point we had been pioneers. Now suddenly we were Danes. And it was about that time my own identity was beginning to take form. I can hardly remember when I wasn't a "Dane."

Two Danish Lutheran churches were formed, one for the hill - rural - community Danes, Brorson - and another for the town and surrounding area Danes, Pella. Both churches conducted all services in the Danish language, and we were essentially a foreign enclave in the MonDak. We were largely self sufficient as well. All our church services - as long as I lived in Sidney - which was until 1921 when I finished high school and moved to Eugene and to the University of Oregon - were held only in the Danish language. Even civic and American functions such as 4th of July celebrations, Thanksgiving Day services, or other American events, were conducted in the Danish language. We even chose where I was to attend college - Eugene, Oregon - based on the fact that a Danish Lutheran church (Danish speaking) was situated there.

But I was the baby of our family and scarcely 5 years old when our family - reluctantly to be sure, but still definitely and factually - pulled out of the Methodist (pioneer) church and became members of the Danish Lutheran Church. We chose to be Danes. But not all of us. I was the only one who made the move automatically, because my parents chose for me. The others - 7 of them - made their own choices and moves - and in doing so, we had a divided family and a hodge-podge of allegiances.

At first there were only visiting preachers, and then Rev. Niels Damskov, who had been stationed in Kenmare, North Dakota, about a hundred miles away from Sidney, became our first resident pastor. Neither area had known of the existence of the other. The experience Dad and Mother had had in Denmark with "The Inner Mission" society and its people, together with the fact that Dad's father was also involved in the same religious movement, no doubt made Dad realize the Danes coming here needed a church home.

The big Danish Bible that Grandfather Anders Christoffersen had given Dad to take along to America was placed in the possession of The MonDak Heritage Center in 1989, as part of our Montana State Centennial celebration events.

Their lives had been so full of problems it was a wonder they held on to the sense of commitment they carried with them to Sidney, Montana from Denmark so many years before, but this they had maintained. Mother and Dad seemed to agree about what they believed and what they considered important. They continued to believe God was taking care of them and it was God's will they had come here. They had no sense of need for a Danish church for themselves because they had become Americans, and they were at home and happy in the Methodist church, but when it got right down to the nitty gritty, and Rev. Damskov came to serve this Danish community, they cut their ties to the Old Stone Church and became a part of the Danish group and church, giving it their full allegiance - no reservations. Because I was only 4 at the time, I remember little of the time we spent with the Methodists. The separation from the Methodist church was hard on our family, but I was so young it was no problem to me. I just went wherever Mother and Dad went.

The Danish Rev. Damskov's family was always very important to me. I was still four when they entered my life. They had four daughters and three sons: Christine, Peter, Esther, Luther, Dora, Ella and Victor. Ella was just my age, and we soon became fast friends. None of them was married when they came here, but when they left for Winnipeg in 1919, all but the 3 youngest were married. Christine married Jim Hansen, also from Kenmare, N.D. and they owned a meat market here in Sidney. Both Christine and Jim had very good voices and had lead roles in the Queen Esther Cantata which the Sidney Methodists put on early in our history. Peter, who had very kinky and tawny hair, married another North Dakota girl, Anina. Esther, who also sang in the Queen Esther Cantata, married Henry Hendrickson, the son of the Danish farm family from Wisconsin having settled in the Brorson area, and was also the brother of Jim Hendrickson, who married my sister Jo. Henry eventually moved from his farm to Sidney, and became custodian at the Sidney public school for years. Luther married one of the Topp girls - the family Dad had brought here to establish and run the creamery that served Sidney for many years. Dora, Ella and Victor did not marry until long after they left here. I believe everyone in that family is now deceased, but they certainly left their mark on our community.

The Rev. Damskov Family

Rev. Damskov was a builder, a mover and a shaker. Under his auspices the two Danish Lutheran churches were built: Pella in Sidney and Brorson in the Dane Flats area, a few miles west of town. Rev. Damskov served both congregations.

For the first couple years the Damskovs lived out in the hills a mile or so west of the Brorson church. Then when Pella church was moved from its original site alongside the church cemetery into Sidney proper, the Damskov family moved from Brorson to Sidney. Pella church building was eventually sold to the Bible Baptist Church. I have not been in it since I returned to Sidney in 1971. I can't help but wonder if the altar picture Mother gave Pella - the Shepherd and the Sheep - is still there.

Every summer we Danes had Danish school for a few weeks in the schoolhouse close by our farm. Nothing but the Danish language was used, and this helped me to become quite proficient in Danish - at least in reading and understanding the language, if not in speaking it. It makes me think back to my first days in school in the Old Log School, the Ridgelawn School, when I came home crying to Mother, asking that she give me reassurance that I was not a Dane, as the kids said I was; and she made me into a Danish convert right on the spot, so that I felt it was OK to be a Dane. I probably was the most Danish of all my siblings - I have always felt Danish, and it is an important part of my identity. I was the only one of my 8 siblings brought up in the Danish Church. I was one of "the Danes," just as P Diamond was my brand - our brand.

Whereas Dad was genuinely concerned for the spiritual welfare of the new settlers, I am sure he also had one eye cocked on the practicality of having a Danish language church in the area, if Danish settlers were to be attracted to the area and settle here. It was probably the most important thing he could have done for Sidney, after the establishment of the irrigation project. The combination of the two was a sure winner. When I left Sidney in 1921 it seemed a safe conclusion that this was a Danish community. When I returned 50 years later, there was no longer any functioning or even nominal Danish church, either at Pella or at Brorson, The Norwegians had largely replaced the Danes in Pella, which now used only English and had members of many nationalities. Few people were left who remembered the old days, and nobody seemed to miss them. It reminds me of the Spanish or Mexican - or Cuban influx - and problems - of more recent times in other places.

I suppose Religion will always be tied to the Danish language, for me. I believe I still can quote scripture in the Danish language far better than I can in English. The many branches of Lutheranism in the United States have been largely ethnic products. Each wave of migrants from Europe built its own-language-speaking-church, and the sect was firmly established for a few generations, until a unification of branches and sects began, and then another and another unification, as the importance of language receded, and everybody became American. It is hard for many people to understand why there are so many different Lutheran churches, but it is simple when one understands the original (ethnic) purpose of their establishment.

The coming of the Danish church was, to our family, a divisive experience. My oldest sister, Mame, married to a Dane from Denmark, and with her own independent family, remained with the Methodists. Niels went his own merry way, belonging to no church ever again. Dalma married an American, a Hoosier, who belonged to nothing other than to the Masonic Order, which Dalma never joined. Lil married a Dane, and they went to the Brorson Danish church occasionally because they lived in the Dane Flats area. Jo married a Dane and they lived at Three Buttes - too far from any church to attend with horse and buggy. When they left Sidney in 1923, for Eugene, Oregon, they attended the Danish Lutheran Church where Mother, Dad and I were members, Emmaus, and later transferred to a larger Danish Lutheran Church, Bethesda, and it has remained her church. Carl had no use for anything Danish, and never became affiliated with any church, but was a devoted Mason and completely satisfied with that affiliation. Christine married an American, but after her husband's death, her family attended the Lutheran church in Pasco, Washington. While I've tried a variety of churches, I'm back in Sidney belonging to Pella Lutheran Church, though I cannot claim I'm active in it. Churches can be extremely important unifying forces, but they can also be very fragmenting. The important thing is that when Sidney needed the on-going assistance of a church home for Danish immigrant homesteaders, the Danish Lutheran church came promptly and met that need.

Rev. Niels Damskov, pastor of Pella Danish Lutheran Church for almost 15 years, was a big contributor to Sidney's development. I am glad his bones as well as those of Sophia, his wife, have been laid to rest in the Sidney cemetery; it's where they belong. They made a very significant contribution to Sidney, as well as to me. There is nothing on their grave marker that would identify him or his wife as the important people to Sidney that they were. When I visit our family's grave site, I often make a little side visit to the Damskov plot and say a little thank you for the memory of the people who meant a great deal to me.

Rev. Niels Damskov, Pella's first resident pastor, and his family filled much of my life. It lasted from age 5 to 15 (1909 to 1919). Ella, and I were together more than we were apart. Mrs. Damskov was a gentle soul whom I saw as an ideal helpmate - ever discrete, competent but never obtrusive. There was a period in the early days when I wasn't sure if she was doing right by letting Victor, her youngest, nurse even when he was running about under his own steam. I was sure, however, that nobody ever baked as good bread as she did. The loaves were heavy, dark gray brown, and the thinnest slices not only stayed together without breaking or crumbling, but each slice seemed to be so filling. They always used wheat they had raised or purchased, and had it coarse ground at the mill for her to bake.

Rev. Damskov seemed equally interested in temporal and spiritual growth. The best word I found to describe his appearance was "urbane". He was the first man I ever knew who wore a beard - a Van Dyke beard - which was always carefully trimmed. The little rocking chair I had in my playhouse had the head of a man with a big beard carved on its back. I told him it was a likeness of him. (I have suspected in later days that it was supposed to be a likeness of Zeus.) He had a great gift of speaking, making everyone feel he was talking to him - or her - personally. I missed them all very much when they moved to Winnipeg, where he had been selected to act as immigration pastor to the endless stream of people who flocked into Canada after the end of W.W. I, in 1919. Mother and I visited them there in 1920.

I dreaded returning to Sidney after our visit to Winnipeg, knowing that Ella would no longer be my "bosom pal", but the void was filled by Ella's cousin, Ruth Damskov, the daughter of Rev. Damskov's brother Peter. Things have a way of working out. Had Ella not left Sidney I would never have discovered Ruth and her family, and to have missed either one would have been a great loss.

While Rev. Damskov lived and worked in Canada the King of Denmark conferred on him a special honor, the Knight of Dannebrog Award, for his service to the Danish immigrants into Canada after W.W.I.

When I was a youngster and came under the spell of Rev. Damskov's persuasive preaching, I would say to myself that if the time ever came when I would wish to be "converted", it would be as a result of Rev. Damskov's preaching. "The plans of mice and men geng aft agley", Burns said, but I still never think of Rev. Damskov that I do not have a warm appreciation for him and his wife Sophia, who never really learned to speak English, and for Ella, their youngest daughter and my first real chum.

The language problem with the Damskovs never seemed to be a problem to me. Whereas I can't recall ever hearing either Rev. or Mrs. Damskov speaking English, neither can I recall ever even trying to speak Danish to them, yet we constantly communicated. I just recall an exception to this: My sister Christine and I were walking down the street and we met Rev. Damskov. He tipped his hat and spoke directly to me, saying he was glad I was taking my little sister out for a walk. She was more than 6 years older than I was, but I was as big or bigger than she was, and he was making special note of this in English, so no doubt he did speak English on rare occasions. I can't even recall hearing the Damskov children of any age speaking to their parents in Danish, but perhaps they did and I didn't notice. The second generation of Damskovs was as American as our family.

Other relatives of the Damskovs made a pleasant addition to Sidney and my life. Rev. Damskov's sister Elsie, (Mrs. Lars Petersen), and her husband farmed just south of us on the Hans Larson place, and raised their family. They had purchased their farm from Peter Damskov, who had purchased it from Hans Larson. I was quite smitten with Pete Petersen, their oldest child, and we often rode to or from school together, Pete on his bike and I on my horse, Kinky. One of the Lars Petersen children, Deborah, contracted an acute disease I had never before heard of, Noma, which was a rare infection of the mouth and throat, and she died of it. Lars Petersen was also a lay preacher who would pinch-hit for Rev. Damskov if he was away. Their children, in order, were: Peter, Lula, Olga, Sophus, Deborah and Mabel. They lived - and died - either in the Sidney area or in Oregon, where they moved later. Only Olga, an R.N.

and widow of a Sidney Hundtoft - remains, living near the shores of the Pacific Ocean at beautiful Yachats, in Oregon.

Rev. Damskov's brother Peter was not unlike Rev. Pearl Blake's brother Bert Blake, in the Methodist Old Stone Church, in that Peter Damskov also was a good carpenter and builder. He contributed much to the Sidney area with his skill. Peter Damskov's family consisted of himself, his wife Marie, and their four children: Ruben, Ruth, Marion and Dora. Marie, his wife, also came from a prominent Danish family, but she was born in the U.S., so the language of the family was always definitely English. When they first came to Sidney they lived in the Hans Larsen acreage just south of our house. Ruben, Ruth and I often walked to school together, a distance of about two miles. We were always looking for rides to town and if we spotted a wagon or a car coming from the north, we promptly put our lunch pails (lard pails) down on the ground and sat down to rest on them until the vehicle reached us. It usually paid off, but occasionally they had no room for us, and we had to trudge on. They remained in Sidney until 1922 and then moved to Oregon as we had done in 1921, but they moved to Portland while we moved to Eugene.

Ruth and I had established a solid friendship before I left Sidney in 1921 and this we maintained throughout the ensuing years. We did not see one another often because we somehow managed not to live in the same city, but correspondence was always sufficiently active so that when we did have face to face visits we were able to pick up where we had left off, and go on from there. It always amazed me that no matter how long we had been apart, we could pick up the threads of our lives and understand where we were "right now," and could move on again from that point. Ruth earned her R. N. degree under the aegis of the University of Oregon Medical School while I began my career in psychiatry in Binghamton, N.Y. In 1931, Ruth had a bout with tuberculosis, which had given me a sense of familiarity with the ailment not to be derived from lectures or textbooks, before my own experience with it (tuberculosis) in 1932. Then Ruth married the son of a Danish Lutheran minister from Eugene, Hart Larsen, and they owned a clothing store for "the smart set" in Eugene called, "Town and Travel". They had no children, but adopted a son and daughter. I was always aware that Ruth could run circles around me in the area of style and taste in clothing.

Ruben graduated from the University of Oregon as an architecture major and practiced his profession with great success in the L.A. area. He died of cancer of the lung only a few years ago. Marion and Dora married and raised families, but because they had been only "kid sisters" of Ruth, I can't really recall having had any contact with them after I left Sidney. Their parents, Peter and Marie, lived to a ripe old age and spent their last years in a retirement village in Oregon.

Imagine my surprise and delight when I received a phone call from Ruth during the summer of 1990 saying she and Marion, now both widows, were coming to Sidney to see if there had been any changes since 1922 when they had left here. It was a busy and pleasant week. Marion, who had come primarily to visit their old time next door neighbors, the Nick Hansens, along with their 2nd and 3rd generation progeny, the Frances Jones family, and Ruth, who had come primarily to see me, insisted on staying in a motel rather than being my house guests.

There had, indeed, been many changes both in Sidney and in ourselves. Both of the Damskov girls were still beautiful, but they now had snow white hair! Ruth, almost a year my junior, was having memory problems which troubled her, particularly because she had such a great need to not let it show, and Marion was no longer just a kid sister, but a very likeable woman in her own right. I - still driving my own car - was able to let them see the changes - and some things that had not changed as much as one might have expected, such as the Brorson church out on Dane Flats, which has had little use in several decades, but we were still able to see it inside and out. They came away from their trip to Sidney with Ruth saying: "I just cannot understand how you can be happy to live in that little town", and Marion saying she loved the whole of Sidney and saw in it a multitude of caring people she would be happy to live among. Beauty surely is in the eye of the beholder.

The Damskov family spanned, participated in and led the activities of all age groups of the Sidney Danish community for over ten years. They left a permanent impact on our area, and I dare say few left a better or more constructive one.

Pella church was moved from alongside the cemetery, to town, and before I returned to Sidney in 1971 it had moved again to a much bigger brick edifice at Lincoln Avenue and

West Main St. But it wasn't just the location that changed. It was the change brought about when several Lutheran churches had merged, nationally, and it was no longer part of the Danish Lutheran Church, but of the American Luthcran Church, ALC. In 1987 there was still another merger, of three additional Lutheran denominations, and this merger created the Evangelical Lutheran Church in America (E.L.C.A.).

The shift from the Danish Lutheran Church to the American Lutheran Church was difficult even for me. I had been mostly outside the church during many of those years, but when I would go back to Sidney for a visit, it did not feel like home or that I belonged. The old and familiar landmarks were gone; the rituals had changed; the songs were different and strange new ones had taken the place of the old ones. The earmarks I grew up with were gone and nothing really felt right. So, because I felt no real need for what it seemed to have to offer, I just stayed away, and each of us went his or her own way. So Sidney has changed, and Pella has changed. They no doubt will continue to change. That's about the only thing one should really count on: Change.

On November 5, 1988, Pella Lutheran Church, E.L.C.A., standing on the southwest corner of our street, had a celebration in honor of its founding 80 years ago. Jan and I had a personal notification of the event. I wore my very best Sunday-go-to-meeting dress - a long and rather gay one for an old lady - I was happy to pay tribute not only to Pella and its capacity for survival and its long history of service, but to honor Dad and Mother who started it all. It was a very nice party. The music was a delight. I'd never before heard Pella's KID'S ALIVE CHOIR. There was a group of old timers who sang a Danish hymn that I remember very well; a flute ensemble that was most enjoyable and an adult choir; nostalgic reminiscences from a church member, Eldon Steffans, who had been brought up in the Danish church in North Dakota, and his shared details brought many an empathic chuckle; there was a long and original poem by a daughter of a founder of Pella, Ethel Johns, that touched us all; and an abbreviated slide show of affairs at Rocky Boy Indian Reservation, in Montana, a new outreach mission program of Pella's. There were special guests with pretty corsages - Jan and I among them. The one thing I missed was even a single mention of Dad's role in the church's coming into existence prior to its founding. Possibly they had never heard of him; but I had tipped my hat to Dad as I strode in.

Among the oldsters and founders honored were Bertha Hall, the daughter of Jens Holl, whose name had changed only slightly by marriage, representing their family who had lived in a sod house northwest of Sidney. Bertha went on to be one of Sidney's very good school teachers and was the person who invited me to become an honorary member of the local Theta Chapter of Delta Kappa Gamma International, for women educators. This was the first time I had been classed as a teacher, but I accepted the invitation and regarded it as an appropriate designation.

There was Sena Joslin, whose parents, the Hundtofts, I remember well. And Ethel Johns, whose parents were Jens and Sophie Jensen of the Brorson community. It was Ethel's brother Henry whom a few of us kids had teased that Sunday afternoon at Pella by the cemetery, by swiping his straw hat, causing him to wail loudly, and his father, Jens Jensen, came out from the church with fire in his eye, scolding us, saying "Fy, skam dig, fy, skam dig" (fie shame on you). There was also Harry Anderson, the son of Anton Anderson from Crane, the brother of my sister Mame's husband. Eldon Steffans I did not know, but I suspect he was the son of the Steffans at whose home we stayed when we attended one of our first Danish church conventions in North Dakota. Then came refreshments and the social hour. The tables had real tablecloths and fresh flowers on each one; the refreshments were pretty to look at and plentiful. Pella's anniversary was indeed, a nice occasion.

There was the church - on display - yesterday, today and tomorrow. The slide show on Pella's new mission at a Montana Indian Reservation, presented by Dr. Gronli, the pastor, certainly evokes new images of mission, and consequently of growth - of Pella constituents as well as those who live at Rocky Boy Reservation. Time will tell its future role. Language is one of the great binders that hold people together - like rivers and roads and railroads and telephones. The same may be said for religion, when beliefs are shared.

I am glad I learned to love Danish traditions. So many situations call for "Tak" or "Thanks." One of the idiomatic Danish expressions I still regard highly is the custom of saying "Tak for sidst" when two people meet and recall a previous pleasant meeting. It means "Thanks for the last time" (that we were together). I like their "Tak for Mad", heard every time one has partaken of food, and means "Thanks for the food." This is followed immediately by the host or hostess saying "Vel bekom dig" (dig pronounced "die") and meaning "I hope it agrees well with you." The custom, a routine courtesy, is just right in my book. It's not fulsome or effusive, but a gracious acknowledgment - and response. I'm for it. I also like their "Tak og I lige maade" (Thanks and the same to you) and their "Vaere saa god" which means "Please be so kind (or so good) as to ..." or "Please help yourself." Excuse me is also prominent: "Om forladelsie," I'm asking for forgiveness.

As a result of Dad's speculating - dreaming - so many good things happened. The Danes began flocking in. Jim Hendrickson, sister Jo's husband, had come from Racine, Wisconsin with his parents' family. Our home was full of people looking for land for homesteads - which were free - and our table almost always had guests for longer or shorter periods of time. Whatever we had was essentially theirs. We fed them and bedded them; we often supplied a team and buggy to take them where they wanted to go looking for land, and eventually, when they moved here to stay, Dad helped them get started by letting them use his equipment or horses. The only one I ever heard express resentment over this was my brother Carl, who developed a lasting antipathy toward all Danes. He never got over his assumption that Danes were to be avoided at all costs, because they were predatory. What he didn't see was that Mother and Dad asked for whatever they got. In fact, they liked what was happening. The negative feelings seemed to belong to Carl alone.

The first really big event that I ever attended was the Queen Esther Cantata, put on by the Methodist Church Choir - with the assistance of other townspeople - several of them Pella Danes - in April, 1912. It was staged in Betty's Hall, the big second floor room over Bert Betty's saloon, right next to the Yellowstone Merc. According to the program reprinted in *Courage Enough*, of the 16 main players listed, I knew well eleven of them, and among the lesser lights I knew 29 more, and I knew all but one in the final grand triumphal march. They were lawyers, shop keepers, school teachers, wives and children of old time ranchers, and members of the town's photographer's family. There must have been 50-60 who had more than bit parts.

No one who has spent Memorial Day in Sidney will soon forget our Flags of Honor Parade and the special way we honor and commemorate the event and the people who have made it a special day. Each person from Richland County who has served in the armed forces, who has died, has his own flag of remembrance, which is carefully kept under suitable climatic conditions in one of our parks - now Central Park Pavilion. On Decoration Day any flag that has a bearer , and there are always hundreds of them, are paraded, with appropriate music, through the Sidney streets. The flags are large, on staffs, and require strength to carry through the parade route. Hundreds of people line the streets, and remember, and are grateful for their services. When the parade is over, all the flags on standards, together with the official information details on tags attached to each standard, fill the park in an organized upright manner and are available for all to see through the day. The parade is beautiful, the park is beautiful. It is filled with emotion, and it is genuine. Few places have anything to match the occasion. We cherish it.

Citizens, Speculators and Contributors

Billy Combes was one of our earliest entrepreneurs, and from all I know, nobody brought him here. His family consisted of Dicey, his wife, and two daughters, Geneva and Esther. Esther was in my class in high-school. Billy had the reputation of having his finger in a number of important pies, particularly telephones and electricity. I believe it was he who generated the first electricity in Sidney, and he had a shop about a half block from the center of town, on the south side of what is now W. Main Street. We had telephones of sorts before Billy Combes came: We had wires strung up on fence posts and we in the valley were connected to one another, so that if there were any emergency or news of note we could communicate with neighbors who would rush to be of assistance, e.g. in case of fire - prairie fire or other variety.

Billy Combes upgraded our primitive system, and formed a telephone company which connected with the outside world as well as with our immediate neighbors. I believe my sister Christine was one of the earliest employees to be working in the Sidney central telephone office which, incidentally, still exists, immediately west of the Yellowstone Merc on West Main St. When she had night shift I occasionally spent the night with her. The room had a bed in it so we could go to bed, but there were generally interruptions, and she would tell me a little about the fascinating messages that were being transmitted through the office.

Esther Combes
High School
Graduation, 1921

Esther Combes and I were competitors in high-school, both vying for the number 1 spot in our class of 1921. She was awarded the top spot - Valedictorian - and I came in second, the Salutatorian. I am rather certain that briefly I was not a very good loser in that I made mention of the fact that whereas Esther had the top grades, I had more credits than she did. She was diminutive in stature, while I was a great big girl, and it seemed to me I should have been able to come up number one. Esther was the only person I was so openly competitive with.

Esther Combes married Earl Vance, a professional airplane pilot, not from out of our eastern Montana area. Esther took up flying and got her professional commercial pilot's license - one of the first women to have this distinction. She died only a few years ago. Geneva never married and has remained in Sidney. As far as I know she has been adamant in refusing to give out information regarding members of her family. There is no listing of the Combes family in *Courage Enough*. It would have been nice if the family's version of the family had been included among the hundreds of other local citizens. Billy Combes was also our first coroner, mortician and casket merchant, and he displayed his wares on East Main Street, almost directly across the street from Kennoyer's Real Estate Office, now the Eagle Cafe.

Geneva, the older of the two sisters has remained in Sidney and lives in the house formerly owned by the W. K. Adams family. As her hobby she has collected all the newspaper clippings presenting the details of the lives of local citizens. She is widely recognized as a very excellent chronicler of the people and events that have made Sidney what it is, but she always kept her distance from me, even more than Esther did, if that was possible, and I cannot recall any social contact between our families.

In early times Sidney had had to depend on doctors from Glendive, or occasionally, in emergencies, on the doctor at Fort Buford, until it was dismantled in the 1890's. By and large, babies were delivered by midwives, who were the women of the neighborhood who made it their business to help one another, inasmuch as the coming of babies was something one could depend on. Dad, in his story, speaks with pride of the fact that Mother had brought so many babies into the world and had never lost either a mother or a baby.

Then Sidney began to get doctors of its own, who didn't have to be fetched. Dr. R.A. Morrill came in 1906 and Dr. John S. Beagle came in 1907. Each one had devoted and grateful followers, and their descendants are still here today. Our family chose Dr. Beagle, a homeopathically trained doctor, who by training used minimal drugs in his practice, (and therefore could do minimal harm). But I never heard the term homeopathy, as contrasted to allopathy which became the common and accepted form of medical practice, until I was practicing medicine in Philadelphia many years later. I found that Philadelphia was the site of the primary medical college of homeopathy - at least a most prominent site - in the U.S. We regarded Dr. Beagle as far more competent than Dr. Morrill because of the single incident during the scarlet fever epidemic in 1908 when Dr. Morrill failed (he said so himself) to recognize that my 2 year old niece had scarlet fever and not just teething problems. We were not a family that sought medical assistance readily or often. Dad was well known in family circles for his half-joking statement: "One can soon enough die without calling a doctor." But whether we sought Dr. Beagle's help or not, he was definitely "our doctor."

He had come from Minnesota and he practiced here for over 60 years, knowing about our many problems and our quirks, helping whenever he could, delivering babies by the thousands and being a strong, continuing and sustaining force in the field of health. Everyone would agree that he had a very reassuring bedside manner. Until I read *Courage Enough,* our area's book about its people and development, I had never heard that Dr. Beagle had known Earl Varco in Minnesota and had had a part in steering Mr. Varco to Sidney, a contribution of no small magnitude.

Through the years, Dr. Beagle was responsible for attracting to Sidney several other doctors, including surgeons, who served our community well, for longer or shorter periods of time: Dr. Goudy, Dr. Parsons and Dr. Benson were known to me, but there no doubt were others. Through the years, Dr. Magruder was the first of our resident dentists and he served us for years, with his office on the second floor of the bank building.

While the supply of doctors was growing, the physical facilities for care were also expanding and improving. My first awareness of any place caring for sick people was when I learned that the Meadors home, near central Sidney, was being used as a hospital that cared for typhoid fever patients in the teens, and then Mother agreed to care for a couple patients at our home who weren't any longer considered contagious but still needed help during their recuperative period. Then came the building of the first "real hospital" with its school of nursing, all under the aegis of the Deaconess organization. It was a tremendous step forward for the area, and the community was thereby medically well served for many years. Modern medicine was practiced even in this little town.

Then came the era of medical service from one of the "H's": Dr. Hyde and Dr. Hannify, followed by Dr. Harper, all of whom exited the scene about the time I returned to Sidney in 1971.

Dr. Harper made one of the biggest medical-surgical contributions to the area that any medical person had made, until his retirement to Billings in the 70's, after the new hospital complex (nursing home, clinic and hospital proper) had become a reality and we were on our way into the modern medical world. The first "real hospital" is still functioning as our Community Services Building, housing offices for County health services such as Public Health, Welfare, Family Services, Mental Health Day Treatment Center, and classrooms and meeting rooms sponsored by the county. A totally new group of doctors, the Eastern Montana Medical Group, has replaced the old guard.

Under Dr. Beagle's benign assistance, Sidney has always been on the move toward good and then better medical care for all it's citizens. Integrating all levels of economic adequacy has not been an easier task here than it has been elsewhere, but we have probably done as well or better than most places, and the new Community Memorial Hospital, in SW Sidney, opened in 1970, has not only office space for all our doctors, but inpatient care that is modern and competent. There is excellent contact with visiting consultation services, on a regularly scheduled basis, from larger centers such as Billings and Williston, N.D., and also a Fitness Center which serves us year round in its assigned and protected-from-the-weather quarters under the hospital. This latter is the brain child of one of our family practice physicians, Dr. Jimmie Ashcraft. Our general surgeon, Dr. Edward Bergin is currently the President of the Montana Medical Society. We are NOT practicing backwoods medicine.

Dr. Beagles and his wife had two children, Melba and Gordon, and they were part of the local scene. Melba went east to study Medicine, got her M.D. degree and practiced - but she had an early death, and that left Gordon, who was a practicing dentist, to maintain the meaningfulness of the Beagle name in this area. After a long illness due to stroke, Gordon Beagle died in 1989, but the Beagle name still lives on in Sidney, not in the health field but in the real estate field.

I wouldn't claim that Melba Beagle was a powerful influence on me toward anything constructive, but the fault, if any, was probably in my willingness to cooperate in doing whatever she asked me to do. This meant I was a party to a variety of ill-advised activities. Left to myself, doing these things would not have occurred to me, because I never took dangerous living as a way of life, but when Melba said "Come", or "Let's do it" I didn't seem to offer much objection.

Melba used to come to our farm 2 miles north of Sidney and not infrequently in summertime stayed for several days. She was older then I was, but smaller. I really wasn't in her class when it came to thinking of things to do, most of them mischievous. We'd climb high up in the barn loft to watch horses being bred by Dad's stallion whose name was Hercules. Or we would break pigeon eggs we found in our barn, usually in the hay loft.

On one occasion during irrigation season Melba and I went out to the laterals or smaller ditches carrying water to the fields. We wore my aprons over our bare skin - which covered us adequately before and aft. Following the laterals, we eventually came to the culvert under the stage road just north of the school. In those days it was called the Anderson school, but after it was rebuilt following the cyclone in 1922 it was called the Hardy school. Melba, being miniature, as compared with me, floated through the wooden culvert to the opposite side of the road without incident or complication. I wasn't so sure I could do it because I couldn't swim. Melba called me a "fraidy-cat". That cinched it. I couldn't let her say that to me, so I headed for the float through the culvert which was the length of the road width.

My shoulders seemed to be too broad for the culvert, but I hunched myself together as best I could, and thought I could make it. Then my hair, which was in long braids, caught on the splinters on the roof of the wooden culvert, and my nostrils came within a fraction of an inch of being at the water level. I was sure I'd never make it out alive - and then my mind raced to the horrible prospect that they'd never even get me out to bury me, because they wouldn't want to disrupt the traffic on the road in order to break open the wooden culvert to extract me. It was surely the longest minute or two I had ever lived - but as you see, I did make it through, though I kept my vow never to try it again.

On a couple occasions while I was in grade school and we lived on the farm, I was invited to stay over night at the Beagle home. I vividly recall one Sunday dinner with them. There were the five of us around the dining room table and Dr. Beagle was at the head of the table carving and serving all of us. It was my first experience with being served. At our house we passed the food around the table and served ourselves. When my plate was placed before me by the maid, it had on it a green vegetable I was told was dandelion greens, which I had never before tasted. I put a forkful into my mouth, and I wasn't sure I wouldn't vomit. But they stayed down. I decided that since they hadn't come up, the best way to proceed was to get them eaten as quickly as possible, so as to have the ordeal over with. So I cleaned them up in a hurry.

Dr. Beagle obviously was aware of the speed with which I ate the greens and asked for my plate to be passed to him. He filled it up again - of course with more dandelion greens. Even then I kept them down, but I was truly miserable. I learned eventually to eat and even enjoy dandelion greens, but at the time it was hard to keep from hating God because He was the one who made the greens available. You perhaps think I could have left the greens on my plate or refused them, but this was not possible because in refusing them I would be saying that their food was not fit to eat, and in my home we had a strict rule established by my father that we made no comments about the food served. If it was served it was good food that was fit to eat - or it would not have been on the table. Additionally, one never left food on his plate - for manner's sake or for any other reason. What we dished on to our plates was what we ate, because it was a sin to waste food. No, the only thing to do with those dandelion greens was to eat what was served!

I recall also a time while I lived in Salem, Oregon in the 1960's and was invited to come to the Southern Oregon College to give a lecture. When there was a pause for refreshments, the President of the college made his way to me and we chatted momentarily. He asked me where I came from. I told him "Montana." He wanted to know what part of Montana. I said, "Eastern Montana." He wanted to know more and I said I was from a little town near the Dakota line - near the confluence of the Yellowstone and the Missouri Rivers, in the MonDak area. He pushed me to tell him just which town, and I said "Sidney." I thought he was going to put his arms around me. He was simply delighted. Then he told me his sister was Fantine Beagle, Dr. Beagle's wife. I had once heard that her maiden name had been Van Loan, but I never connected that with my host at the college. I certainly had not expected to meet someone who not only had heard of Sidney, but had such tender connections with it.

Still another man came out of Minnesota and settled in Sidney, leaving a permanent mark. In 1906 Augustus Vaux and his wife arrived here, and they remained here until they died. Mr. Vaux was a very tall and spare man - perhaps 6 ft 3 or 4, and always dressed immaculately but conservatively. He, like Mr. Varco, was a merchant, but Mr. Vaux owned and operated a lumber yard. I am quite sure I never heard him speak a word in the many years I had occasion to see him, but his influence was felt in a wide spectrum of activities. I can see him walking through our streets, with his long, measured strides, never seeming to be in a hurry. The Vaux's had only one child, Florence, who went away to school for several years and then she returned to head the Department of Home Economics in the Sidney High-school. She later married Sig Anderson, who was employed at the Yellowstone Merc. as manager, after Mr. Varco was unable by reason of his Parkinson illness to carry out that job.

Mr. Varco, along with other boosters of Sidney worked to have this area separate from Dawson County, of which we were a part. Richland County was established in 1914 by a vote of the people - local option, it was called - and then Sidney won the right to be it's county seat. We no longer had to travel to Glendive to get official as well as other business done. This necessitated providing the physical trappings for being a County Seat, and Mr. Vaux figured in this prominently because he offered his rambling frame building, which had served as office space for his lumber yard, to the county on a rental basis as our first Court House. It served as Court House until a new and more suitable structure was built in 1928. It was long before the time good roads were established, and early in the life of automobiles, so trips to Glendive (50 miles away) were regarded as wasteful of time and money, and we chose to remedy this. We'd have our county government right at home!

Mr. Vaux was Sidney's first mayor. He was such a quiet person it never occurred to me he was one of the important movers and shakers in Sidney. He not only provided lumber for local people to build whatever they desired, but he had several "satellite" lumber yards in small surrounding towns, and he figured out a way of making Sidney's needs pay off for himself. Grain raised in the area needed a market, so he established a system wherein wagons hauled sacked grain to the railroad terminal at MonDak for shipment, and then used his empty wagons to haul lumber back from MonDak to Sidney. He also acquired numerous pieces of land, which was forward-looking both from his own personal standpoint and from Sidney's various developing needs. He had a wonderful eye for the future. He owned and operated a ranch only a couple miles from Sidney, through which Lone Tree Creek wandered, and he made it into a recreation spot for the area; it even included a place for swimming, dining and dancing and other recreational opportunities.

Florence and Sig Anderson had two children - a son Hugh who earned his M.D. and became a urologist living in Great Falls, and a daughter Ruth who married a Mr. Witt. Mr. Vaux probably had his fingers in more pies than any other person in Sidney has had, before or since, but it was all done unobtrusively and with an eye to enhancing Sidney. He was just as good at anticipating and meeting Sidney's needs as he was at furthering his own interests. There's no doubt as of why his efforts worked so well and so constructively.

Mrs. Vaux died in 1944; Mr. Vaux died in 1953 and both of their grandchildren have died during the last decade. When the obituaries of Hugh and Ruth appeared in the SIDNEY HERALD, nothing was mentioned of their part in our local history. I had an urge to write a letter to the editor of the paper filling in some of the "interesting" details I felt were getting lost, but I decided against it. Mr. Vaux, I have heard, developed a circulatory disturbance which necessitated amputation of both his legs some time before his death. The family served Sidney well.

There was another detail which occurred after I left Sidney, having to do with the marriage of Florence Vaux to Sig Anderson. What I know about it is pure here-say, but I regard it as worth mention. As I understand it, Mr. Vaux, together with his son-in-law Sig Anderson, developed their Lone Tree acreage near Sidney, building a dam in Lone Tree creek and impounding the water. The surrounding site became Lone Tree Park, which provided a recreational area for local citizens. (As a child, long before the area was developed, Lone Tree creek area had been the site of picnics and wading and 4th of July or other group outings.) Then eventually the time came when the dam burst, sending water cascading to the Sidney area, doing great damage and costing Sidney much money, both in actual loss and in cleanup. The citizens did not soon or easily forget or forgive Sig Anderson, whom they held as responsible. The pain and the memories were enduring.

My mother was never one to mention resentments, but I recall a visit I made to her here in Sidney a year or two after the flood, and she said that if she ever again had the opportunity to choose, she would prefer to be assaulted by fire rather than water or flood, because fire allows one more time for escape.

One of the phrases I picked up as a child but had no idea of its essential meaning or all the ramifications of life it would lead me to, was "The Minnesota Clique." I am quite sure I never heard my parents use the term, and they certainly never clarified any aspect of it for me. I have asked relatively old timers still living if they ever heard of it, and I get a variety of responses. Some think it was a group of less than savory people from Minnesota who lived in Sidney and exploited the area people. Many never heard of them. My impression when I was a child was that it concerned a group of people from Minnesota who were the elite of Sidney. Not only were they models for the rest of us, but they also regarded themselves as better than the rest of us. It certainly did not include any Danes, who were just ordinary people. They were brighter - smarter - than the rest of us, and often sent their children to college in Minnesota. They knew how to do things, including make money, and one could count on whatever they did to be done well. The Minnesota Clique were people who were better than the average. I wasn't in their class.

I also had the impression that many people I knew were part of the Clique and Sidney was lucky to have them in its population. Whereas I have not found the term mentioned in our local history book, *Courage Enough*, studying the book has given me a clearer idea as to exactly who was in this select crowd, and why it was important to understand their role if one would understand the development and nature of Sidney. I think they provided a unique pattern of success for any nascent city to follow if at all possible, because it provides the ingredients and the how-to - the fine print - that would insure success. If my deductions are correct, it was no wonder Sidney emerged from nothingness to real stature, and very early in the game.

Sidney, it seems, did not just happen to attract or accumulate a lot of people who just happened to be exactly what we needed. The people came from Minnesota, and they knew one another to some extent while they lived in Minnesota. Each one was known to at least another member of the Clique. I have no idea who first put the idea of coming to Sidney into their minds, but from the first, it was one person influencing another person to move here, apparently with a common or shared purpose: there seemed to be a very logical pattern to the inclusion. The town was scarcely in existence, but there seemingly was attributed to it an extraordinary potential for future development. The terrain as well as the water for irrigation were exactly what could mean renewable riches for all who lived here, indefinitely, and the more intelligently and realistically they supplied their input - from the beginning - the better it would be, because there was little about Sidney that had to be discarded. It was like starting with a clean slate. In retrospect, their talents and assets, ready to be used, covered the spectrum of needs of the area.

As far as I know, Earl Varco was the first of the Minnesota Clique to arrive. That took care of supplying the on-going needs for a wide variety of essential but smaller items. But it was Dr. Beagle who steered Mr. Varco here. Dr. Beagle could meet health needs that did not fall into the surgical field. This included delivering babies, an essential service. Then came Mr. Vaux who by training and experience knew lumber, and was ready to help newcomers build or maintain homes, another essential. He also brought along an interest in as wide a field as is implied by the term building, and he foresaw and encouraged these to open shop in Sidney.

Although he had not lived here, Burton Adams, an assessor, had been making sporadic contact with the area for a long time and believed in its future. This was important because when the "Clique" brought in its banking expert, Axel Nelson, along with his wife's relatives, the Gleasons and his brother Art, Burton Adams helped induce his brother Walter K. Adams, another banking man from Minnesota, to come and join the bank. I am not sure whether they were all part of the "Clique," but they certainly would have qualified. W. K. Adams had four grown daughters, Georgia, Mabel, Mary and Winifred, mostly school teachers, who taught in the high-school and acted as role and fashion models to many young students. They also went to college - back in Minnesota where they came from - and Mabel became the History instructor at Sidney High School and taught me whatever I learned about the world that had been. Whenever I watched her walk, I was impressed with how well she held her tummy in - but it also had the unfortunate consequence of making her rear end protrude. It was not easy to come to terms with both these facts. But they always seemed to me to be so sure of themselves, and I saw that as a real asset.

No one has ever made me privy to information that would explain how the Minnesota Clique originated. The best guess I have is that it started with Burton K. Adams who was an assessor and therefore understood land values. I understand he had been here several times before he moved here and as an assessor he surely must have known about and recognized the economic potential of the developing irrigation system to the area. He no doubt shared his impressions and assessment with acquaintances in Minnesota and remained a catalyst, encouraging "the right people" to consider investing their lives in a place that was comparable to a high quality mineral find - and they did. They would be getting in on the ground floor.

It was quite a while after Sidney was well started that Burton K. Adams also moved here. His interests were more in the social field; his background in assessing brought him in contact with the old time settlers here, and definitely would have provided input that was helpful to the new citizens in running successful businesses, and he could give valuable information to the bankers. He served as one of Sidney's postmasters. His daughter, Lorena, married into the Rounce family and became a social worker - I believe Sidney's first - residing in Portland, Oregon for many years. Her younger brother Walter was one of my high-school classmates. I vaguely remember Dad being unhappy because the First National Bank, which Axel Nelson headed, went under, and Dad had bought shares in it. It was reorganized under a new name, Richland National Bank; it still is the largest bank in Sidney. Axel Nelson's picture hangs prominently on its walls.

As the world, including Sidney, moved inexorably away from horses and their power, and toward automobiles and mechanical power, car dealerships and repair shops began to appear. This was another blow to Dad, in that he bought, sold and raised horses as one of his sources of income. He did not give up easily, but continued in it until after W.W.I, when they were selling horses for dog food. It helps account for Dad's continuing sense of poverty, even after a period of seeming affluence. The Minnesota Clique got in on the new industry, bringing in first Axel Nelson's brother Art, who was first into hardware and then into cars, and then they brought in Roy Rounce from Minnesota, who built Gem City Motor Co., which still exists and has the entire line of General Motors cars, sales and service

The Valley Hardware Store was established and run, first by Art Nelson, Axel Nelson's brother, one of the Minnesota Clique, and then by Jack Johnson, another Minnesota Clique member, and it continued in business from 1907 until the 1970's, when it's site became our present Village Square Mall. The Johnson Hardware store, owned by two Johnson brothers who were not related to Jack Johnson of Valley Hardware, and who were not part of the Minnesota Clique, also carried furniture. It was an early competitor of The Valley Hardware, and it seems still to be going strong despite newer chain store competition, such as Coast to Coast. I believe that in the early days the Valley Hardware Co. sold such large items as were carried by John Deere Company under it's own name.

I always believed Turner Brothers were part of the Minnesota Clique. Their drug store was right next to the Bank, but I have come to doubt my conclusion even though they seemed to be qualified as leaders. They were Jack, Hank and Jim, until Hank died in the 1918 flu epidemic. Their drug store not only had a soda fountain but a commodious ice cream parlor which made it a popular gathering place for youth. It went out of business shortly after my return to Sidney in 1971, and Johnson Hardware took over that space.

The Topp family, whom Dad induced to locate here, provided Sidney with a good creamery, which served Sidney for many years, and served the local farmers who brought their milk and cream there to be processed. The last remnant of that family in Sidney is the FLOWER TOPP, a florist shop. The Snowflake Bakery supplied us for years with good white bread and delicious goodies. We had a jewelry store where they not only sold diamonds but repaired clocks and watches, owned and operated by William Orr.

No one should fail to visit Sidney's current jewelry stores, successors to Mr. Orr's shop, even though the one I especially wish to call your attention to is not even listed in the phone book. It is located in the same block as the MonDak Heritage Center and Mr. Sissel, the proprietor, will give a personal tour of his establishment. He has a most interesting collection of agates - the best I have ever seen; I think many are of museum quality. He also repairs clocks. When you go there be sure not to be in a hurry. Gary Morken owns and operates the Stockhill Jewelry Store here, a well stocked, modern emporium suitable to Sidney's real needs.

Among children, magical thinking is not uncommon. They are not aware of the many details which have worked together to bring about the present scenario. I am sure I thought the railroad came to Sidney in 1914 because it decided this should happen. But in reading our history in *Courage Enough*, it is clear that many people participated in getting the desired event to happen, and that people in the Minnesota Clique tended to be active and effective. The establishment of Richland County, the coming of the railroad to Sidney, and the building of the Holly Sugar Company plant appeared to be only a few of the successful projects they supported.

One of the patterns of the Clique that was especially helpful in getting things done was teamwork. They pooled their funds, establishing companies in which they held shares, so that capital was available for building over and beyond what any single individual could have raised, and borrowing money for new ventures was minimized. They also had money to loan, and this also increased their "take," or at least it increased good will in the community. Projects which were regarded as worthwhile to undertake tended to have the backing of not only the individuals, but of the establishments they represented or involved.

The religious affiliation of the people in the "Clique" seemed to be important enough so that I could say with reasonable assurance, "That person was not part of the Clique." I cannot place a single Methodist or Danish Lutheran in the "Clique," but it abounded primarily with Congregationalists, and Catholics came next. In fact it was "Clique" members who started the People's Congregational Church. The "real" members of the "Clique" tended to stay and spend their lives here, with their heirs maintaining the businesses even into the third generation. The only one in our family who clearly felt put-down by them was my sister Christine, who refused to continue in the newly opened high-school after a couple weeks because she felt discriminated against because her wardrobe did not measure up to their standards.

SIDNEY GROWS

It was taken for granted that Sidney was going to become a town. Buildings made their appearance, and in 1907, the same year we started moving into the big house, Sidney had its formal birthday. It had been named Sidney, at the suggestion of Hymie Otis, for a boy, Sidney Walters, the son of a man who had lived here briefly. On October 22, 1888, six months before my parents came to Sidney, it was designated as a U.S. postal station, so that the stage could drop off and pick up mail. In November, 1889, Montana became a state; at the turn of the century the old stone Methodist church, together with the parsonage were built on the site that was to become Sidney.

Eddie Kenoyer's Land Office

In 1911, Edgar Kenoyer set up a real estate office in the building currently housing the Eagle Cafe, right in the center of town. He had laid out the streets - on paper - and had the town platted. Lots were sold and the town was booming. After the town was platted, the Post Office address no longer shifted from place to place depending on who was willing to do the necessary job, and one could count on it to be at a designated location.

Eddie Kenoyer is the person directly responsible for the planning and the original platting of Sidney. He bought the square mile site and made it conform to the location of the original stage road, which lay in a general north-south direction as it ambled from Glendive to the south, to Fairview, the Montana - North Dakota Line. But that road did not agree with the points of the compass, so Sidney's streets were laid out slightly askew. I never heard of anybody objecting to this. When the time came to make Sidney larger by several specific "additions", the decision was made to make these abide by the points of the compass - rather than by the old stage road, so, on a map, the transition from the original townsite to the addition involves a bit of a bump, and the same is true for the added streets themselves. In some instances the jog, which could not accommodate a residence, would turn into the locus of a park.

The east-west roads were streets and the north-south roads were avenues. In the early days all the streets were called by the names of "important" local personages, thus giving them status and honor - their day in the limelight - but this lasted for only a brief time and then the decision was made to scratch all the names and give each street and avenue a number, and divide the entire townsite into north, south, east and west segments. There was great disparity between the size of the 4 segments, and this fact was determined by the prominence of the already established road and its usage. Main St., running from the hill-country on the west to the railroad station on the eastern-most border, marked the separation into north and south Sidney, while Central Ave., the original stage road, running north and south, separated Sidney into east and west segments. Thus, there are northeast, northwest, southeast and southwest sections in Sidney.

In the midtown area the streets are especially wide, but at no point are the streets narrow or cramped. Every block has its designated alley, thus making access to the back part of the lot, as well as for absence of garbage clutter on the street. Originally Kenoyer sold the lots with the written - and signed - stipulation that no alcoholic drink would be sold on the premises, but both Bert Betty and Andy Mercer, our two saloon keepers, surmounted that hurdle by utilizing the alley behind their lot for the place of actual sale of the drinks. It has always been that where there's a will there's a way. But Eddie Kenoyer tried, and tried sincerely, to make Sidney an alcohol-free town.

Except for the establishment of the People's Congregational Church, the Clique had only indirect influence on the cultural development of Sidney. Probably the highlight of all our cultural history was the presentation of the Queen Esther Cantata in 1912. Year after year we listened to some new series of lectures by men or women who were visiting guests for a one-night stand on the Chautauqua circuit, or some other circuit. I recall being greatly enamored of one man - a Welshman - whose picture I kept on my mirror for a year or more, and I felt sure he was greatly influencing my life for the better.

Mostly we brought in outside talent, but Sidney has always been one to appreciate and even to develop local artists, particularly in music. There was the Quilling family, Walter and Amy, who from the early years have sung freely, and whose daughter Brenda achieved international recognition for her voice. Her father's sister, Jennie Quilling, was my high-school classmate and we sang together in the Girls' Glee Club.

Sidney has had many excellent teachers both of voice and of instrumental music who were attached to our school system or to our churches, as well as operating as individuals. Olin Strom and Howard Hunke were two I know who taught instrumental music in our schools for many years and made their mark for music; and Don Gratz, who also taught, endeared himself to thousands of people who were helped by his singing. Each one enhanced appreciation of music and stimulated learning for great numbers of people in the entire area during many years. In the past year our new Central Park Pavilion for the Performing Arts has been named in honor of Milton Anderson, a local longtime attorney and talented pianist, who entertained and inspired our people with his generous gift of musical talent.

There has been no dearth of talent in the broad field of arts and letters. The MonDak Historical and Arts Society, the predecessor of our present MonDak Heritage Center, has been part of Sidney's life for decades. Appreciation, preservation and development of talent has long been its goal. Some from this area have made a name for themselves in painting, notably J.K. (Ken) Ralston, (who follows after the tradition of Charlie Russell and his Indian and Western art), and who is usually thought of as coming from Billings, but who certainly also belongs to Sidney. His sister, Bess Ralston, was our county superintendent of schools during my youth, and his wife, Willow Arthaud, was one of my classmates in high-school. Our MonDak Heritage Center gives attention and space to local artists as well as others.

The area abounds with people who write: history, fiction, poetry and all sorts of books to delight the spirit. It is time well spent to get acquainted with them. We also claim another distinction in the education - cultural field: Barry Petersen, son of Holger Peterson, who bought our farm in 1917, and nephew of our cherished next-door neighbor, Astrid Petersen, has long been CBS Radio's overseas reporter and coordinator. He has served for years in England and Russia and now in

Japan, and may be heard by turning on the radio. He does Sidney proud.

It may be easy or it may be difficult for radio stations in our land to keep the music coming into our homes reasonably free of obviously objectionable smut. Our radio station, which was one of the earliest on the air in this part of the world, did a commendable job of connecting us with the outside world, until suddenly and without warning, it went off the air and to our conservation has remained off since then. I have no slightest comprehension as to what needs to be done to correct this eventuation, but it is a grave injury to the entire region.

Ira Alling, an early resident of Sidney, built the big, nice looking home he and his family occupied just west of the Yellowstone Merc. They lived in it a few years and then on July 21, 1914, Sidney purchased the land on which the house was built, from Mr. Alling for $3000 and the house had to be moved away to enable Sidney to begin plans and construction of it's Court House, since it was the County seat of the new Richland County. On June 11, 1914, Sidney had leased from Augustus Vaux the rambling frame building, which had served as the business office of Mr. Vaux's Valley Lumber Yard for several years, to become the temporary - and first - Court House of Richland county. That frame building was used as courthouse from June 11, 1914 to May 4, 1928 when construction of the permanent brick courthouse was completed and dedication of the building took place.

The new Court House was a distinguished looking building (though not particularly well planned with regard to function) but still serves our needs. About 1988 it was modified to eliminate the huge windows on all its 4 sides (which had been the appropriate way for windows to be made in past times), miniaturizing them, but not destroying the overall attractive appearance of the structure. Meanwhile, the heat-loss from such vast window space could well help put the county into bankruptcy if maintained indefinitely. I have speculated that the designer of the building could have believed - along with my parents, as they set sail for Sidney from Denmark - that Sidney's climate would be comparable to the climate of Paris, France - given it's latitude and longitude. That belief doesn't conform with the facts!

The Court House together with the County Jail and the County Library now occupy the entire block and form an attractive as well as functional unit right in the center of the city. It was a well thought out purchase of land the new county made from Mr. Alling, and was obtained at a very reasonable price. Fred Hurst, our longtime "city cop" was the brother of Mrs. Ira Alling.

Not the least of Mr. Alling's claim to importance in my book was the fact that he and Dad were born on the same day, and they often exchanged birthday greetings. I never knew what Mr. Alling's occupation or business was but I assumed he did important work because he was always so immaculately dressed. He was not like Dad, who never dressed up for anybody but God, when he went to Church on Sundays. I learned quite recently that the business of Mr. Alling, as well as that of his sons later, was probably money - investment and managing.

Mother and Mrs. Alling also were friends by reason of their both belonging to the W.C.T.U. (Women's Christian Temperance Union). Despite this, she got on my rejection list on an occasion when she came to visit Mother on the farm. On this particular occasion I was riding a saddle draped over a sawhorse out in the front yard, and Mrs. Alling commented that I was a tomboy. I felt the disdain which was in her voice so I informed her that I WAS NOT A TOMBOY! I'm sure I did not convince her, but I was smart enough to let the matter drop. The Allings had three sons; John, Bob, and Frank. They were part of the fabric of Sidney, and some may still remain, though I never hear of them. When the Court House was built, the big noble Alling residence was moved south of town. There it became the first County Poor House; then the County Pest House, and finally a flower shop. Now, I understand it has been moved again, but it never again became the grand mansion it was originally.

The recent (1990) acquisition of Thogersen Motors by Gem City Motors was occasioned by Ed "Honest Ed" Thogersen's retirement from his Oldsmobile sales and service establishment. He sold me my last car, a used Oldsmobile Cutlass in 1976, and I trust I'll not be needing another. Ed's father, Jim (Jens) Thogersen, was one of Sidney's true entrepreneurs: he harvested enough ice from the Yellowstone river to supply the whole of Sidney for a year, stored the ice and delivered it as needed throughout the town. This was, of course, before the days of electricity and refrigerators, and it was a basic service, as is all refrigeration. Ed told me not long before he retired that his father's ice business had one of the biggest payrolls in the area, and added significantly to the economic well being of the whole community. Both men were part of the Danish community. The Danes had tended to remain in the agribusiness sector. I feel sure I am correct in believing that refrigeration has saved more babies from dying, particularly from the scourge of "summer complaint" than the efforts of all doctors combined. The eventual arrival of refrigeration in practically every home in our land has been a great boon to everyone, and it's development was not unlike the construction of roads. The steps we have gone through to get where we are now!

In the early years before horses had gone out of style, one of the important shops in Sidney was the "Cy and Joe Harness Shop," built on what is now N. Central Avenue. They constructed and mended harnesses for the area horses. Cy Bock's family still has representatives here, and John Bock is a very skilled craftsman - not in leather but in wood.

The Ed Easley's lived on the same street, it seems to me, as the Beagles and the Combes families, and they were important for many reasons. Mr. Easley was an animal doctor - a Veterinarian - and we called him "Doc", not Doctor, because he did not treat people. He belonged to the horse era and was accorded appropriate status. I never saw him when his cheek did not stick out because of the big chew of tobacco he always had in his mouth. His wife was Mother's friend because both of them belonged to the W.C.T.U., but she interested me because she always was so nicely dressed, and seemed so pleasant. Their daughter Eva (pronounced Evva) was my classmate both in elementary and in high school, and once during grade school she invited me to stay over night. I felt more comfortable at the Easleys than I did staying over night at the Beagles, because the Easley's let me dish my own food on to my plate, and did not serve me dandelion greens.

Ira Bendon's livery stable, which must have covered a block or more in the northwest segment of Sidney, served a helpful purpose for several years. It was now possible for people to drive to Sidney and stay for several days, because we had a hotel for horses. One did not have to worry about the horses behavior or remember to feed or water them. It added significantly to comfortable communications and to the ease of doing business.

For a long time there had been provisions for people staying over night, but not horses. There was the small building on the southwest side of town, run by the Al Kelch's, I believe; Billy and May Ball had a small hotel and finally the 3-story Valley Hotel near the city center where even the stages stopped to let people off and take on passengers. The Valley Hotel had a dining room, which made life very simple and easy. Eventually came better roads, and the construction of the Lalonde Hotel and dining room by the Lalonde family, which is still an important asset to Sidney. Mr. Lalonde was State Road Commissioner and had lived through all the painful steps in road building know-how. The Valley Hotel eventually was razed to be replaced by Kentucky Fried Chicken Emporium with parking space for customers.

Mixed up in my memory of the special event of the Queen Esther Cantata in 1912 was that it was spring, and the roads just couldn't have been worse; horses were mired up to their bellies in the muck, and were scarcely able to lift one foot past the other. It was also my first real awareness of the horribleness of our scarce roads. When it had been possible to remain at home and still have no sense of missing out on anything, roads were not all-important.

I remember the roads gradually changing. The road trails were gone before I came, so I was used to real roads, with barbed wire fences on either side, from my very beginning. Eventually, these became almost impossible to use because of the clay muck which prevailed, and whenever it rained, the horses could scarcely navigate because they were in thick gumbo-like muck up to their bellies. When we began trying to improve them, the roads were made with a high center crown sloping to each side, to encourage the water to run off, but they gave one the feeling of being perched on top of it and it would be easy to slide off. It didn't drain very well there because the soil had too much clay in it. Later, deep open or covered drain ditches were scooped out along side of the main or well-traveled roads, into which excess water could slowly drain, but the open drain ditches were a constant hazard. Next, we got macadamized roads, with an almost impervious surface of gravel and oil. Years later came miles of asphalt, or paved roads, properly engineered for curves, and passing lanes, which made us feel we were part of the outside world and no longer hinterland. Good, safe roads enabled people to travel under their own steam, and helped bring about the demise of trains, not because it was better, but because it was more convenient travel. It also brought pollution.

Sidney's Golden Rule Store was replaced by Penney's Store; the Princess Theater built next to the SIDNEY HERALD building was replaced by the Center Theater, which was close by our hotel, The Lalonde, and that seemed a logical move even to me. The Russell Miller Milling Co., which made Occident Flour from our grain, went out of business and Holly Sugar Co. which makes sugar from our sugar beets took its place in the world of commerce and of real significance as a source of jobs. The railroad, which is at the east end of Main Street is still right where it used to be, and still runs trains. It carries no passengers, but it does carry freight. Long ago, we had to make peace with the idea that the railroad was pretty much on the way out. This was a sad day for us, and I suspect it marked the beginning of the fading of our dream of Sidney going places and doing things, because it aggravated our isolation.

It has seemed to me that when the federal government stopped subsidizing railways for carrying mail, and opted for air mail service, we all lost something very important. The small and isolated areas no longer counted. Most of us don't need our letters carried faster than the trains would do the job, and plane mail service has hastened the day of the twenty-nine cent postage stamp. The Northern Pacific Railroad - which was our southern route across Montana - and the Great Northern Railroad, our northern route - have been replaced by Montana Rail Link to the south, and Burlington Northern to the north. I just suspect it was all in the name of progress, and that it was all a big mistake - at least for rural people including us here in Sidney. We have nothing but private transportation now - no bus service, no taxis, no railway passenger service, and a precariously funded plane service - to anywhere. It would be hard to assure greater isolation. It reminds me of a human body having suffered a lack of blood supply to one of its parts by an embolism or clot. The unimpaired flow of life blood is essential to health, whether it is a body or territory or a nation.

It might seem we have everything we need, but that isn't quite true. We are incredibly isolated. Once we had both passenger train service and bus service, but for many years we have had neither. We have managed with subsidies to hang on to plane service once daily - to Billings - but fares are truly outrageous as compared with emplaning from Williston, N.D. There is no way of getting to Williston, North Dakota, a distance of about 50 miles, or to Glendive, Montana about 60 miles away, both of which are mainline railway centers, other than by private conveyance. We take good paved roads for granted now. There is just no way of going any place except with private transportation.

We have lots of TV channels available to us both through regular TV as well as Cable TV so we do not lack for information or entertainment. Our recently expanded library has access to endless information, but what we really need is better access to public transportation. Railway facilities would serve us better than air because at best the cost of flying is prohibitive for all but the wealthy.

There was another family that came to our area too late to be considered early settlers or entrepreneurs, but they touched my life in a variety of ways through many years, even to the present moment, so I shall include them. I refer to the Brown family. My first contact with one of the Browns was when I first started taking music lessons from Mrs. Isham, who was one of the Browns. I have no doubt I was not a very good or dedicated pupil, and I finally got Mother to let me stop taking lessons. I really think it was a waste of her money, and my memory tells me she charged only fifty cents for a lesson lasting an hour. Her son, Carlos, was one of my high-school classmates. I'm quite sure she brought me farther than brother Niels had on the pedal organ, but it wasn't as much fun.

My second Brown contact was in high-school, when "the Browns of Savage" sent their daughters Vera and Blanche to high school and Vera and I were classmates. I always felt closer to Blanche than to her older sister, and Blanche and I sang together in the high-school glee club and girls sextette. When I returned to Sidney - from San Diego - for Sidney's first high-school reunion, in the 60's, who should be there but Blanche. She also was living in San Diego! Our coming together again was the beginning of a most pleasant relationship, and lasted until I retired and returned to Sidney permanently in 1971. I visited them when I drove from Sidney to San Diego in the 70's. She had married Harry Shierson, a school psychologist from Lodge Grass, Montana, not long after her graduation from Sidney High-school.

Then Blanche developed Alzheimer's Disease, and life became a veritable nightmare for both Blanche and her husband. It was necessary to have her cared for in an institution rather than at home, and Harry died, from overload of work and caring, and Blanche lived on for a few more years, with little of her normal and regular personality left. She finally died this past year. It will be a wonderful step forward when the cause of Alzheimer's is discovered and progress made towards cure or amelioration. Alzheimers was never heard of when I worked in hospitals with mental patients. This might lead one to think it is a disease of modern times, but that would be hard for me to believe. To me it seems more likely that this malady was just part of the diagnostic group labeled "senile psychosis" or "senile dementia."

I also came in contact with the Browns in the Sidney public schools where Elmer B. Brown was the head janitor. He had had some injury to his nervous system which left him with a one-sided flaccid (not spastic) paralysis, but he never seemed to let his disability interfere with whatever needed to be done. I recall he was always good about getting the cooperation of kids. He had several children - all very intelligent and attractive with social orientation.

My last contact with the Browns was after my return to Sidney in retirement. Here were Mary and Ed Hardy. Ed Hardy was the son of Loren Hardy and his wife, who was a Brown. Mary was the manager of Sidney's Sears Catalog store outlet, and Ed was ever in demand as the best repair man in our area. Everything had to make complete sense to Ed, and everything had to be strictly honest for both Ed and Mary. We got along famously and became friends. I was a part of the Study Club that Mary nursed along and that gave me pleasure for years. There were always new ideas cooking. Then Ed became ill and died of a circulatory disturbance, but only after he had had to have both is legs amputated. Intermittent claudication was what it was called, but I had known only one such prior patient, Augustus Vaux.

Mary, remaining, and as loaded with energy-to-be-expended as ever, has helped me have a vicarious family in the tales she tells of her son Mark, his wife Rita and their three children, who are always good for a chuckle or a nod of approval, and serve to help keep me in touch with the world as it is. I am aware of my good fortune in this turn of events because not everyone at soon ninety has this opportunity. After Ed died Mary began to take courses in car upkeep, in tax reporting and quilt making, among others, because she had learned from Ed that everything has to make sense. She probably knew this even before she met him. Mary's occasional blow by blow sharing of her life with her family, and her 2 dogs and cats calls to my mind it would be nice if she started writing - or recording - these treasures that surely will be lost - and soon - if they are not captured promptly. I have called them "I books" or "I stories". They are too precious to not share with others.

Mary is also from an old time family, the Irish O'Connors from nearby Sioux Pass area, who certainly must have been here when the Andersons came in 1889. My brother Carl used to ride for horses with Mary's uncle, Dan O'Connor, so in a sense, whether with the Browns or the O'Connors, we are almost kinfolk.

Mrs. Arthur Cherry was also a Brown. I think I might recognize her if I saw her, with her dark hair streaked with gray and parted near the middle, but my only actual memory of that family was that her son, Earl Cherry, was one of the first of Sidney's casualties in W.W. I. He was tall, handsome and well liked. The very first of Sidney's casualties was George Ahlquist, who had been a commissioned officer before he was 17. Now we have almost finished the Persian Gulf War. One wonders how many wars there will have to be before we stop fighting. It wouldn't be hard for me to picture human nature prevailing as long as there are people. Some of us are bound to have very strange ideas about what is right and what is wrong! But I'm grateful to the Browns for many things and many people.

Sidney had several very important, once in a lifetime days: the day in June, 1912 when the railroad came to Sidney; the day in 1914 when the voters approved our separation from Dawson County, making us Richland County, followed by the acceptance of Sidney as the County seat. Then came the construction through Sidney between the Northern and Southern main line railroads; (Glendive, Sidney, Snowden). This meant we were connected to the whole world! Sidney had big celebrations on both occasions, and we felt liberated from bondage. We were on our way. Nothing could stop us now.

It was the same sort of feeling we got on that first Armistice Day in 1918 at the end of W.W.I when we believed we had become liberated from any further or future threat of war. The celebration was wild and genuine. The only thing that dampened the Armistice Day celebration, November 11, 1918, was the memory of the terrible Flu epidemic of 1918 which had killed so many of our citizens. Mother, along with many, many other women, had taken care of dozens of friends and relatives, with their families, who had fallen ill from the Flu. Fortunately she did not get sick herself. She was essentially gone from home for several weeks, and it was the first time I had tried being chief-cook-and-bottle-washer in my home. I was just past 14.

The establishing of Richland County out of part of Dawson County, and Sidney becoming the County Seat of the new Richland County was one of the important details we integrated on May 16, 1914. We finally had our own County Court House, our own county officials, and we no longer had to go to Glendive for all the details needing attention. Now we hear rumblings of future fusing of counties to cut down cost. Even what we do gets recycled.

I can remember the night in 1914 when the election returns were coming in on creating Richland County. Everyone who could, came to town (Sidney) to be there to hear the latest election returns. Of course we were in town with the rest, for Dad had been a most eager supporter. Finally the clock in the saloon on the east side of the street said it was time for the closing of the two saloons - one on the east side of the main street and one on the west side. The roller curtains, which pulled up from the bottom, rather than down from the top, were about 3/4 closed, shutting out seeing from the street who was inside, but from the street one could still see the clock on the wall above the curtain. It said midnight. The next thing we saw was the hands of someone, obviously standing on a chair, reaching up and carefully moving the hands of the clock back to 10 - so it meant there were still 2 hours left before closing time, for celebrating. And a big celebration it was, because Dawson lost, and Richland, the name of the new county, won. None of us went home until success was assured.

Sidney seemed to keep right on growing: streets were paved; and the old "speed limit 10 miles per hour" sign that greeted us as we came into town from the north was removed. Cars were everywhere. Fairview, 12 miles to the North, for a while attempted to compete with Sidney: It put up it's own sign as one entered Fairview - "Speed Limit 9 miles per hour."

Sidney seemed to retaliate by failing to assign space in the Sidney Herald for Fairview news. Rivalry was not especially pretty - or even helpful.

Our Daily Lives

But let us go to more mundane events. Every year there was the search for fruit - berries - to provide us with jelly for the year. There were choke cherries early in the season, wild plums later, and buffalo berries after the first frost. We tended to know where to look for them from our experiences last year, but there were always surprises. I still think these jellies top all other jellies. Delicious! Mouth watering! In our back yard we grew currant and gooseberry bushes which provided excellent jelly, but they couldn't compete with the wild berries for flavor.

Our family was no doubt more rigid and impatient with - or intolerant of - pure fun than most families, but we were never long-faced or even pious. Communication was encouraged, and evenings were spent playing dominos, playing flinch, playing whatever else did not involve regular decks of cards; other families danced and had basket socials and were members of the baseball club group, in the summertime watching their kids perform at the school play. In the winters, or later, they would be cheering them on at inter-school events. Sports have always been a rallying point that enlivened ordinary lives. But when one has conversation, reading and work, he truly has a good start on a good life, roads or no roads. Probably had there been deep hostilities this could have been a different story. No doubt the absence of TV was one of our great blessings.

News was ever very important in our family. Everybody read. The old - original - *SATURDAY EVENING POST* had been our main source of world contact for years. But let us take a look at some of the events that filled our lives and kept them from becoming monotonous. I'll never forget the sinking of the Titanic and how everyone's mind was riveted to every news item available in the paper. It was the prime subject of conversation for what seemed like weeks. Reporting the events occurring in Desert Storm had some of the same quality. The discovery of the Titanic's buried grave and presentation of the relics on TV a few years ago certainly brought back memories of its proud maiden voyage.

It was through Dad I first experienced - or even heard of - radios. He had purchased a little "crystal set", about 3x4 inches in size, with a lump of stone, the "crystal" attached to its flat metal surface, and another movable part, "the cat whisker", which must be manipulated so as to touch the crystal. If one was lucky, the cat whisker evoked some sound when it touched certain points on the crystal. As I recall, an electrical cord connected the "set", to the wall socket. Dad was fascinated by the hour trying to touch just the right spots on the crystal so some sound would emerge. My memory says it was probably about 1921 or 1922, and we lived in Oregon. Had radio brought only music, Dad would never have accepted it. He was all for NEWS.

We tended to have lots of special "times," rather than special days. Branding time was lots of work, came every year, and could not be done haphazardly because it had to be done according to the specifications of the law. These laws have been in existence since Montana's earliest days, 1887, I believe, and was especially helpful to settlers who let their stock roam freely in this land without fences. If the animal strayed and got into the hands of someone who wanted to sell it for a bit of cold cash, it had to be accompanied by a legal bill of sale signed by the owner of the brand, or it was confiscated and a check sent to the brand owner. It certainly discouraged thievery. Calves and colts were branded when they were very young - and the brand grew or stretched with them as they grew, so it was a permanent identification mark.

Dad was one of the early owners of a brand. He was delighted when he was assigned the P Diamond Brand - a diamond with the letter P atop the diamond, like this  Every one in the family was very conscious - and proud - of belonging to the P Diamond family. A fee is paid every few years to keep it registered in Helena and in force. We would hate very much to lose title to the brand, or to let it go by default through negligence to pay the fee. P Diamond means the Peter Anderson clan, and nobody else. This is our unique and distinctive emblem, like some cultures have the coat of arms of the various families. *I am a P Diamond person*, in perpetuity. With a P Diamond brand, the product is distinctively mine (ours). It belongs to our immediate family. After Dad died, my brother Carl, our cowboy, took over the brand and maintained it for years, even though he really no longer had any need for it. Then when Carl died, his daughter Mary took it over. When she left this area and her husband was in service, it was transferred to my great nephew, LeRoy Anderson, who lives in Montana and still maintains it.

On horses, the brand is smaller than on cattle, and is placed on the right shoulder. It is only about 5 inches from top to bottom on a full grown animal. Our cattle were branded on the right side and the brand is about 8-10 inches from top to bottom. The P Diamond brand is displayed at our MonDak Heritage Center, among many other local brands. The size of the brand, its location on the animal as well as the precise pattern or design of the brand are all stipulated by the state registry of brands maintained in Helena.

Branding time was a yearly event. Every rancher aimed to have all of his stock branded. There was a roundup of all the new stock born since last year's branding time, together with any strays that had been missed at the previous branding. They were kept in corrals until, one at a time they were brought to the branding area. There each one was lassoed, tripped - or felled - by a couple of additional ropes to front and hind legs, then immobilized by someone sitting on their head while the white-hot branding iron, from the adjacent coals, was applied to their hide in the proper position until it would make a permanent burn scar. Naturally there was a lot of bellowing and protesting by the animal, but this shortly subsided and the job was done for good. No animal could carry more than a single brand.

Branding time at the P Diamond

Along with the branding, other necessary surgical procedures - castrating and dehorning - were carried out at the same time. The testicles removed were facetiously called "Rocky Mountain Oysters," which reminds me of Carl refusing to eat scallops with me in Philadelphia because he thought they were testicles.

Branding and roundup time remind me that in 1989, Montana's Centennial year, we had a variety of special events throughout the state to commemorate this special year. The most spectacular of all was "The Great Montana Centennial Cattle Drive," which was a real success and did Montana proud. It started Sept. 4, 1989, and took a week to cover the distance of 60 miles, beginning at Roundup and ending at Billings. Involved were 3337 horses, 2812 cattle, many of which were Texas longhorns. 2397 people participated in the roundup, 105 of whom were drovers and 79 were wranglers. There were 208 covered wagons. Every conceivable hurdle to success had been carefully prepared for, such as use of weed-free hay, so no new pests would be introduced along the way. Feed and water for all the animals was provided, along with food for all these people, and nightly entertainment on the way. Most of the Drive was off road and on the prairie. There were no casualties, and medical services were provided by doctors who gave their services for the privilege of being able to participate. Several calves were born en route. If animals could not finish the trip, they were hauled by truck.

All the cattle in the Great Montana Centennial Cattle Drive had their own registered brand, and also an additional brand, an M over 89, as a mark of distinction which made their hides of special value. As they entered Billings, their destination, they were herded to livestock auction blocks for sale and slaughter, if that was the wish of the owner, or they were detoured for return to their regular home. The proceeds from the auction of the cattle went into a "rural community foundation" to assist rural Montana youth to go to college.

In addition to newspaper coverage not only throughout the state and beyond, there was media attention on TV networks, and it was shown in many foreign lands. Books about the events of that week were published in living color, and are a splendid memento of the occasion. The books created by the Billings Gazette are excellent and in 1990 are still available. The audiovisual cassettes also put out by the Billings Gazette are a delight. Oscar Anderson, my nephew, shared both the book and the TV cassettes with us twice, and they reinforced the pleasure. It made the whole event come alive. It was truly a celebration.

Sidney participated directly in The Great Montana Centennial Cattle Drive through three of our physicians riding along and giving medical assistance as needed throughout the entire Drive. They were Dr. Edward Bergin, Dr. Gregory Faul, and Dr. Raymond St. John. I talked with Dr. Bergin about the experiences, and he said it was the experience of a lifetime, and he would not have missed it for anything. They rode their horses on the trail but could be quickly summoned by car whenever any medical emergencies arose.

The great cattle drives from Texas to Montana with its lush prairie grass had been going on for years, mostly prior to statehood. The cattle were present everywhere when my family arrived in 1889, but disappeared shortly thereafter. There were no fences to get in the way, but this also changed by the turn of the century. The cattle were considered a menace for anything planted, and for children going to school afoot or horseback, through trampling.

Fire danger was a constant threat to the settlers in our grass-laden prairies. A stroke of lightning or an inadvertent moment of carelessness with a match or a cigarette could set off a blaze that would sweep miles of prairie grass in just no time. Thank goodness it was before the days of packaged cigarettes, and even rolling our own from Bull Durham sacks was not common. High winds - of which we have plenty - fan small flames into big conflagrations. People had their own methods of protecting themselves and their log homes: they plowed furrows around and around whatever they wanted to protect - their homes, their outbuildings, their pastures, their fields. The breadth of the plowing varied from a couple of furrows to several feet, to impede the sweep of the fire as it relates to the pattern of the prevailing winds. Whenever there was a fire it was a community problem and community project for putting out the fire. Families kept barrels of rain water on hand, ready to douse any blaze. If the fire was big, everyone got into the act. The women soaked the brown gunnysacks they had accumulated and stored against such an event, in the barrels of water. Someone would rush the wet sacks from the barrels to the men on the "fighting line", and they would pound or beat the fire line with the wet sacks, putting out the flames in the grass.

If things seemed to be getting out of hand, there was another tactic they used. A calf or mid sized steer would be quickly killed, and ropes would be tied to fore and hind legs. Two men on horses grabbed the ends of the ropes and with each men riding in his assigned lane, they dragged the animal carcass rapidly over the smoldering fire, squelching it as they went. It was like stomping out the fire, only more effective. I never heard of anyone getting seriously hurt in these "volunteer fireman" activities, but they performed valiantly and served everyone well. I haven't seen fire-furrows for many years.

It must have been sometime around 1910 that I can recall there being terrible forest fires in western Montana. Even here in eastern Montana, the skies were darkened for days with smoke so thick we had to light our kerosene lamps in order to see, even in midday. Mostly, our skies were clear and the air was fresh and unsullied by any foreign particles. Settlers lived so far apart that the burning of coal from the coal seam probably on one's own land - summer and winter - made no appreciable impact on the quality of the air. Then horses faded away and were replaced by cars, but while the population was so sparse, cars scarcely accounted for pollution. No mountain barriers and plenty of wind also help.

Another important event, threshing time came every fall. A great big threshing machine, perhaps 30 - 40 feet long, pulled into our yard after it had threshed for this and that neighbor. It parked just northwest of the barn and the threshing job began. The rigs varied in size. I don't know how big the crew that came to our farm was, but my memory says it was bigger than 10 or 11 men. Some ran the threshing machine, others hauled in from the fields the bundles of grain which had been shocked, or placed in shocks, made up of 6-8 tied bundles standing upright against one another after cutting. The bundles would dry out well and be maximally protected from rain, from cutting or harvesting time to threshing time, a matter of days or weeks.

The bundles of grain that had been tied by the binder with hemp binder twine were hauled from the fields in big hay-wagons or hay-racks and tossed into the threshing machine with pitchforks, bundle by bundle, where they would be mechanically separated in the threshing rig's separator - the kernels of wheat, or other grain, from the chaff and straw - and the straw was then blown out onto the ground through a great long pipe about 6-8 inches in diameter and 15-25 ft long. Depending on the size of the rig, the straw blown out gradually formed the strawstack which served the farm and farm animals in a variety of ways through the year: for shelter by burrowing, for windbreak, for animal bedding; for fiber, and it also filled many a bed mattress to sleep on.

The kernels of grain, cleaned of chaff, a fibrous covering, were poured in a steady stream from the bowels of the threshing machine through a big spout in its side, into triple-box wagons or into big light brown "gunny sacks" that required no bins, and were hauled either to the elevators in town, for storage and railroad shipment, or were stored in our own granaries until time for selling, through the grain dealers, or were used for planting one's own fields in the spring, or feeding one's own stock.

Threshing time might last a few days or even a couple weeks, depending on the cooperation of the weather. If it rained, everything came to a screeching halt. Close neighbors who were part of the crew went home, and those who couldn't go home stayed and the family having the threshing done accommodated them. Feeding the threshing crew was a huge job, and the appetites the men brought along with them were phenomenal. It was good that farmers depended on their own larders to feed the crews and not the grocery store. It is no wonder Fall, which was threshing time, was an important time in all farm homes. The same outfit tended to do the threshing job year after year, because there were not many threshing rigs to choose between, and the job of moving the rigs from one farm to another was cumbersome and time consuming. The farmers tended to be signed up by the owners of the rigs from year to year or months ahead, so whole localities could all be done in logical progression. Grain ripening took place simultaneously all over, and to have had to backtrack would be too costly, so it was always a planned undertaking.

Progress, however, was all pervasive, even in farming. Binders, the machines that farmers owned and used for harvesting grain when I was a child, began to be replaced, by the time I left Sidney in 1921, by new machines that were bigger, more complex and more efficient, as well as vastly more expensive. They were called Combines because they combined a variety of functions not previously incorporated in one machine and one operation. The former "binder" cut the grain stem a couple inches above the ground, arranged and directed the stalks into like-sized bundles, bound and tied the bundles with hemp twine, and eased them out of the binder-carrier onto the ground, as the binder, pulled by two horses, moved along. Helpers gathered the bundles from the ground, stacked them upright in shocks with the cut ends of the stalks down to the ground. In due time the bundles would be transported to the threshing rig for separation of the kernels from the chaff and straw, and final deposit of the grain into storage bins was accomplished.

The new machines - the combines - cost an arm and a leg, but they eliminated several steps, namely, bundling, binding, shocking, carting, hauling, and separating or threshing. One medium-sized machine now did it all. No threshing machine was needed. The cutting was made just below the heads and terminal kernels thus eliminating most of the straw, and chaff was blown away as the combine moved along in the field, making it one continuous process from start to finish. It eliminated the possibility of wind, rain or hail damage while the bundles stood on the ground in shocks, or of damage from mold or mildew if dry weather did not prevail. It was threshed right in the combine, in the field, as it was cut, and the kernels deposited into wagons or trucks moving along beside the combine, for storage or sale. It could be accomplished by fewer workers, more quickly, and with minimal loss as occurred when it rained or with high winds. Each farmer owned (or was paying for) his own equipment to do the job. The old time threshing machines have completely disappeared except for nostalgic exhibition purposes. Farming equipment is truly remarkable.

The sickle was probably one of the earliest machines for harvesting grass or grain with long stalks. It took only one arm to accomplish its mission, and consisted of a short wooden handle attached to a curved metal blade, whose shape correlated with the sweep of the person's arm as he walked along felling his crop. This was followed by the scythe, which took two arms to make it work, so the handle, still made of wood, was much longer and was attached at its far end to a much longer and heavier blade which was also curved in harmony with the swing of the person manipulating it so as to bring it in forcible contact with the stems to be cut.

Eventually the blade was incorporated into a blade pulled by horses, and the blades were made of numerous pieces of sharpened steel, like teeth, attached to the basic bar, which moved from side to side rapidly, depending on the speed of the horses. There were machines which did only cutting, and let the cut grass lay in the path of the machine. Then came the era of the binder, which operated with the use of horse power, but added another dimension, namely bundling together a given quantity of stalks and tieing them together with twine before the bundles were permitted to drop to the ground as the binder moved along in the field.

Then came the era of the combine, which was horse propelled in the beginning, but evolved to being equipped with a gasoline engine which accomplished all the duties formerly carried out by people or by horses. Threshing machines which were used in my day had donkey engines about the size of a modern automobile, that provided the propelling force for movement of the rig on the highway, from one farm to another, and supplied the power for threshing, separating the grain from the chaff, pouring the grain into some vehicle and blowing the straw into a pile. The energy to do these jobs came from steam. It was a steam engine that led the procession and had to be liberally supplied with water for conversion to steam throughout the entire operation. So it really was a 3-unit operation - the water being hauled to the engine in a tank. The only place where human energy was necessary was in pitching the bundles of grain into the maw of the threshing machine.

The imagination and ingenuity of the ones who fashioned the machines is almost beyond belief. Now that threshing machines are obsolete, one sees them only in shows that keep alive the memories, and entertain with their nostalgic reproduction of events of times long past.

The machines doing the combining have grown to be such monsters that custom combining has become the rule because to own one's combining machine is cost prohibitive. In the beginning, they cut a swath of grain 6 ft. wide and they were pulled by 2-4 horses. Now the swath is up to 30 feet wide and they are power-driven with such wide swaths and horsepower, it is no wonder farms need to encompass thousands of acres to make them pay. The small sized farm has largely disappeared. In 1991, Georgia and Oscar Petersen enabled me to watch them combine their fields of barley. They were spared any hail or drought damage, and they estimate their dryland farm operations will average over 60 bushels per acre.

All the fields both in the valley and in the hills tended to raise winter wheat or spring wheat, depending on the time of planting as well as on the nature of the wheat, barley, and oats planted; but now in the valley it is sugar beets, some safflower, canola and beans that are planted. We are in the hard wheat belt where I understand we grow the finest quality that exists.

The Montana Extension Department of the State University at Bozeman has a research station right outside Sidney, the Northern Plains Soil and Water Research Center, which is in the lead role as teacher in planting and production. They are constantly busy experimenting with crops, developing new varieties with greater suitability to soil, weed and weather conditions, and keeping farmers abreast of progress in all aspects of agriculture. The Montana University Extension Service is helpful in the dissemination of information.

I'm sure someone in the area also raises flax, but I haven't seen such a field in years and years. The beautiful light blue fields in bloom in spring were a sight to behold, against the dark green stems and leaves, waving and undulating in the wind. I'd recognize a field of flax immediately any place I saw it. No doubt this shift stems from the demise of interest in linen as a fabric. We also raise corn and soy beans, and recently we are playing with asparagus, which grows wild here, but is not yet a cash crop.

During the years I was away from Sidney, 1921 to 1971, the vegetation on the prairie changed. It was always a short, native prairie grass; now it has become a darker, raggedy-looking plant that gives a rougher more uneven appearance, but I am told it resists drought better than native grass, and provides more dependable fodder for animals. Personally, I don't appreciate the change. I like the old-style grass better, but then, I'm not an agri-expert, nor am I consulted! I have asked if loss of the native prairie grass is responsible for the fact I don't see or hear meadowlarks around any more - with the big black V on their bright yellow breasts, and their glorious song which, incidentally has changed too - because nesting on the ground as they do could be hampered by the new grasses. I am told I don't see the meadowlark because these birds don't like towns and people-congestion, and that the birds are still here. Additionally, I wear hearing aids!

Dad's dream of irrigation wrought a miracle - but only for the valley. The surrounding hills still have to rely exclusively on the bounty of the skies. As far back as I can remember, Sidney has thought it was special and was going to do great things. The irrigation project encouraged us to believe it was inevitable. I cannot say for sure how far we have come, but being here has been mostly a pleasant experience.

Stock raising has been a profitable enterprise in the non-irrigated dryland acres, and when we have adequate moisture they raise good grain crops in the hill country too. The year of 1988 was my first experience in a truly desert climate. When the grass doesn't even sprout, it's really dry. It makes people worry lest there could be a repeat performance next year, or the next. Being in the Dust Bowl is no fun.

There are many things I always think of as typical Montana. There are the distinct seasons, the big unpolluted sky, the rolling prairie with its grasses, boundless space, the wind - often too much of it, the welcome absence of congestion, and the presence of quiet; the beauty of the night sky when one is away from lighted towns, the shimmering Northern Lights, and the beautiful Milky Way. Of course I have learned that this is not the Montana that people in Western Montana know, but to me this, not the mountains, is Montana. Living here in the MonDak is truly pleasant. But we had the dust bowl years and the dirty 30's and then 1988 - when we had Washington D.C. weather with heat and humidity both very high by the first of June. Then we had no rain or other precipitation for months on end, and the normally lovely prairies were ugly and grayish and never greened at all. Everything turned dark and pessimistic.

In 1989, I am happy to say it decided to rain a little again. Nothing seems quite as important as that fact. There are other details that are becoming everyday experiences once again, and every time I go outside I marvel once again at the beauty of the sky. It is like it was when I was young - big and clear, delicate blue, filled with tumbling cumulus clouds racing all over with the wind, never the same for a single minute. The sky and its beauty are too vast to overlook. When I was a kid lying on the prairie grass, perhaps listening to the song of a meadowlark keeping watch lest I disturb her nest nearby, I would keep busy watching the sky endlessly. The clouds were my movies, and they kept me busy making up stories to match them as they rolled all over the sky, ever changing.

Montana is called Big Sky, but that must have been named by someone who never lived in eastern Montana in the MonDak. It is not only Big Sky, but it is the unbelievable, matchless constantly changing beauty of the sky. That beautiful sky seems to be back! I don't know whether it is here to stay, or only for a while - but I cherish it every moment I am outside. Come to think of it, I believe it really wasn't here the years I have been back home since 1971. I hadn't missed it until it came back! - and then I realize how important it always was as I was growing up. It was one of the most distinctive features of this area. I cannot tell you how glad I am to see it again. The clear blue sky, with cumulus clouds ranging from dark blue-black, through all shades of blue, gray and white, plus some pink and gold not just at sunset or sunrise. And the cloud formations! They take my breath away. I love it.

Dad loved Sidney and its land - the valley - the MonDak - with a passion that never diminished until the day of his death. We were brought up to love it like we loved our lives.

Oil is also here as part of the Williston Basin formation, but Dad died before he heard of its presence. It might bring economic well-being too, but there is a big difference - to me - in the type of reward the two systems - agriculture vs. oil - bring to a region. Agriculture is a total citizenry involvement. It is a way of life. Oil brings in strangers and "foreigners" - no matter what their nationality - and they leave again without ever having been slightly integrated into our society. The same may be said for tree fellers. Farmers are family people, having been here for generations. They belong. They are a part of everything that happens. Oil people come in from elsewhere, bringing crews and hiring locals. The well is drilled and it produces or it doesn't. They take their leave and go on to the next drilling site. The oil may keep flowing, but the oil people are gone. They never become part of us. There is only temporary sweat and worry. The oil people's place in the community is always that of strangers and sort of foreign bodies that are only partially tolerated. Locals are glad enough to have oil money flowing through the community's veins, but there is a sort of sigh of relief when they are gone. Oil people are here today and gone tomorrow. Farmers don't come and go - they are part of us forever.

On Oct. 22, 1987, I went to our beautiful MonDak Heritage Center almost in the middle of town, to see their new display commemorating the 100th anniversary of the establishment of the Sidney Postal Service. As usual, I was richly rewarded for going to the Center. Not only was the display excellent, but there were some special surprises for me. There was a letter giving the dates and terms of all the Post Masters Sidney has had in its 100 years of existence, a picture of Hymie Otis, the man who brought my family from Glendive to Sidney that Easter Sunday 1889. I had heard of Hymie Otis farther back than I can remember, but I had never seen a picture of him before. I can visualize Mother and him singing Danish and English hymns as they lumbered and bounced along the prairie trail. The other surprise was a picture of Sidney Walters, the boy for whom Sidney was named, quite a while after he and his family had moved away from here. I had never seen a picture of either of them before.

The biggest surprise was that Sidney Walters' picture was taken - soon 40 years ago - with Beverly Anderson Peterson, my great niece, sister Mame's granddaughter. Bev's 8th grade teacher in Sidney, Jo Rogers, a Delta Kappa Gamma member, had had her students write a letter to Sidney Walters, to help bring him up to date on what had happened to his namesake and invite him to visit. The best letter was chosen and sent to Mr. Walters. It was Bev's letter. Mr. Walters responded graciously, and actually came to Sidney to visit the town - and Bev. I had never before heard that Mr. Walters had been Sidney's guest, or that Bev had helped bring this about. There was a snapshot picture of them together.

Jo Rogers was a teacher of singular quality who taught two generations of Sidney students, being an excellent role model in basic self esteem and in being ever oneself. I can well recall the last time I saw her: We were attending a Delta Kappa Gamma luncheon, with our seats all around a long, narrow table. We had stood for the Collect, and in the process of reseating ourselves, Jo and the rest of us had leaned toward the center of the table, where there was a row of lighted candles. Jo's hair, which had been sprayed with hair spray, caught fire. The rush to be helpful came from everywhere. The fire was put out promptly, but it was still a nasty burn. Shortly after that Jo left Montana, not to return.

I learned a couple other things at our Heritage Center: Eddie Kenoyer had bought the land he platted as Sidney for $3.50 per acre in 1904, and since he had bought a square mile, or 640 acres, - or section - he paid $2,240 for the townsite. It was Kenoyer's purchase of this tract of land and chiefly his platting it and offering lots for sale, that constituted the actual beginning of Sidney, for that made it an actual, factual locus and no longer a moveable spot centered in a name and a stage stop. So Sidney and I are the same age - born in 1904. I also learned that Kenoyer was Sidney's 4th Postmaster and he took his office in 1904. That might account for the fact he knew everybody, and that included me. I recall being highly pleased because he always called me by my full name: Camilla May. If one is going to be a real-estate salesman, it is helpful if he has an outgoing personality.

It was Mary Mercer, whose family, the Hammes, were early settlers considerably to the west of Sidney, who has been largely responsible for our displays, and who always seems to have her hand in helping those who visit the MonDak Heritage Center to be more conscious of our heritage. Her husband, Russell Mercer, now retired, is the son of Sidney's earliest saloon keeper, Andy Mercer.

It was the fact that Sidney had an official name and Mother could send a letter to that address and it was received by Uncle Charlie in due time, that enabled the plans to move to Sidney to become concrete and attainable. It must have been very soon after the U. S. Government established the postal stop that the correspondence between Mother in Denmark and Uncle Charlie in the MonDak began. The postal service was established on October 22, 1888, and my family was here on April 22, 1889 - scarcely six months later - which seems to me phenomenal speed.

Just as there were early settlers for the MonDak as a whole, also there were early entrepreneurs, who settled the newborn town of Sidney. Noting which ones of the people who came made the smaller and which made the larger contributions to the development of Sidney has been an interesting exploration. They all dovetailed and intertwined and left their various and combined footprints. Only a few have been mentioned.

Sidney had moved from the point of having not much of anything besides space, wind and weather, to having doctors and even a hospital where babies are born and surgery is routinely done. Whether Mr. Varco who established the Yellowstone Merc was more important to Sidney than was Dr. Beagle, or Rev. Damskov, leaves room for argument.

As long as I can remember, Sidney took for granted that it was important, and therefore it was never comprehensible to us that we never seemed to get recognition from the people in the western half of the state. It was almost as though we did not exist. They seemed to have a blind spot toward us. This was brought home to me with great force when I spent several months in Helena in the 1970's lobbying the legislators and

Governor Tom Judge, to extend mental health services - a mental hospital - to Eastern Montana, so we wouldn't have to travel over 500 miles to Warm Springs any time we needed psychiatric care. Transportation being what it is, it seemed to me so obvious that we needed a mental hospital at our Eastern end of the state. It should not have been hard to see that.

One legislator told me he couldn't see why Montana should not be cut off just east of Billings, and the eastern end of the state be annexed to North Dakota. A visitor at a legislative hearing said to me after I had made an impassioned plea for recognition of our needs, that she had never before really thought about Eastern Montana at all. Montana had always meant to her the western end of the state. Well, Sidney never saw it that way. We counted too.

Sidney reminds me of people. We all take our worth for granted. We expect concern and respect. In fact, we feel entitled to it. Yet, as I retrace my own patterns I am surprised at how easy it was to devalue "kid sisters" and growing boys. What we are or what we do or think is always special. And that's the way it always was with Sidney.

Sidney - Now on the Map

So many things about Sidney have been done right. Only today I had a conversation with a man born here but who has been away from Sidney for several years. As he returns he is full of appreciation for the magnificent planning job that was done by the early Sidneyites in arranging a townsite that was excellent as a little town, and yet was completely suitable for development into a larger city. It has a central well-positioned business district including both governmental and municipal services and private enterprise. It has a simple and rational street-naming pattern. Available parking space provided by its wide downtown streets is suitable to the transportation needs and there are no parking meters. There is room to grow in all directions, yet the town is not thereby fragmented, but has merely been extended. Churches of many denominations are situated primarily with regard to traffic movement patterns and available parking area. Educational facilities are realistically placed, and numerous parks for a variety of designated functions are scattered throughout the town.

The railroad is at the edge of town rather than in the center and does not impede traffic or constitute a hazard. Livestock accommodations for marketing are related to the railroad, as they should be, as are the grain elevators and the sugar factory. The County fairgrounds are just beyond the west edge of town, with ample parking space. To the west of the fairgrounds is the Country Club, with very good golf links, and our airport which is ever being upgraded to provide better and better service. Practically in city center, the library, the jail, and Court House make a pleasant appearing unit, and it all makes for an attractive city. All of the townsite is watered by 2 large water towers that store the water from wells. Whereas there has been no problem with contamination, there has been a problem with the hardness of the water and iron discoloration. Sidney's long battle with this problem seems finally to have been successful.

The Lower Yellowstone River Irrigation Project, under the U. S. Department of the Interior, has been a godsend not only to the farmers but to the entire community. It has set our area apart and given the MonDak an economic stability that is to be envied. It surely changed so many things. Intake, the point of diversion of the water, has become a tourist attraction as well as the source of water. One of the items of interest one finds there during certain seasons is the Paddlefish, reputed to be the oldest big animal surviving in North America - a "prehistoric" fish. Aside from its home base in the Mississippi River Drainage Basin, the Yellowstone and Missouri Rivers, chiefly Montana and North Dakota, they say, it is to be found only in the Yangtze River drainage area of China. It is a huge essentially scaleless fish, with a long paddle-shaped snout, living chiefly on plankton. It was known here early in the 1900's but I never heard of it until long after I returned to Sidney in 1971. It may attain a weight of more than 100 lbs. and a length of over 10 ft.

Just as Puxatawny, Pennsylvania is notorious for its Groundhog, so Sidney has made claim to the Paddlefish as its mascot. Since 1963 it has been fair game for all anglers. It is plentiful around Intake, between Sidney and Glendive, during spring months, and only this year have I braved eating this ugly looking monster. The texture of the baked fish reminds me of eating scallops, and I regard it as delicious. There is considerable fat directly under the rather tough outer covering, and extending into the texture of the fish muscle itself, but aside from providing most of the oil for its own preparation, I cannot see that it is a deterrent to classifying it as a dietary treat.

It was one of our local citizens, Gary Torgerson, who helped put the Paddlefish - "Peter and Paula Paddlefish" - into our local repertoire of important dates. May 1st each year is Sidney's "Paddlefish Day." The abundance and quality of the paddlefish eggs in the Yellowstone Valley, from Intake to Glendive, has generated plans to market commercial-grade paddlefish caviar through a firm in Glendive. Current news says the fish is to be federally assessed as to its suitability for placement on the endangered species list.

We started here in the MonDak having Prairie Methodists and Roman Catholics. We now have forty-one churches listed for Richland County in the *Sidney Herald Leader*. Twenty-two are in Sidney, nineteen are elsewhere in the county. In Sidney there are four Lutheran churches and one Roman Catholic church. Among the officials of our local government we have both a Mormon (Latter Day Saints - L.D.S.) and a member of the Baha'i faith. We have a well used Masonic Temple, but we have no Moslem, Greek Orthodox, or Jewish houses of worship.

In the field of education we moved from a one-room log school beside the stage road near Ridgelawn, staffed by Professor E.C. Hicks, to having Sidney's own school - a frame building that was rather soon destroyed by fire - to a single brick building for both elementary and high-school departments under the benevolent guidance of very tall and skinny Principal and Superintendent, Joe Nevins. He truly bridged the gap between the old times and the new and led us into modern educational goals and practices. The Nevins family still lives here.

The growth in enrollment, facilities and faculty has kept pace with Sidney's growth and with the times. Whereas Montana students have always ranked high on performance scores as compared with other states, Richland County students also compare favorably with those from other Montana counties, but we have not exactly set the world on fire, although we manage to hold our own. Faculty and Principals tend to remain in these positions of leadership for long periods of time, and this seems to have been helpful in maintaining a high level of "quality students." Our sports teams constantly rank at or near the top, statewide, and team loyalty and civic pride abound.

We are affiliated with and make use of Dawson Community College, attending its classes both in Glendive and in Sidney, and many get into regular colleges through this route who might not otherwise do so. We are even getting set to try out distance-learning with the aid of TV arising out of Miles City Community College, coordinated with Dawson Community College in Glendive, specifically to assist in the area of Health Care and supplying nursing school graduates for our area. Many of our high-school graduates complete college in Montana's University system, or go to college in schools throughout the nation. Our area prides itself on being education oriented. Computer skills increasingly are taken for granted. We now have two large elementary schools, a Middle or Junior High-school, and a large Senior high-school, which is the home of the Eagles, repetitive sports champions.

Schools have grown in size and number but many basic problems have never been solved, such as "How does one choose a good candidate for a teacher?" or what is more important - order or self expression? Naturally, we suffer along with the rest of the nation from the effects of the Spock-generation of permissiveness with its tiresome assertiveness and poor manners - the me-generation. This doesn't mean we have produced a group of youngsters we might as well scratch - even though sometimes one would like to - but I am reasonably sure the pendulum will continue to swing in a variety of directions, and out will come lots of fine young men and women who will make their constructive contributions to society in the future, as their predecessors have done in the past. Perhaps we have lost or wasted time, but even that is questionable. Everything takes time, and one of our unreported but perennial problems is being in a hurry. Speedy progress is probably not only painful but questionable.

I may have firm convictions that educational priorities should be establishment of order (authority), simplicity (to make learning possible), and a benevolent atmosphere (to ensure a sense of security), but I am neither an accepted dictator nor a trusted consultant, and probably each teacher will spend valuable time discovering what are his or her priorities. People play out or enact whatever their priorities dictate, but correct law and the dictatorial powers of established Religion often have determining power over what schools teach.

Sidney is a nice place to live and bring up kids, or for retirement, but it is short on diversified industry with significant payroll. There are limited sources of income, especially if one doesn't own land. But there is room for imaginative and patient entrepreneurs.

Herds of cattle used to graze freely - from here to eternity, almost - and then we got fences - barbed wire fences - and now there is essentially no free grazing. Animals roaming free on highways are a hazard and therefore not tolerated; so we have laws which put a stop to freedom to munch the grass along the roads. Animals must be contained.

We take more and more service for granted. Then along comes news of planet Earth's many environmental threats from so many sources, and one cannot help but wonder if we have not been far too smart for our own good. Our water system (wells) has been so adequate we haven't had to curtail sprinkling even in this recent drought period, but the water is so hard, water softeners are almost a necessity of life for Sidney residents. There are also wells that provide soft water, but these are not part of the city system. Nature is seldom easy to decipher through foresight. The unpaved roads are a clay muck, while the fields beside the roads grow lush crops of grain. Figure that out!

Changes were made so gradually that they were often scarcely noticed. Our town was laid out providing not only nice wide streets but with practical alleys, so we can place our garbage in dumpsters in the alley rather than having it on our sidewalks, and for years we have had garbage disposal trucks to haul it away from the alley, just as they do in big cities. We also have a landfill to dispose of the garbage "properly." Now in 1991 it seems there has arisen a question concerning the suitability of our land (soil) for a sanitary landfill.

The new high school, southwest of town, with adequate parking space not only for students and faculty, but for visitors as well, serves the public in many ways: as a voting place, as a community center for a variety of activities both on the playground and in its Gym. Sidney has an outdoor swimming pool where swimming meets are held, an armory, and lots and lots of churches of many varieties. Pella is now big and beautiful and stands at West Main and Lincoln Ave. on our block! The old People's Congregational Church was replaced by a new one. The old building years ago became a designated "historical site", but in 1989 it was badly gutted by fire and has been razed. Until then it was used by senior citizens as a place for socializing. I'll never forget the part it played, through its impressive first baccalaureate service for nursing students graduating and getting their R.N., in my own decision to become an M.D.

It took us a long time to learn to play. Some of us haven't learned yet, but fortunately, we're in the minority. The schools with their sports and athletic programs have led the way and the media all help to keep us reminded. By the time I graduated from High-school in 1921, girls were being included in the sports program, but girls were at a disadvantage for a very long time. I played basketball but we played no games with girls outside our own school. It is hard to keep track of how many sports are now part of the school or other scenes: baseball, basketball, football, volleyball, ice hockey, swimming, wrestling, horse shoes, bronc riding and barrel racing are at least a beginning.

We are seriously learning to live with and make use of computers. Those who don't, will find a big segment of their population as "Illiterate" in this area as if they had not learned to read and write.

We had essentially no winter sports. Skating was almost nonexistent because there were no lakes or ponds, but occasionally now there is an indoor rink to be used, and roller skating attracts many, as does bowling and tennis. Sports help to generate and maintain local loyalty better than anything I know. It also helps to bring about multigenerational involvements that might otherwise get totally lost.

The present emphasis on achieving and maintaining health through regular attention to nutrition, fiber, and exercise is all in the right direction. Sometimes it looks as though our longevity has increased beyond our capacity to make good use of it, but again, everything takes time, not only to accomplish something, but to find out what we actually accomplished and what effect it had. The need for rest, relaxation and exercise still needs better understanding, but is worth exploring.

We had an inflatable dome for a hockey rink, sponsored by the kids' hockey club, which provided shelter from the winter blasts until a big wind storm in 1995 demolished it. We still need a single central place for holding large crowds of people who wish to attend a variety of functions, other than the high school gym and the middle school auditorium. Edgar Kenoyer had lots of good foresight. He planned well. Finding one's way is not a difficult problem. There is also a superbly helpful and well-used Senior Citizen's bus five days a week, but transportation remains our most pressing problem, whether in the city or outside.

We also have our school drug - including alcohol - problem, although it seemed to me that for too many years it was well swept under the carpet through the mistaken notion that if we didn't dignify it by noticing it, it would go away. Or perhaps we believed our kids simply would not be a party to such an involvement. But we were wrong, because drugs do matter, in a negative way, no matter how we got into using them. It will be a long time before we will have finished paying for this unfortunate aberration in our value system. Many promising people will have been lost permanently before the song will have played itself out, and society as a whole moves toward greater sanity.

There really is no shortcut to constructive, safe, dependable self esteem. We'd no doubt have it in the palm of our hands if we only didn't have to try out the short cuts. Some experiments are not lethal; they just waste precious time. Making use of drugs, however, is comparable to cutting off one's head by the centimeter. And there is little possibility of putting it all together again. It may not be as spectacular as the Humpty Dumpty story, but just as final. It will, I believe, be impossible to erase it fully. Occasionally, there is a lucky person but I wouldn't plan to tempt fates. In the process of trying to raise our self esteem we seem to be losing our chance for everything worthwhile. Any addictive drug is very dangerous.

I am well aware that our home was a tee-total home. We never had alcohol there; it was never served on any occasion, and not drinking was literally part of our religion. Mother and Dad agreed 100% on this. I can still remember Dad telling me about the unfortunate people of China who freely used opium. It would never have occurred to him to think that Americans might ever have drug problems, and be as unfortunate as those people in China! I'm grateful to Dad and Mother for their strong feelings.

For retired people, and for the developmentally disabled who have "graduated" to independent but sheltered living, a large, attractive separate unit, Crestwood Inn, is on the same block as the Community Services building, (the old Sidney Hospital). It provides a practical link between illness and health, particularly for the elderly, with it's three story apartment building, spacious dining room and meeting room fostering socializing, and available nursing monitoring night and day.

Holly Sugar factory near the railway converts our excellent quality sugar beets to sugar and is one of our largest employers in the area, along with Community Memorial Hospital - Richland Homes, and the Eastern Montana Medical Clinic complex. The educational system and local governmental offices provide other major contributors to our economic health and well being.

When I left here in 1921 Sidney had its own creamery, but it disappeared many years ago. We have many large chain stores - like hardware and drug stores, Penney's, I.G.A., and John Deere farm equipment - but mostly, the stores represent individual enterprises; like the Homestead, the Toggery, Modern Lady and the Yellowstone Merc. We have a Chamber of Commerce, modern motels, a hotel, and it is entirely possible to live here without lacking for anything. The big names in cars are well represented. In fact, we could survive without going elsewhere. We are primarily farmers and ranchers, both of the dry land and the irrigated lan d variety. We used to see field after field of beautiful fragrant alfalfa growing or cut for hay. Now we see beautiful lush green fields of sugar beets.

One of the delights of Sidney is the abundance of trees of many varieties literally lining many of its streets, which are clean and broad. But Sidney seems to be moving from the days when it took “going places” for granted, through a rather long period of feeling sorry for itself and somewhat picked on, to a new stage, wherein we are attempting to make some realistic appraisals, and setting the stage for moves that may propel us in the direction we think we want to go. The oil boom bubble that burst several years ago, and that kept things busy and humming for a decade or more, has been a sobering event. Little oil drilling has gone on for several years, but there still are wells pumping oil throughout much of Richland County.

The Chamber of Commerce has built suitable office space right beside the highway coming into town from Glendive, and has been an active force for progress, but greater emphasis is being placed on GRCEDC (Greater Richland County Economic Development Corporation) for making more significant studies of problems and potential actions than on any other official or unofficial organization. It is doing less singing in the dark. It seems to be a respected and trusted agency. More recently it's name has been changed to Richland Development and it gives promise of being viable and functional.

One of the interesting buildings in Sidney is the MonDak Heritage Center, at 120 3rd Avenue Southeast; it is only a few years old. It is an outstanding building both in design and size and the museum features are delightful and functional. I have not seen any small local museums that compare with it, anywhere. It is a wonderful addition to Sidney, and one of the special things about it is that it’s offerings to the public are constantly being redone, with new arrangements, new emphasis and new exhibits. Yet it has successfully preserved the historical highlights and flavor of the area, past and present. It promises to be adequate into the foreseeable future. Charley Evanson, who was an indefatigable worker in its development, died this past year and will be sorely missed. Don Rees, the son of our late talented artist, Charlotte Rees Gabisch, was the prime mover, when design was under consideration. He has been the

President of the MonDak Historical Society, and has made a splendid contribution, as have Board members, and many others who are given the title of Docents, or helpers. It is always a pleasure to be there. The old passes into the shadow; we miss it and try to preserve and recall it, but we move along and things are still very good.

The *Sidney Herald*, a weekly paper from its beginning under publisher Harry Ketcham, now comes out twice a week as the *Sidney Herald Leader*, and publishers have changed many times. I think I note policy changes and I find clip-able items in almost every issue. Surrounding areas get greater attention than they used to, and local people are more often presented for interesting things they have been doing, than who attended whose party, but they totally missed reporting a recent severe hail storm - the first in over 20 years - that affected every Sidney citizen.

Our streets are in fairly good repair, and the roads in and out of Sidney - in every direction - have never been so good. But that is almost the only good thing we can say about our transportation system, which carries the trade and commerce - the life blood - of our area. We lost our passenger train service years ago, but we still have freight service. We lost the bus service we had to Plentywood as well as to Glendive, and the only thing that we still have, other than private conveyance, to any place in the world is a plane a day to and from Billings, and a plane a day to and from Bismarck, which few average citizens can afford. No big-line buses come through here. This would appear to be unforgivable negligence on the part of the state as a whole. No body can afford to have circulation cut off to any of its parts, or the body as a whole suffers. To permit it to happen is gross ignorance of the facts of life.

People who started where my parents did, would scarcely be able to recognize Sidney today. The many changes were unpredictable. There were quite a number of nationalities present at that time: German, Irish, French, Americans and we were the first Danes as well as Scandinavians. Perhaps there were some other ethnic groups I did not know about. Today we have a sizeable Mexican population as well as a German-Russian group who came when workers in the beet fields were first in demand. Some Mexicans still come and go, but many have opted to remain and become a permanent part of our scene - attending our schools, graduating from high-school and running for office in local government - and not infrequently winning the election. Those who call themselves German Russians are not truly Russian but were Germans living in Russia for numbers of years and displaced by the Revolution.

Now we have most of western Europe represented - some having come directly from France and Italy, as well as from Holland, Germany, England, Norway and Denmark. There are few from lands that have had little kinship with us and our ways, or who shy away from harsh climates. We are not exactly in the sun-belt. We are a relatively homogeneous society. One of our doctors is from Tunisia. I often see Native Americans in our grocery stores, but I know of none who lives here. There are many half breed - or less - Indians who have already melded with Whites, whom we do not recognize as Indians. As far as I know, we have no one who claims to be Aryan, and I know of no White Supremacist members. I can't recall seeing any Afro-Americans or Orientals.

I have just learned that just beyond Richland County's borders there is an active White Supremacist movement group. I said to myself "At least Richland County had sense enough to reject it;" and in so-saying, I fell into the same pit with them: feeling smugly superior for something for which I could take no credit. We're all very human; all wanting to be "better than;" all tarred with the same stick - our felt need for pride, or vanity.

Our voting average is higher than the national average. No official figures exist as to the population of Richland County in 1889 when Montana became a state, because Richland County was then still a part of Dawson County. Perhaps there were 100 to 150 people living here then. On July 1, 1982, the year of Richland County's maximum population, the official projected estimate was 14,900 people. Since then there has been a bust in the oil boom bubble, and a continuing dearth of moisture, so there has been an out-migration of people, so that the post-1990 census gives the official population of Richland County as 10,644, a drop of 4,236, or a decrease in population of over 25% in 8 years. This has been a serious loss and affects the tax base adversely, and this determines what one can and cannot realistically plan to do. It calls for reappraisals.

It is quite possible that we are suffering from a constellation of problems and not just a couple. We suffer as a nation from the belief that if something is good or would be nice to have, of course we ought to have it; and without adequate deliberation or record keeping assume that "buying it on time" is the way to go. We find it difficult to postpone gratification. We also do little assessing or pondering to see what we might do with our own might or resources, but think, instead, of someone providing us with a job with a paycheck, or with a ready-made project. This tends to stifle individual initiative and swells the need for unionization and becoming little other than a blur or a number. But who thinks in other terms? It takes comparable effort for an individual to move toward maturity as for a territorial or political segment to do it. It is always difficult to get out of ruts or to change gears. Fortunately life is not set up on an either-or basis, but tends to provide both - and choices particularly if one can use postponement of gratification, and has a modicum of capacity for assessment and appraisal. Some pioneers had a goodly supply of both of these qualities, and I suspect there are still some who have good habits or good genes to supply some of the vision and go-power we need. This may be the time to make more intelligent use of computers.

I am convinced that having things handed to us or done for us is rarely productive of growth or of maturation. Movement, change, unfinished business is normal. To be sure or to have safe answers may not be what we need. Living is unpredictable. Sidney was good in the past; perhaps also in the future.

Since the end - or interruption? - of the oil boom in the 80's, Sidney has suffered a sizeable out-migration. If I should try to act as a lobbyist in the cause of establishing Sidney's preeminence, what would I feature? That would depend not only on the product under consideration but on the "buyer." Some buyers would not consider it as a place to live because it is "too fur off"; some wouldn't consider it because it's public transportation system is not only a far cry from the ideal - it almost doesn't exist. Some wouldn't consider it because it has Montana's extremes in climate; others would not consider it because it is too small. Some others would say we have a climate hostile to labor unions - or to business - or too this or that, or not enough of one thing or another.

But none of the objections is the whole story. One of its on-going assets is its image of itself. It may be small but it thinks of itself as "up and coming." It has never considered itself a follower - because it is a leader! It is a survivor; all these years it has survived the failure of western Montana to recognize its worth to the state. Because we are off the beaten path and passenger trains don't come near us any more - or buses or taxis, or main thoroughfares - nobody knows that we are a beautiful oasis in the vast stretches of space around us. We have changed from the arid land with it's Lone Tree Creek to a very fertile valley with bountiful growth, abundance of trees and busy farmers, surrounded on one side - the east - by "badlands" with their beauty and industry, and on the other side - the west - by rolling hills that invite stock raising and even permits farming.

Our people emphasize education. We have a low crime rate. The town itself has been well planned and developed. There has been an abundance of city and county administrators that have left a legacy of responsible decisions with benefit for everyone. There is room for expansion, both industrial and commercial. The population has been so stable that many descendants of families who were here from the beginning - 100 years ago - are still here today - not as recipients of Welfare, but as contributing members of the area. Our streets are wide, clean and lined with trees.

Sidney has its own modern and competently staffed hospital and excellent "Fitness Center" serving us both summer and winter, together with office accommodations for the entire medical staff as well as visiting staff from larger centers such as Billings, MT and Williston, ND.

We have our own newspaper, and we have both regular channel and cable TV. The Billings Gazette arrives here early every morning of publication date. We do not lack for news. We have a commodious hotel, numerous motels, eating houses and stores. Our roads are excellent. We have survived an oil boom and bust, and oil still flows from our wells. We have a sugar factory (Holly Sugar), Grain Market, and Livestock Market facilities. Other than private individuals, income for our tax base has been fairly stable and is primarily derived from Education, Health, Utilities such as gas and electricity, Government, Agriculture and Livestock. There are few sources of appreciable employment in industry, and this is truly regrettable because we have a much better than average labor supply. Recently we tried - and failed - to become the locus for a new Women's Prison. Our citizens are our greatest assets. As my friend Marion Damskov remarked, "You have more than your share of caring people."

Sidney hosts tournaments of a variety of sports: swimming, boxing, wrestling, horseshoes, high-school sports, and recently welcomed the coming and grieved the loss of a hockey dome which promised year round events. MDU - Montana Dakota Utilities (natural gas and electricity) - provides not only excellent service but an excellent source of employment. Sidney has a Heritage Center that would be hard to beat. It has an annual community-wide Medical-Laboratory service that would do any center proud. We are innovative as well as conservative.

The climate is actually far better than in many places, and we take the activities of nature in stride and without publicity. There are lots of people who would be surprised and delighted not to live in the hot muggy weather of the central states or the South. Obviously, I like it here.

We have much to offer - even absence of smog and a reliable Senior Citizen's bus - but we still have room for innovation, imagination, cooperative endeavors, vision and dedication. Our eyes are still on the future, even though our feet are planted deep in the past.

We are not too far off track, and we are not seriously ill. We are still innovating and doing things on our own - finding our own ways to do them. We cry about being overlooked and bypassed, but we are not and never have been paralyzed. We rarely spend time being bitter or feeling injured. I'm sure we need to devise better ways to obtain continuing input from many overlooked people - which probably would produce something comparable to making use of free association, discovering thereby that we have unanticipated goodies available from sources we'd never considered. Putting our heads to work needs to be the name of the game, not resentment because we have not been better cared for, or self pity, or depression or a bigger handout.

The most futile - and destructive - thing we could do would be to spend our energies feeling sorry for ourselves. We are luckier than most people in being right here. But there's no harm in making it even better. That might even be fun.

As someone has asked, "Wasn't life in olden times boring?" No TV, no radio, no drinking, no card playing, no sports events, no dancing, no cars, no decent roads and no place to go. Wasn't it boring to the point of desperation? No, we weren't bored, and life was never a pain in the neck. Boredom is for those who won't work, or who won't tackle what needs to be done. Our situation may not be perfect, but it is not far from idyllic. Our crime rate is low, suicides are few, our Welfare rates are not staggering, and our obituary columns attest to the fact that more and more of us live to our 80's and 90's, and many of us have lived here all our lives.

But what about our census falling, and there being out migration, and it is hard for our young people to find jobs, and there is no doubt we lack public transportation facilities. Doesn't that sound like we are in serious trouble?

Maybe a percentage of our growth and development problem stems from our self image of specialness. It's hard to feel fondness for a person who emanates smug superiority. We give to the obviously needy and withhold from the obviously affluent. Maybe we need to make more squeaks and creaks. At least we need to be aware of how we move in our own way.

It is 1996, and we are already well into the second century of Sidney's existence. it will be a very different picture from the first century. The free land is gone; there will be no further open sesame experiences, such as when the ditch and irrigation became a fact of life. Statehood, the building of the old stone church, the establishment of the townsite, the building of the ditch, the coming of the railroad, and the portioning of Richland County were all major events in our local history.

Then came the flour mill, advances in education and health care, improved roads, with some degree of assurance that the sky was the limit - nothing less.

But the wheel turned: we lost railway passenger service, lost bus connections to the outside world. Very abruptly, we even lost our radio station that did its daily job of binding us together. Our young people felt they had to leave the area to get ahead. It was not easy to learn that things don't happen automatically or last forever.

few who live here yearn to be elsewhere. Climactic extremes are not at all intolerable, and most of us like it better than other places we know. But it is about as isolated a place as one can imagine; and it is hard to get anywhere except by car. But the old hardy stock that took hardship for granted without feeling sorry for themselves doesn't make loud noises, so dissident voices are not common.

Maybe Sidney and the Mondak are like beings in any usual lifecycle. They are born, they mature, they live, and they die in a relatively patterned fashion. Times have changed and what is now necessary for a community to survive and beat the odds isn't too clear. The goals change and the forces for continued survival change, and at this point, nobody can say what these will be. The things that made Sidney possible will have to be redrawn and implemented.

I believe it can be done, but probably not without some agony and some implementation of new leadership criteria. Very good and qualified people still come out of Sidney - and it may yet find its way to leadership - not necessarily broad leadership, but leadership that fits into the broad spectrum of things.as they are and as they work in the computer age. Even there, there is need for such basics as integrity, caring, sharing, self reliance, ability to postpone gratification, ability to perceive relationships, imagination and trustworthiness. In fact, if one really thinks straight, the sky is still the limit, and change is the natural order of everything.

Would Peter and Bertha Anderson have thought their trek to Sidney, Montana Territory was worth the effort? Would they have felt satisfied that the move had provided them and their family "a better life?" I'll let you answer that for yourself.

CHAPTER 2 - FRUIT OF THE WOMB

I was the youngest of eight siblings and I was so much younger than they were that I grew up feeling they were much more important and competent than I was. I also took it for granted they were more important to me than I was to them. Translation: They didn't love me very much. There was one exception to this. I felt sure my oldest brother Niels cared for me. The result of this was that throughout my early life I idolized him and thought he could do no wrong. He was almost 19 when I was born, and we had a love relation going since I was a baby. But he was the only one, aside from Mother, who paid any attention to me or made me feel special or wanted.

The sibling next older than me, Christine, was six and a half years my senior, and whereas we slept together and on rare occasions played together - paper dolls - there was a certain rivalry and competition between us which shut out a sense of closeness. The rest of the siblings had their lives, their patterns, and their goals and their interests well established, and I was merely an unimportant tagalong that their lives scarcely touched. They certainly had not been yearning for a baby sister to fill their lives, and I cannot recall that any of them ever took any interest in what I had on my mind. There was the added detraction that I was definitely Mother's pet, and this never served as one of my assets.

I don't remember spending any time thinking about this state of affairs or brooding over it. This was the way the world was: Some days it rains and some days it doesn't. It is not easy to miss what one has never had. I know I felt I was well supplied with love, and it came generously and without any conscious effort on my part, from Mother and Niels. I had no gnawing hunger. My cup was full. It didn't occur to me to pine for more. I never really took it all out and looked at it until I began writing this book, and this helped bring a great deal of clarity to many hitherto fuzzy aspects of my life.

In the order of our arrival in the Anderson family, the P-Diamond outfit, we were six girls and two boys: Marie, Niels, Dagmar, Lillian, Josephine, Carl, Christine and Camilla. The oldest one was past 20 and married before I was born. All but the first three were born in the old log house.

Marie - Apple of her Father's Eye

Anna Marie Nielsine, or Mame, born in Denmark on May 21, 1884, was nearly five when she came to Sidney. Almost as soon as she arrived she was given the job of being responsible for the two younger children, Niels, three and a half and Dagmar, almost one, whenever Mother and Dad were away from the house, which stood on the West bank of the mighty Yellowstone River. Perhaps they were gone to round up from the prairie the twenty cows Mother would be milking, or while they were crossing the river on the ice so they could find cedar trees to cut down for logs to build a corral, or for fence posts, or to sell to other settlers for cash income. Mother always had complete trust in Mame's ability as well as her trustworthiness, because whenever she left, she left them all not only in Mame's hands, but in God's hands. I never heard of Mame being "a problem," or disobeying either one of her parents. She knew exactly what was expected of her, and the bond between them was strong - perhaps even stronger between Dad and Mame than Mother and Mame, if that was possible; Mame was Dad's girl.

A small voice inside me says I better remember to tell of the one specific occasion when Mame did cause quite a problem. The kids were alone at home, and perhaps a bit bored, when they decided to do some planting. That was a splendid idea because they had found some kernels of corn they could use. The hitch was that Mame decided she would plant a kernel or two in Niels's ears and see if they would grow there. They hadn't figured on it hurting, but within a few days it did. Mother and Dad, Mar and Far, tried their best to pry the kernels out, but they were stuck in real tight. They decided it called for expert medical help, so they drove to Fort Buford, at the confluence where they sold dairy supplies to the soldiers, and the Fort doctor was able to remove the kernels. They never tried the planting game again. It was apparently the only time Mame ever misbehaved, or at least that was my understanding.

Necessity molded Mame into a very competent as well as comely person, whether that be in managing, in care of her own family, in food preparation, housekeeping, sewing, decorating a home, or looking out for the needs of others. She loved school and learning. She learned to speak English quickly and

I never heard her carry on a conversation in Danish. As she matured, she never failed to be involved in a variety of social activities of her church and her community. In her later years she enjoyed shopping at the Yellowstone Mercantile for new clothes, and then giving her old ones to some needy person, more than likely her own relatives. She was the one of our family who remained permanently in the Methodist Church, after the Danish Lutheran Church, Pella, was chosen by our parents in 1908 as their church home.

A month before she was twenty, April 1904, she married Peter Anderson, also a Danish immigrant, who had the exact same name as her father, even to having no middle initial. He decided to remedy that by adding a middle initial, and so became Peter M Anderson. People kidded him that he chose M for Marie. They first lived on their homestead in a log house west of Sidney, under the brow of the western foot hills. Within a very few years they built a large beautiful frame house which still stands on the northwest corner of Holly Street and Cemetery Drive. It remains an attractive landmark house now owned and occupied by members of the Beagle family.

To our family, Mame's husband was always Peter M. To outsiders he was "Little Pete", contrasted with Dad, who was "Old Pete". Eventually, and for no valid reason, he became Peter M Anderson Jr. Some newcomers took it for granted that Dad and he were father and son. To my astonishment I discovered recently that their youngest son, Glenn, now retired, had always assumed his name derived from his Grandfather, my Dad, and not from a totally different Anderson lineage. He felt shock when I attempted to set him straight - almost as though I was trying to disown him!

Peter M had come from a large family who had migrated from Denmark to Sidney about the time I was born. Three of the siblings, Peter M, Andres and Marie (Mrs. Niels Rqasmussen) had homesteads just below the brow of the encircling foothills northwest of Sidney. His sister Katrina, who came here in 1899 together with my mother's remaining relatives, had just married Mother's younger brother, Uncle Louis (or Ludvig) Josephsen, and settled just north of our farm/ranch. Another sister, Anna, married a Sidney merchant, Arthur Bird, and they moved to Wyoming. Arthur Bird was the first person I ever knew of to have Huntington's chorea - from which he died. Another of Peter M's brothers, Anton, settled a few miles south of Sidney, and his youngest brother, Christian, was killed in a barnyard accident at our farm. All but Anna remained in the area and made solid contributions to our community.

Sister Mame clearly had a double relationship to the other "Anderson family", in that she was both sister-in-law and niece of Aunt Katrina (Teenah) and Uncle Louie. There are still quite a few third and fourth generation members of that family remaining in our area. During subsequent years Uncle Louie and Aunt Teenah came to be of a pivotal significance to me, i.e., that they determined where I would get my medical education.

Peter M had excellent acreage both above and below the ditch, which had been built after he filed on the acreage, and he was also a superior farmer, so that he and his family were financially "comfortable" early in his marriage to Mame. In addition to straight farming he had other activities: He operated Sidney's first home delivery dairy, which kept everyone in the family hopping, and he was also involved in the banking business at the Sidney National Bank, one in competition with the First National Bank, where my family did its banking business.

I cannot recall any time when I did not sense lots of tension in their home. There were no open battles - just glares or snide remarks. Nor did I ever see them sit down in the same room to discuss any matter. They were strangers living under the same roof. Peter M ran a productive farm and Mame ran a competent family and social center - with her prime interests being her children, her house and flowers, and her involvement with her church and Eastern Star.

Mame's children Ervin, Glen, Myrtle, Dorothy, Oscar

Peter M and Mame had six children: Myrtle, Gladys, Ervin, Oscar, Glenn and Dorothea. There were many problems and heartaches associated with these children. Myrtle, born January, 1905, was just half a year my junior, and was born with double harelip, though not with cleft palate. The gene for this deformity was contributed by Peter M. Myrtle's problem involved not only the actual difficulties in feeding her, but the emotional strain on Mame in that her beautiful child was a cripple. It was also a costly financial problem through their trying to provide an adequate corrective job on her mouth, which meant repeated trips to Mayo's in Rochester, Minnesota for surgery. Despite her defect I always thought Myrtle was beautiful. She was well built, had beautiful long blond curls, lovely big blue eyes and the fairest skin.

She started college in Missoula, Montana, after graduating from Sidney High School, but developed St. Vitus Dance, and it was determined that the high altitude of Missoula was a contributing factor, so she discontinued at the University of Montana and returned home. Then she came to stay with us in Portland, Oregon, where she went to business college. She also met and married an emigree from Denmark, Alfred Johns. After a few years of battling the Great Depression following the 1929 stock market crash, and trying to make a go of things in Oregon and then in California, they moved back to Sidney and started their own business, the Sidney Greenhouse, which they operated for many years, until their retirement. They never had any children, and Myrtle died of cancer in 1982. Although we were the same age, I cannot recall ever playing with her or even talking with her meaningfully until she was about to get married.

Mame's second child, Gladys, born in 1907, was as perfect as Mame had wanted all her children to be, and she was very welcome to the household. Our family had moved into the brand new big frame house and the log house had been torn down in 1908. The irrigation project was becoming a reality, and Danes kept flocking in. Mother and her girls were hosting a social affair at our house and everybody came. I was under the weather - sick in bed - and confined to the bedroom on the first floor - the sitting room. Through the afternoon many people wandered in and out of my room. This turned out to be a disaster, because, unbeknownst to any of us, I had scarlet fever and passed it out liberally to many people. Gladys, age two, caught it and died. Aileen Kelly, the teenage daughter of our good friends, Mike and Bridget Kelly, also contracted scarlet fever from me and likewise died. I believe there was still another person who died.

I recovered from the scarlet fever without difficulty, but Peter M. who also had it, developed a mastoid infection, a common complication of scarlet fever, which laid him low. He eventually had to have mastoid surgery for it. This was done on our dining room table by Dr. Hathaway of Glendive. After the surgery was completed and Peter M. was recovering from the effects of the chloroform anesthetic, he kept complaining about his foot, saying Dr. Hathaway had operated on his heel. Everyone thought he was still out of his head. When they finally got around to checking, they discovered that he really had good reason to complain: the flatirons they had put under his feet to keep him warm during surgery were too hot and had caused a deep burn on his heel. It took him much longer to recover from his burn than it took for his mastoid surgery to heal. Mame's cross was almost greater than she could bear.

Such epidemics were new to Sidney and management of them was a most onerous necessity, with each detail prescribed by law. The house had to have a big "quarantine" sign posted on it so people would stay away. There could be no public funeral for Gladys; not even Mame could go to it. The minister had to attend by stealth, and anything that could possibly have been touched by the baby had to be burned. Mame was inconsolable. I now wonder that she tolerated me at all, because I had caused Gladys' death.

In 1909 her first son, Ervin, was born, and as far as I know he had no imperfections. He went to Sidney High-school and then to business college in Portland. He married Dorothy Johnson and they built a lovely little home practically in Mame and Peter M's back yard. Ervin ran a gas station a while, and then worked for several years in the lab at Holly Sugar factory. They had three daughters, Beverly, Shirley and Billie Lou, and no major problems, but Dorothy, Ervin's wife, developed cancer of the uterus, and had surgical intervention. She made a complete recovery and still lives with Ervin, mostly in Yuma, Arizona, though she and Ervin drive back to Sidney every summer for a brief visit. Their oldest daughter, Beverly, still lives here and is married to Ivan Peterson, D.D.S., son of Ivan Peterson Sr. D.D.S., who practiced dentistry for many years here in Sidney. Bev's husband,

Ivan Jr., eventually got tired of being a dentist and became involved in staffing the Sidney Ambulance Service, and also serving in several capacities at the Richland National Bank. Their oldest son, David, graduated in medicine in California and practices his profession there. David and I are the only members of our family to have earned our M.D. degree. Beverly is an accomplished pianist, and she and her husband Ivan add to the beauty and grace of Sidney. Ervin and Dorothy have fourteen grandchildren and three great grandchildren.

Mame's fourth child, Oscar LeRoy, had no physical handicaps either, and this was a great relief to Mame who feared another harelip with each pregnancy. He resembled our side of the family - tall, straight blond hair - but he resembled his father, Peter M in his interests: economics and finance. When he was still a baby he developed "Bright's Disease", a kidney disease, and for months and months he was on a strict dietary regimen prescribed by Dr. Beagle, which might well have floored an ordinary mother, but which Mame carried out with complete devotion. Fortunately, his recovery was good and he was able to participate in most of the activities life provided. More recent modern diagnostic tools suggest that it is doubtful he ever had any kidney disease, but he does have arthritis.

I have a very clear memory of him and his propensity - from early childhood - to spin long yarns. With a perfectly straight face he would tell about his amazing experiences of the day. He invariably presented them as gospel truth. Then this pattern was gone as quickly and completely as it had begun.

Oscar worked on the family milk route, finished highschool and then went to business college in Portland. He returned to Sidney and was employed in the bank his father had a financial interest in. He married Helen Utterback from Glendive, an attractive, intelligent and competent school teacher, and they had three children, LeRoy, Judy and Caryl. He was an indefatigable worker, a stickler for details, and gradually he became part owner and eventually President of the Sidney National Bank. He was elected to the position of Mayor of Sidney and was a delegate to Montana's first Constitutional Convention (CON-CON) and was actively involved with its section on Local Government.

After his retirement from the bank, Oscar and Helen moved - for winters only - to Sedona, Arizona. Health problems have continued to plague him.

Sometimes it is hard not to think of Oscar as like his father or a chip off the old block, but he isn't a sadist, as Peter M was, even though it often appears that way. He doesn't get pleasure out of people's discomfiture, but out of being able to set them straight. Oscar's thinking is always precise - and often accurate. He is didactic. He cannot tolerate people who say something that does not meet his criteria for accuracy. He spends a lot of his time getting precise answers, and he would not be discussing the subject if he hadn't done exactly that, so presentations that differ from that are not tolerated.

But in the midst of his precision - his perfectionism - he also has the habit of being unexpectedly kind and thoughtful, like his transplanting a five foot seedling horse-chestnut from his back yard to mine the year I returned to Sidney, that has now grown into a beautiful tree; or his taking me and my guest from San Diego to visit the newly opened Bourgeoisie House at Fort Union; or his tipping me off that a suitable house was available when we were planning to move to Sidney. Then there is that other compelling evidence of his basic goodness: Helen stays married to him, and she has both good taste and good sense.

Oscar and Helen's three children, Lee, Judy and Caryl, all now moving rapidly toward senescence too, may seem different from one another, but probably are more alike than different. The oldest, Lee, has sat at high places and bogged down in troubled waters. He has had three marriages and two divorces. He also has two children and a grandchild. He came to see me a year ago and I got the distinct impression he was beginning to mature and grow up, no longer giving his high intelligence the number one spot in his life. Judy spent years demonstrating her ability to succeed at whatever she undertook, in shedding a marriage, and taking pleasure in the high intellectual attainments of her son. The youngest, Caryl, has spent her life running away from any situation that might end in her having status or being considered a success. Her marriage of many years has been terminated and there are no children. One wonders just what factors are most important in each one's life. Helen seemingly accepted all her children, and they in turn seem to trust her acceptance of them.

Helen, Oscar's wife, is one of my favorite people: intelligent, personable, with no need to be a star and seemingly in competition with nobody; maintaining her poise and her inner strength and her ability to keep her own counsel. I would like very much to listen to her analysis of the various patterns her family members present, and who played what part in establishing the patterns. Everything I know about her says she is on the beam, but to really understand, I'll have to know a lot more than I know now.

Mame and Peter M had two more children: Glen and Dorothea. In retrospect, Glenn, the 5th child, seems to me to have been burdened with dyslexia, a problem in speech and communication, right from the start. He seemed to have his own brand of speech, and his teacher in the first grade could not understand him, so she would send for Myrtle, in a higher grade, to come and interpret. I remember that on an occasion Mame had said that something "was the limit" at the same time she put a new outfit on him. That outfit became invariably his "limit dress". In World War II he served as a Military Policeman. He married Gertrude Kopp and they had two children, Georgette and William - whom Glen always called "Willie". Gertrude, Glenn's wife, worked steadily in a bank in California and Glenn worked in a large industrial firm in San Francisco, where he was involved, I believe, in servicing equipment. He had a problem with alcohol, and had psychiatric treatment on more than one occasion.

On several occasions I have tried to have meaningful conversation with him, but never succeeded. My last contact with him in 1987, I believe, was more rewarding and with better communication than any I can recall, but it was on this occasion that he appeared quite incredulous when he learned his father was not my brother or my father's son. Dyslexia is often an indicator of more extensive neurologic problems. I know Oscar has had real difficulty knowing what to do in business situations where Glenn is concerned. Both Glenn and Gertrude are now retired, Glenn is seemingly free from the monkey on his back, and life is a bit more serene.

Georgette, Glenn's oldest child, was married and has two or three children. Her first pregnancy turned out to be a family disaster in that she contracted measles early in the pregnancy, and her son was born handicapped as a result - causing deafness and other problems. She was young and hardly equipped to cope with the difficult situations this entailed, and after a few years she became physically worn out and medical opinion was that she had developed Addison's disease. The marriage was dissolved and her husband was awarded the children. After many years she began to recover physically, and then remarried. Recently she sent me an announcement of the marriage of her deaf son. It has been a long, hard road to travel.

Bill, Georgette's younger brother, whom Glenn called Willie, and whose profession is in the field of horticulture, finished college in California, married and has two children, both of whom are fine looking and bright. I have never been apprised of any problems, so I'm hopeful all's well. Glenn and Gertrude do not anticipate leaving their home in San Francisco, which faces right on the ocean, or returning to Sidney. They like being near their children and they like California.

Mame's sixth and last child, a daughter, Dorothea, was a heartache for many years. I recall her well when she was an infant: normal appearing, normal acting - absolutely nothing unusual about her in any way. Then, when she was about a year old she grabbed an open hot oven door on the kitchen range to pull herself up and burned both her hands very severely. The extensive scars persisted throughout her life, giving evidence of the severity of her injury. Following the burns, she had a series of unrelated yet consequent problems: mastoid, worms - the big ascaris lumbracoides variety - which she expelled out of her nose and mouth and which created terrible problems. She had one disability after another. The upshot was that she turned out to be "retarded". To my belief, she never was a "retarded person" in the common or genetic sense. Rather, she was a brain damaged individual. She had EBD - or early brain damage or a developmental disability, and the original culprit was her being severely burned, followed by numerous health sequelae. I have tried to help her family set this straight, but I've never had much success at it. "Dr. Beagle said she was retarded," and that settled that. She was always a problem, always immature, never having adequate comprehension, never able to be a fully responsible adult; yet she had none of the commonly recognized physical stigmata associated with mental retardation of the D.D. type.

As long as Mame was alive, she was able to care for and supervise Dorothea. Then, in 1972, on her 88th birthday, Mame died of cancer of the floor of her mouth. This meant Dorothea was without any parental supervision, inasmuch as Peter M had died many years previously of heart trouble and this left Myrtle, her older sister, to take Dorothea under her wing. She was moved to a little house next door to Myrtle's, and whereas Dorothea lived alone, she was never able to assume any normal responsibility for her daily living. Everyone was grateful she constituted only a family burden and not a major social or community burden. She died a few years later of cancer of the breast. Her death occurred several years before Myrtle's death, so she had continuity rather than fragmentation of responsible care.

Despite the fact that Mame seemed to have numerous medical disasters, her home was a pleasant and comfortable place to visit. But I hated to be there when Peter M was at home, particularly at mealtime, because he seemed never to fail to make someone at the table cringe. His sarcasm was honed to a sharp edge, and he spared no one. The fact of having guests at the table never deterred him one bit. In my parent's home this never occurred, and I was grateful. I guess it takes all kinds of people to make up a world, but living with someone who delights in cutting another person down never appealed to me. Sarcasm is, indeed, a potent and very hostile weapon - most destructive, and Peter M was a past master at it. I never envied Mame, despite the fact there always seemed to be plenty of money. She no doubt had her share of blemishes, but these were not as hard to live with as her husband's.

And how she enjoyed keeping up with the Minnesota Twins! She rooted for them with the enthusiasm of a youngster, even in her eighties. She would have loved to watch them play in the World Series game this coming weekend (1987. Incidentally, the Twins won the Series)!

A role that Mame played for most of her adult years was to pass along an endless stream of gifts, mostly clothing, to her own siblings' families, and to her husband's siblings' families. She practically clothed many of them, I am sure. Did she have a huge checking account? I doubt she had a checking account. But she did have a charge account at the Yellowstone Mercantile, that long antedated charge cards, and sufficed to let her act out her largess, or perhaps her hostility toward Peter M. I sometimes used to wonder what went on behind closed doors - since Peter M was not one who was inclined to give much away, and it was he who had to pay the bills. Perhaps the fact that her gift list included not only her family but his family as well, provided some grease for the wheels. Whatever it was, Mame never was cowed or dissuaded, and nobody said her nay when it came to gift giving. In looking back I cannot remember that she ever gave me anything. Could this have been unrecognized resentment, related to my having given scarlet fever to Gladys? It's possible. I could understand that, or maybe it was my being Mother's darling, and my having little time for Dad?

I cannot recall ever having had a single "heart to heart" talk with Mame - about anything. I was well aware I never ceased being her baby sister - lacking in skills and in judgement - but mostly tolerable. I never for a moment would have wanted to change places with her. She loved fashionable clothes, and she did a myriad of things very well. She exuded competence and took a back seat to no one. She was a manager. She was inordinately good to Dad: every year from 1921 to 1929, when he left Oregon and came back to Sidney for the summer, he stayed at her house, and they got along fine together. She was also good to Mother for years, with her blindness and advancing age, but her kindness also carried barbs. Methodist church functions and Eastern Star and Masonic activities peppered their lives - her's and Peter M's, but they seemed to have little in common besides that. She never complained, or tried to change him, but neither was she cowed or subservient.

Not a negligible pleasure in being a guest at Mame's was her abilities as a cook and purveyor of delectable food. I suspect she was the best of my siblings in that area of competence, though that would have to mean she was truly outstanding, because all of them were tops. Mame, however, seemed to take the time to do that little extra something to make it special and memorable, even on ordinary days. The fact that she always had a "hired girl" to help with the work, plus an open ended charge account at Yellowstone Merc and never ending dairy farm products, made it possible for her to accomplish the superlative culinary feats that impressed me. She was truly a worker, but she was so well organized it never seemed to be a burden to her. She just got things done.

Another delight was her green thumb. She not only raised a vegetable garden, which was never obvious or even in evidence, because it was out back of the barn, but she loved flowers, and she raised innumerable types and varieties in her huge flower garden, that surrounded the front of her big, comfortable home. Their front, as well as their back yard was fenced with woven wire, and every inch of this front yard was filled with color from early to late. In those days a wide circular porch, mostly screened in, against flies and mosquitoes, surrounded the front outside of the house, and made it more possible to enjoy the beautiful grounds. Now the porches have been deleted by the present owners, and a more prim and precise house is the result, but I still miss Mame's flowers.

Even today, the house itself, is a pleasure to look at, and it surely was a delight in those early years. A high board fence across the front now obscures the road and makes privacy possible, but no lovely flowers arrest one as he enters Sidney from the West. I feel sure her involvement with flowers was a symbol of her affectionate involvement with Dad, and he no doubt taught her a lot about gardening.

I should make mention of the fact that one of the big laterals from the canal to the lower (eastern) farms went right past their home, and served as the northern boundary between the town of Sidney and the country. This lateral lay right along the south side of their farm, and therefore it was important that they should have maintained a fenced yard. To walk to town, a few blocks to the Yellowstone Mercantile, which Mame did almost daily, meant they would have to cross "the ditch." A heavy plank bridge two to three feet wide spanned the ditch, and it was encompassed on both sides by heavy planks and woven wire fencing, so that no one could inadvertently fall off the bridge into the water. In all the years they were there I never heard of a single person coming to grief with the water, or in any other way being injured. It attests to the meticulous care they took to make their place safe. Their home was always swarming with kids - their own and those of visitors - but nobody was ever hurt. Mame seemed to never miss a trick. No doubt Dad played a part in her love of flowers, and she passed this love on to Myrtle, who, together with her husband Al Johns, provided Sidney with the best in flowers at their greenhouse, a couple blocks from where she was raised.

Mame was also a Tournament-quality Bridge player. It is no wonder Dad was partial to Mame, though his partiality was never offensive or blatant. Mother, on the other hand, also had her favorite, but she was not as discrete as Dad was, so she engendered no hostility in others toward those she favored. I have been most fortunate in that I have largely escaped a potentially unfortunate legacy.

From beginning to end Mame was my big, adequate sister, but we never, ever shared any part of our lives. She was Dad's girl and I was Mother's, and nothing ever changed between us. Her main contribution to me was probably a conviction that I'd never measure up to her, but I always knew I didn't have to, so it was no open sore.

Yesterday, July 1991, I attended the funeral of Ervin, Mame's oldest son. He died in Yuma, Arizona, after battling for several years with Schwannoma, a type of cancer I had never heard of before. I had assumed it was a sarcoma, involving primarily muscle, but my knowledge is infinitesimal. Numbers of things seemed to come together for me at the funeral: Although Ervin and his wife Dorothy had lived away from Sidney for many years, the church was packed with friends who represented a cross section of the past and the present. There was a warmth of feeling for both Ervin and Dorothy which was touching and genuine. Oscar was there, but Glenn from San Francisco could not be reached. Each one in the family has been hard for the others to accept or even tolerate. Estrangement has been the rule.

This brings me to the point of considering the values that made each of them behave as he or she did, and that made them intolerable to one another. There was a lot of resentment and frustrated entitlement among them. Ervin seemingly felt due deference did not accrue to him by reason of his being the firstborn son. Oscar knew he was more precise and knowledgeable and persistent in effort and accomplishment than the others, and had thereby earned the right to be the acknowledged leader among them. He abhorred imprecise thinking and impulsive reactions, and deserved - felt entitled to - cooperation rather than criticism.

It reminds me of the story of Mary and Martha: Martha the competent, orderly, methodical person, and yet Mary with her spontaneity and lack of forethought still won the approval of Jesus. Mary's public relations job was more effective than the well planned production - competence - of Martha. It is obviously not something in the black/white category, but of the and/or.

I always liked to go to Mame's home because she was ever pleasant and jovial as well as responsive and efficient and her house was always filled with good food, friends and acceptance. We are whatever we are, and there is a place for us. There is room even for Glenn, who could never compete with either of his brothers in intellectual adequacy or human relations, but managed - even with alcohol, plus a helpful wife - to live out a whole lifetime of steady work, to retirement age and a retirement pension. This is no small accomplishment for a basically handicapped person.

Why are we so ready to discard the other fellow who doesn't have or live by our values? Moralistic judgement tends to prevail when our reality judgements are in short supply. Obviously we need to understand the factors in the reality situation better.

NIELS - MOTHER'S PRIDE AND JOY

Niels was born in Denmark, the second child and the first son of Peter and Bertha Anderson, on September 25, 1885. He seemed to measure up to everything Mother could want in her son. He was healthy, handsome, bright, interested in everything, he could fix or repair anything; he seemed to understand how everything was made and how it worked, and despite his being somewhat of a dreamer, he was also active and a doer. He and his older sister Marie, or Mame, were close, but he never got along well with his younger siblings, except for me. There was a certain hostility toward him from almost all the family except from Mother, Mame and me - probably because of his obvious egotism, which endured throughout his life.

Niels, cc 1918

Mother also told me that he, at eighteen, was not pleased that she was pregnant AGAIN with her last pregnancy, and even when I arrived, he made no moves to accept me or to include me. It was not long before she had the opportunity to put me in his arms while she was climbing out of the buggy, and this broke the ice. From that time until I was in my fifties, he was ever my very special person, my idol, and I was his "Toodles." I adored him; everything he did was beyond criticism, and I accepted his values as my own, e.g., his breadth of interests, his vast area of competence both with ideas and with things, even though I soon learned it was not an easy thing to be very knowledgeable in so many areas. Considering the fact that by the time I was 5, he no longer lived at home with us, his influence on me has been remarkable.

It seemed to me there wasn't anything he didn't know, and since he was very verbal, he was always telling something interesting and not generally known. By trade he was a carpenter, so he understood all sorts of things such as dimensions, surfaces, textures, grains, size, composition and suitability. One has to know these things when one is a builder or a fixer. He read everything he could lay his hands on. He wrote poetry, and sometimes when he was away from home a while, he would send me one of his poems instead of a letter. He liked to grow all sorts of specialty trees and plants. He kept up with the latest hit songs - even though it was long before the day of radio or TV. We had an organ that had to be pumped with one's feet. He coached me in singing the notes of the scales, and then in finding out how to read notes on paper. He drew cartoons and he painted, and he had one of the first cameras I ever saw - one that stood on a tripod. He built a darkroom in the cellar at our new house and developed and printed his own pictures. Probably his specialty was stereopticon exposures and pictures that had to be mounted double and looked at in a certain way to get depth perception.

He could knit - so could Dad - and he could sew, and his singing voice - tenor - always seemed very pleasant to me. He was intensely interested in politics and he gave me Karl Marx's COMMUNIST MANIFESTO when I was still a very young child. He tended to subscribe to its teachings. I was too young to have any opinions, but I still have this book on my shelves. He loved horses, and I can recall how he mourned when his horse had been put into the livery stable in Wolf Point, Montana, for the night and it burned to the ground and incinerated his horse and many others.

He had been hired by the local school board to assist Professor E.C. Hicks teach school in the one room log school south of Ridgelawn. I have no idea how long he worked at this job, but he was my first school teacher. The only incident I can recall was my resistance to having to call him Mr. Anderson, when I wanted to call him Niels. I was only four going on five years old at the time. Mother wanted him to go to college and encouraged him to enroll in Montana State College at Bozeman, then called Montana Agricultural College. He soon ran out of money, dropped out and failed to notify anybody what was going on or where he was. Mother was very worried and got the President of the college to help her locate him. It seems he had joined a threshing rig somewhere. He was ever her pride and joy.

He would always rather have something he had made himself, than a more prefect item that had been bought. He could always find a good reason for downgrading the purchased item. This pattern was present in his joining nothing - not even the Communist Party. He always found his own reasons for rejecting something. Whatever he produced or made was better than what was for sale. To have joined any organization - no matter how much positive value it might have for him - would have been too demeaning. He was seemingly unable to accept even the idea that anyone could be his leader or teacher. But he had infinite patience and tenderness with children - even handicapped children. One could go on and on about his talents, but there was one area in which he had no skill: He could not accept anyone who did not regard him as the leader and teacher. I didn't realize this until I was a middle aged woman.

This pattern included his attitude toward Dad, who knew a lot, was an avid reader in a few fields such as agriculture and domestic politics, and basically was an intelligent but non-verbal person. But Dad could never win an argument with Niels. The two of them could never be together, even briefly, before Niels would be making some sneering retort to Dad, and show his contempt for Dad's puny mind quite openly. Both their faces would be contorted with hostility, and another impasse would have arrived. I understand that once Dad took after him with a pitchfork, but as far as I know, Father never, ever, touched or hurt him. It must have taken tremendous control on Dad's part not to have beaten him to a pulp. It is also true that Mother gave Niels unstintingly of her love, approval and acceptance, for she thought of him as almost too wonderful for words. She surely encouraged him in his vanity, narcissism, and egotism, and in regarding him as in a class by himself, and thus superior to Dad. This must have been bitter gall for Dad to keep swallowing year after year. Let's agree that Niels was intellectually superior to Dad. That does not make Dad a no-account person, nor wipe away Niels's impossible behavior. Through the years, most of my siblings covertly took sides: against Niels and Mother and for Dad.

By 1909 Niels was largely gone from the family home, but Mother, Niels and I were clearly on one side. Mother was also almost - but not quite - as overtly partial to me as she was to Niels. She was perhaps part of the source of the veiled rejection of me by my siblings. I never really saw the picture until I was old enough to be a grandmother. Likewise, I never had the same handicap Niels had, in that I was not greatly impressed with my specialness, while he apparently was. Also, I no doubt had less factual basis for feeling superior. I had no need to be the leader; I was happy to be taught, and happy to be loved, and being contemptuous did not come easy for me.

These factors probably spared me from the active hostility of my immediate family as I got older. Mostly, I just did not rate very high with them, but at least they did not actively hate me like they did Niels. It was the easiest thing in the world for me to accept Niels as the teacher and leader, so it was natural that we should have been so enamored of one another. Niels was also blessed with a delightful sense of humor, and more often than not he wore a twinkle in his eyes. He could find the outrageousness in almost anything - even in himself - if he were approached right. When he was beginning to lose the verve and vigor which had characterized his approach to life through his many years, he would say, with his twinkle, that adequacy should be measured by a man's ability to put on his pants without holding on to anything.

To this day I cannot understand or subscribe to what was essentially a habit with Niels and me. We would stand together at a ninety degree angle from one another, and then he would start clapping me very hard with both his hands - on my chest and my back. This would go on until one of us got tired of it. No one ever said "STOP!" I held my breath to be able to stand it. I have no idea if it ever did me any damage; at least I was never aware of any bleeding from it in my sputum, and I always assumed that since Niels did it, he was sure it would do no damage, and he probably was trying to strengthen my lungs. But I never asked him.

In later years, after coming out of my "fallow period" in 1986, and again in 1991, when chest X-rays were taken and I was told I had an enlarged heart, I have wondered if my holding my breath until I felt like bursting for long periods of time could have had a bad effect on my heart. I was never told I had a valvular problem and I never had high blood pressure. It would be interesting to know if this might have been possible.

I had minimal contact with him since he had left home about the time the big irrigation ditch was built - completed in 1912. On one occasion I had "run away from home" and gone to live with him in his little homestead shack just west of and above the ditch and about three quarters of a mile from our house. I really cannot remember anything about it except I stayed a while, maybe even overnight, and then he took me back home. It all seemed correct and proper. He didn't scold me, and neither did Mother.

Niels & Johanna

Additional memories are of Niels going to New York to escort Peter M's parents from Sidney, where they were visiting, to shipboard in New York for their return to Denmark. Also, he was away from home in 1909 when he went to Seattle to attend the A.Y.P. (Alaska, Yukon, Pacific Exposition), and from there sent me small gifts : a tiny glass cup with my name cast or poured right into its side (along with "1909"); a miniature aluminum picture frame with his picture, and AYP 1909 etched into it. On this same trip he took a picture of Uncle Charlie and his wife, Camilla, for whom I was named. This is the only picture I ever saw of her.

In the early teens he left home for good, and acquired some land in the Prairie Elk country and built a 2-room tar-paper covered shack which was home to him until the end of WWI, when he was married to Johanna Amundson from Circle, MT. Johanna was from a large family of Amundsons, Norwegian's, and was a person for whom I later came to have genuine affection.

Although they never had any children of their own, both she and Niels were naturals in the child-caring business. They kept the wolf from the door during the long dust-bowl and depression years by caring for "Welfare Children" in their home, which he, the carpenter, had built on the exact site of our old log house.

The time came, in 1945 while I was living in Washington, DC, that my needs and his needs meshed, and we were able to coordinate and synchronize our living situations for the good of all of us. We all survived a difficult and bitter period of years together. They needed financial assistance to survive, and I desperately needed someone to help our family have reliable caretakers of our beloved baby, Janet. At ten months she had suffered sunstroke and cerebral thrombosis, or clotting of the blood in a blood vessel of her brain. This had left her essentially with cerebral palsy. One of the chief cogs in the wheel who ran the show for us and accomplished what was necessary - substituted for me - while I worked and earned money to keep us all afloat, was Niels' wife, Johanna.

Johanna was neither beautiful nor brilliant, but she was endowed with an abundance of goodness, common sense, good judgement and stability. After some of the things we went through in Washington, I could say she was - they were - truly like manna from heaven. God surely must have had me in the palm of His hand to have teamed us up together, just as Dad and Mother felt they were in God's hands. I had no idea this would be so when I asked them to come, after their cow had strangled to death by a freak accident. But the days and the months and the years were to show me how fortunate we were in having gotten together.

Our household at that time consisted of my husband, Len Friendly, Jan, our only child, Len's aunt, Aunt Bertie, in her mid-seventies, Niels, Johanna, and their seven year old foster child Rosie, who also had cerebral palsy and was quite retarded, and myself. So, we were seven people who needed to get along with one another well enough so that being together would be tolerable for all of us. I had become convinced that we were desperately in need of help if we were going to provide Jan with even the semblance of a therapeutic environment after the acute problem was over. As far as I was concerned Jan had suffered sunstroke as a result of the horrible Washington weather, and the term - or the concept of cerebral palsy never occurred to me until years later. I had found little to read about sunstrokes that helped my ignorance.

Our pediatrician didn't attempt to clarify very much of anything. He had told me long before her accident that doctors' children usually turned out to be major headaches, so I had been hopeful we would be an exception and that we wouldn't bother him very much. We didn't. He had effectively closed the door on me. Every new aspect of her massive and seemingly progressive symptomatology was a complete surprise to me and I never seemed prepared for it. It actually was not progressive. It was merely the unfolding of the scars of her illness as time marched on, and showed up in new and unexpected ways. No doctor we consulted clarified what we were dealing with, and it was not something I had learned in medical school - although Dr. Lawrence Selling, my professor of Neurologic Medicine had taught me many other things! Perhaps they didn't clarify because they expected me to know! At any rate, we didn't seem to move any faster than I could learn.

I continued to work at the Washington Institute of Mental Hygiene, the Red Feather Public Mental Hygiene Clinic of Washington, D.C., where Dr. Rex Buxton was the psychiatric director, and I was his assistant. I could not adjust to the outrageous uncertainties associated with available household help. We needed stability coupled with a sense of responsibility and commitment.

When Niels and Johanna came, it was like one could begin to live again in some semblance of order. They were there. I didn't have to worry lest they not show up. And they had unfailingly good judgement and perpetual love and evident caring. I could trust them like I trusted myself.

To the love for Niels I had in my childhood, I now added an enduring gratitude. They were surely what all of us needed. We were also what they needed. They explored Washington, delighted in it's offerings. Rosie was enrolled in a Special Education School, Jan found out how it was to have a child companion, and Johanna began teaching her the rudiments of sharing. For the first time they had money enough for the things they needed. They got used to all of our ways - even those of Len and Aunt Bertie. We found there were things to be enjoyed everywhere, even at home, where we relaxed with cribbage and whist. We didn't even have the perpetual hassles that had come up between Len and "the help." After two or three years had passed and things had gone so well, I thought I'd like to try dropping my practice and assume responsibility for Jan myself, so they returned to Sidney. Only after they were gone did I discover I was neither as capable nor as durable as I had assumed. My survival drive began to insist I return to my profession. We moved to Salt Lake City, and again, when we called on Niels and Johanna to come back to us, they did just that. We spent another six to eight years together - equally as good years as the earlier ones in Washington. All of us assumed our arrangement was permanent.

Then in one year - 1955 - we had three deaths: first, Mother, ninety-three, who had come from Sidney to Salt Lake City to live with us; Aunt Bertie, Len's "Tante," who was well along toward her 80's, and finally Johanna, who died of cancer of the pancreas. This terminated everything we had counted on to go on indefinitely. Niels was inconsolable. He tried Sidney, but that didn't work. I felt that I could not manage Niels without the help of Johanna. Our plans changed radically. We gave up our home, including my office, that Niels had been building for over eight years, and moved from Salt Lake City to Seattle. Within a year, Niels returned to Salt Lake City, bought a little home somewhere at the end of the line, and entered into what he called his "flippety flop years." We visited him from time to time.

Niels in San Diego, 1970

In 1969 he broke his hip, and while he was hospitalized in Salt Lake City for hip surgery as well as for a prostatectomy, we came to see him from San Diego, where I had newly retired. I suggested he come to live with us for an indefinite period - as long as he wanted to stay - and this he did. He stayed for about a year, then returned to Salt Lake City - to his flippety flop days - and within two days of his departure from our home, he died suddenly, apparently of an acute cerebro-vascular accident in September 1970, when he was almost 85. His funeral was here in Sidney, and he is buried right beside Mother, Dad and Johanna. He remained ever an important person to me and my life. In some ways he was a father figure to me, but I think he was more of a male figure, a male figure who clearly accepted me, and this was different from the way Dad came across to me. I think Niels, a male, helped me believe in my own acceptability. I never saw him as replacing Dad in my life.

He and Johanna never had any children. There were no pregnancies during their many years of marriage - thus no descendants who might carry on the Anderson name.

As far as I know, Niels had never needed nor sought medical attention for any problem until he fractured his hip when he was 84 years old. He had had many years of partial disability due to a large inguinal hernia, but I doubt that he ever gave serious thought to having surgical repair. He remained handsome, alert and involved with the affairs of living up until his seemingly abrupt death. He maintained a breadth of interests to the moment of his death.

He had an awareness of his uncommon intellectual gifts and often said that it was his belief that people who were privileged to have such gifts were also burdened by an equally strong negative quality. I was all too familiar with his negative quality so I never asked him to elaborate, but it would have been interesting to know whether he was aware of the same detractions to his functioning as I was.

His egotism and his distorted paranoid thinking were a permanent part of him. I knew I would never change him, and that these aspects would make it impossible to live with him. But I loved him despite his handicap, for all the good things he had helped bring into my life during many, many years.

His death was also the direct cause of my returning to Sidney. The problems I had by reason of his death occurring just prior to Labor Day weekend, with no railroad transportation for his body from Salt Lake City to Sidney, and the mortician advising me that if I expected to return to Sidney eventually - to make it easier for others I better come now. And that is what I did, because I knew this is where I belong.

Dagmar - Born To Work

My parents' third child, and the youngest of those who came with them from Denmark to America, was Dagmar Antonia Margareta, or, as we all called her, Dalma, or more precisely, Dowma. This is the way it sounded when her name was pronounced by Danes. Dag-mar was altogether too hard and cumbersome. The Danes always softened harsh tones thus, unlike the Norwegians, who retained the hard d's and g's even though they shared a common written language with the Danes, e.g., the written word for God is Gud in both languages, but the Danes pronounce it "Goo (as in moon), while the Norwegians pronounce it "Goo-d", Table - Bord, in both written languages, - is "Boor" to the Danes, but "Bord" to the Norwegians.

When we wrote her name we wrote Dagmar, but we pronounced it Dowma. Finally, after her marriage she had her name legally changed to the way Ira, her husband, pronounced it: Dalma. So now we never use the original spelling of her name, either in writing or in speaking. The Danish spelling was discarded, but the Danish pronunciation was the winner.

She was born May 27, 1888 and thus was 11 months old when she arrived in Sidney in April, 1889. The trip from Denmark to Sidney had not only been unpleasant but downright hazardous for her. She had learned to depend on a reliable supply of nourishment, and she enjoyed it as babies do. Then the supply was abruptly cut off at the source, as a result of Mother being seasick, and there was no acceptable substitute to appease her hunger pains. Mother was so seasick she could not retain any food for days, so her milk supply vanished into thin air, and her baby was starving right before her eyes. If she wasn't exactly starving, at least she was a most unhappy youngster. She was beginning to learn early that life is real and life is earnest. Not surprisingly, she had no memories of the trip. Her earliest memories were of people coming to the log house beside the river to talk to Dad, and invariably, when strangers would come she would hide under the bed until they were gone.

She was never demanding or assertive. She accepted what was provided, and minded her P's and Q's. Undoubtedly, she learned that Mame was Dad's girl, and Niels was Mother's boy, and she had to find some place where she seemed to fit in also. Because she was bright and quick to catch on and able to use her head and her hands simultaneously, she soon found there were all sorts of things she could do. She got status and security as a result. This reinforced her natural aptitudes and skills, so she became the one who can do things - the worker. She was unbelievably competent in so many areas. Whereas I had always thought of all my sisters as hard workers and very capable people, I think Dalma's aptitudes would have taken first prize, outshining all the others. She was much like Niels in this, but then, she was a GIRL! She did a man's work as well as she did a woman's. She could build a fence - or a room, and accomplish anything thought of as "women's work," with no great sweat. She organized, she cooked and cleaned and sewed with great skill, and she kept things orderly. Her capacity for self-abnegation was vast.

The folks wanted to help her acquire even greater skill, so they sent her to Kenmare, North Dakota to take a course under Mrs. Isaacson's tutelage which would make her into an expert seamstress. Mrs. Isaacson surely succeeded in her endeavor. By coincidence, many years later, both Mrs. Isaacson and I lived in Portland, Oregon at the same time and attended the same church. She was a woman of real quality and competence, and I would be the first to say that Dalma had had a true expert for her instructor. I was told this repeatedly by many people. Dalma could sew ANYTHING: the most intricate, the most beautiful, the most utilitarian. She turned with seeming ease from the finest pin-tucking to repairing binder canvasses for the harvesters. She used patterns if these were available, or she made her own from newspapers. She never wasted an inch of cloth, and everything fit beautifully. I doubt that she ever had to discard anything she made because it didn't fit right. Whatever she did was well done, whether it was sewing or cooking or whatever, and it seemed to me as though it always came essentially out of nothing. She taught scores of people how to sew.

I can scarcely remember anything of Dalma prior to her marriage in 1910, at least nothing from the days in the log house, but in the "new house" I recall her once leaning over the upstairs bannister to shake a rug, pitching forward and breaking her collarbone. I also remember her sewing and sewing, upstairs in the southeast bedroom where the Minnesota Model A sewing machine stood - with its foot pedal. She made beautiful things for all of us. Suddenly she was making wedding dresses for herself and Lil, my sister just younger than Dalma, and for all of us, so we could be all gussied up for their double wedding.

It was a big affair, June 1, 1910, the first really big celebration we had in our new home. I had never felt any concern about Lil being left an old maid, but Dalma had given me moments of concern because here she was, almost twenty-two, and not married yet! So I was relieved, as any caring sister should be, that finally she was going to be married. Shortly I would be six.

Everyone was invited to the wedding, and about that many came. They came on horseback, in buggies, and in wagons. Cars had begun to put in their appearance, but were about as scarce as hen's teeth. Two huge tables were set up, seating possibly thirty to thirty-five people at a time. Dinner was served for several hours - from noon to nightfall, to new groups continuously. Everyone wore his Sunday-go-to meeting best, and in our family, Dalma had sewed them all. I never before saw so many gifts. I can still see the wedding cake, a round, three tiered fruit cake baked right at home, which was about twenty-six to twenty-eight inches in diameter and weighed maybe thirty to thirty-five pounds. It was appropriately decorated and I thought it was beautiful. The bottom layer was baked in our biggest dishpan which could just barely squeeze into our great big oven. Each layer was perhaps four to six inches thick.

Ira Albin, the man she was marrying had been one of Dad's "hired men", and had come from Indiana. That was about all I knew about him, except that Dad thought he was a good worker. He had filed on a claim for a homestead of 160 acres in the Girard area. Their marriage had been performed in the big parlor at our home by Rev. Damskov, and in the Danish language - with faint efforts to translate for Ira's sake. It is quite possible Ira had resentment over "all this Danish language stuff" - but he didn't mar the ceremony. When they took off for Girard in his lumber wagon the morning after the wedding, they seemed to shed the family, as well as the Danes - with all the patterns and traditions that accompanied. They seemed no longer part of us. It was almost as though we had lost our sister.

I recall how chilly it felt the day of the wedding even though it was the first of June. The night after the wedding there was a very heavy snowfall that left deep snowdrifts everywhere. Nobody attempted to leave that evening, and by the following day the snowstorm was over and all they had to do was to get through the drifts on their way to their new homes - Dalma and Ira Albin 20 miles westward, at Girard; and Lil and Thorvald Jensen 10 miles west at Brorson, or Dane Flats. Each couple had a little 2x4 shack to move into, and their wedding gifts from so many well wishers surely took up most of the space. But they survived and started their new life.

Dalma's family. Front row, Dalma, Ira Jr., Rose and Ira. Back row: David, Donald, Paul and Effie.

I visited Dalma and Ira in at their one-room home later that same summer, and stayed a couple days. I'm sure times were really tough for them, and we had little or no variety in diet, but we did have plenty of baked beans and home made white bread. I tended to have a week to spend with each of these two sisters every summer vacation. Meeting Dalma's specifications was not too difficult, but Ira was a different matter. Cutting the prairie grass for hay was a necessity in order to feed their livestock, which constituted not only food for the coming year, but their cash crop as well. Cutting the prairie grass with a mowing machine pulled by two horses, involved keeping the cycle - the blades - for cutting the grass, razor sharp. Everyday, when the mowing was finished, Ira had to sharpen the cycle blades on the grindstone, a big round sandstone wheel about eighteen to twenty inches in diameter, which was turned with a foot pedal or by means of a handle. That was where I came in: Ira always wanted me to turn the handle while he held the blade against the grindstone. I would stand there turning, turning, for what seemed an eternity, but probably was not over an hour at a time. After a couple years they built a larger three-room house and eventually there was another expansion to house their growing family.

When her family had grown to the point where she decided they needed more room, she contrived to open up the attic through a hole in the kitchen ceiling, building a ladder with flat steps rather than rungs, attached to a pulley arrangement she built, which provided a stairway, giving access to a hitherto inaccessible attic. It still took up no room because the ladder was built and installed to be pulled up and down, and put to rest flat against the ceiling in a matter of seconds. The two levels of the house could be separated or connected simply, easily and quickly. The ladder was placed at such a point it interfered with nothing when it was lowered into the kitchen. The hole in the ceiling had a trap door lid which was lowered at will so the kitchen had a "finished" look, and nobody needed to fear falling out of the attic. The arrangement worked so well it functioned for years.

She converted the attic to bedrooms for the kids, and heating it was simple: open the trap door and let the heat from the kitchen warm the space, like a pipeless furnace. Still later she added another couple rooms to the house, built a real stairway to the attic and dismantled the ladder. She seemed always to be able to devise a workable plan to provide what she deemed was necessary. Asking for help was not in her scheme of things.

It was essentially unthinkable that Dalma would ever get angry or raise her voice. She simply was never assertive and certainly not in her own behalf - ever. Nor did I ever hear her complain. I thought she had a lot to complain about, but I am sure not complaining was one of her most cherished virtues. She never said outright to me that Mother was a complainer or whiner. By the time I arrived on the family scene there had been so many changes in the family that I wasn't aware of, so it would be entirely probable that her perceptions of family members and family situations were correct, even if different from mine. I believe she always felt superior to or better than Mother because of her own "not-complaining". I never heard her criticize or disagree with her husband, and she certainly never nagged or thwarted him, as Mother had done. Once I heard someone say that at night after they went to bed, Dalma helped Ira make up his mind about things, but she surely never did this in the presence of others.

I am sure Dalma had contempt for women who try to run their husbands, and she had contempt for Niels and his arrogance, and his readiness to let others know how much he knew. The difference between Niels and Dalma seems to me not so much in abilities but in the way they used them. In addition to being non-assertive, Dalma was completely practical. She would never have done anything merely for the pleasure of doing it. It had to serve a practical goal. Nor did she ever gloat or openly disparage. I recall her telling me about a time, early in their marriage, when Ira came in to the house in mid forenoon and found the dishes unwashed, and her reading a story in a magazine. He just looked at her, but said nothing. She never again, she said - and I believe her - indulged herself in reading. I'm sure I never saw her reading anything - until later in her life she often read her Bible. She had the capacity to stop doing something she dearly enjoyed, so that nobody - even herself - could point an accusing finger at her. Her feeling of smug superiority because she had no guilts whatsoever really must have been overwhelming.

I became aware of what hard work was as I visited Dalma year after year. I really took note of her one year during my vacation. Her day began early with milking the cows. Then would follow separating the milk in the separator. Next came making breakfast for five of her family and for me, as well as for two or three men who were helping with the harvesting. In between, she got the kids up and dressed, fed them and herself, washed the dishes, swept the floors, tidied up the house and made the beds. By this time it was mid forenoon and time to bring forenoon lunch to the men working in the fields. So she made and packed a lunch, and took it to them in the buggy, a mile or more away. While the men ate sandwiches and drank coffee she filled in for them by shocking - putting into shocks or uprights stacks - the bundles of cut grain lying on the ground where the binder had dropped them nearby.

Then came making and serving noon dinner for nine or ten people, washing dishes and getting the younger kids to take their nap, bringing afternoon lunch to the men as had been done in the forenoon, and then starting to make supper for the large family. After supper it was getting the two little ones to bed and washing the dishes. After everybody was bedded down she started mending the binder canvases that had become torn during the day - sewing by machine, patching expertly. Then to bed to get ready for the next day. I never saw her sit down to rest or even to read. Life was hard, but she seemingly did everything well and willingly, with never a complaint or a grumble. She stayed well, so it must have agreed well with her.

After decades of complete abstinence from any kind of church affiliation, Dalma became a convert to a new type (to me) of religion, which had no name, she made clear, but the believers called themselves "Friends of Jesus." They say it is a worldwide congregation, without a name, without headquarters, without churches or edifices, or collection plates, and without ordained leaders. Their preachers are both men and women, and they go about their business two by two, meeting in the homes of believers. Nobody is paid any money for any service. Everything is freewill giving. When I first knew Dalma in her new role as churchgoer - except they never use the word church - she wore a dark, simple garb; but that no longer is true. The women do not cut their hair, and there is never any ostentation. They regard themselves as the most elite of the elite because they are carrying out the New Testament-ordained patterns of worship and living, and therefore are the ones who practice the truth, the whole truth. They never question their certitude.

They eschew all signs of vanity or religious politics. It was the first - and only - thing to which Dalma ever gave her complete devotion, other than to her family. It served as a wonderful outlet for her need to be useful, together with a sense of belongingness and status which she had never before had. It superseded and encompassed her never criticizing her husband. To her dying day she was ready and eager to participate fully in the life of her group. In behalf of and in the name of her Religion she could for the first time in her life make a few demands, such as going to any and all of the services, routinely twice a week, rather than as someone else pleased, and participating in whatever there was to participate in. I have felt deeply grateful she had this opportunity. She finally had the right to make a few demands because they were not ostensibly for herself but to carry out God's plans.

It was only when she was old and I had returned to Sidney that she sometimes would express thoughts and feelings to me that she no doubt had had since she was a young girl: She was severely and quietly contemptuous of Mother for her nagging Dad; and toward Mother and Carl for Carl's never learning to work hard; and for his being permitted to loll off to sleep in the kitchen every evening when he was a child, and not being able to wake up and go to bed on his own, but had to be carried there - and apparently she was elected to carry him. Probably she had volunteered for the job. And she was hostile toward Niels for his overbearing manner and his egotism. I'm glad she could get it off her chest. She had harbored it for too long. It is almost impossible for any of us not to be smug when we consider the terrible sins and failures of others. Another version of the same sentiment has graced my desk everyday for many years: "It's hard to be humble when you're as great as I am." One has to supply himself with reminders, lest he forget.

If Carl had his non acceptable forms of behavior, Ira surely had his too, but she refused to see them. It bothered me to no end how he could swat Dalma's bottom - or pinch it - laughing gaily as he did. He did it so hard I know it must have hurt - dozens and dozens of times a day - and year after year she never made the slightest effort to stop it! Another habit of his was to come in from the outside, go directly to the bed or buggy or crib where one of his kids was asleep, wake up the child with a loud swat, hug and kiss him or her for a few moments, put the child down in bed again - crying lustily - and then leave Dalma to get the child back to sleep. It was routine. And Dalma never said him nay! Her need not to criticize her husband was, to me incomprehensible. But it was the warp and woof of her life.

A memory crosses my mind: Since being back in Sidney and seeing her frequently, she told me she used to hold my eyes shut when I was a baby when it was her turn to get me to sleep. Another memory comes to mind of when I was perhaps seven or eight. A buggy load or two of family members had gone for a drive out in the hills to pick chokecherries for making some good jelly. I don't know where we went, except that we went west, and in the various draws and coulees we found plenty of berries to supply everybody. It was a hot summer day. Ira and Dalma joined us with their wagon at their home at Girard, some twenty miles away from Sidney. Most of the way, there were no roads and we drove on the open prairie. Maybe it was the heat - I cannot say - but something caused me to faint. Since I couldn't walk, and no one knew how long

I'd be out, somebody had to carry me back to the wagons, perhaps a quarter mile away - up and down the hills. I was always a huge and heavy child, and just thinking about it now sort of tires me out. Who carried me? Dalma, of course. She always did what was the hardest job. How she managed I never could understand, but whatever she undertook, she finished. One could always count on her. Mame was Dad's girl; Niels was Mother's boy; and what or who was Dalma? She was "the worker."

I recall another time I fainted. This time it was Spring break-up time, and Mother and I were visiting Sister Jo and Jim Hendrickson's home at Three Buttes. Again I was completely unconscious, and I fell smack into the coal bucket, generally messing things up in their kitchen. Thank goodness nobody had to carry me anywhere.

There are so many unrelated memories that come back to me: Ira's booming voice, singing to the top of his capacity as he worked outside, and the songs always having a totally different kind of lyrics and flavor than I was used to. I thought he must have brought them with him from Indiana. I remember several of my nephews, Lil's sons, who had worked for Ira, and always liked it because so much was going on there. They described Ira's approach to his various and sundry enterprises as, "Haywire it together, and let's get going."

I also remember well one summer I was spending my vacation week there. Late in the afternoon, Ira decided he would head for Sidney and take me along to deposit me back home in Sidney. It was during that period of a year or two, in the third and fourth grades, when we were living in town. The sky kept looking more and more ominous, and the thunder roared and the lightning flashed. Even the horses didn't like it, and we had a twenty mile drive ahead of us. When we got to the Brorson Church, out there on the prairie, about half way to Sidney, Ira turned the horses and wagon into the church yard. The rain was pouring down and the lightning flashes and the thunder were incessant. We made it to the long barn, built to accommodate those who attended church. It was open and Ira quickly unhitched the horses and led them inside and tied them up in a stall. He found one stall with clean straw on the floor, and the two of us bedded down there and went sound asleep. After a couple or three hours Ira woke up, and thought we might as well get going inasmuch as the storm was over. So we drove on to Sidney, arriving at about two a.m. I can assure you both Mother and Dad were surprised to see us. It was the only night in my life I ever spent in a barn. Another time I slept UNDER a barn, but that's another story.

I should not forget to make mention that Ira, Dalma, and their last two little ones were the only ones from Sidney who came to Portland to help me celebrate my graduation from Medical School in 1929. Their coming was a total surprise to us, but we were happy that they had thought enough of us to make the trip, close to a thousand miles each way. The car trip to see us was as hard on the two little ones as crossing the Atlantic had been on Dalma so long before. She spent her entire vacation taking care of her babies, Rose and June, (Ira Jr.) and trying unsuccessfully to reconcile them to being away from home. Added to that, in my attempt to show them around, I drove our car far too fast for them to follow me comfortably, and they were extremely critical of my lack of awareness of their difficulties in following me. I was used to driving in a city and they weren't. It is quite probable that I showed no adequate concern for their predicament. No accidents happened, they survived the trip, but my behavior only increased the tensions that were already present.

Dalma and Ira had seven children. The first one, a girl, died in process of birth in 1911. Dalma had been attended by a nurse-midwife, Mrs. Taylor, who had delivered lots of babies in the Girard area. As I recall it, the baby was the second person to be buried in the new Pella cemetery beside the Church, that eventually became the Sidney cemetery. This whole plot for church and cemetery was given Pella by my parents - a chunk of land out of their homestead. Grandma Maren Josephsen was the first to be buried in the cemetery, a few weeks before Baby Albin. I was told that the baby had been baptized on her little bottom while she was still alive, by Mrs. Taylor, and therefore she was sure to go to heaven. Baptism was an essential to Nurse Taylor, who was Catholic. Many others in our family are now buried nearby. Grandma and Baby Albin lie side by side along the west fence, close to the northwest corner of the cemetery. The other 6 Albin children were Effie, Paul, twins David and Donald, Ira Jr., and Rose.

Twice during the ten years I lived in Sidney prior to her death, Dalma told me the story of her decision to wipe Carl off from her close personal relationships. Years ago, long before

Carl was married, he had dropped in to the Albin place on horseback, not long before time for dinner. When dinner was served, he was part of the family and ate with them. Then he continued visiting through the afternoon, and it looked as though he expected to have supper and stay all night, as well as have his saddle horse fed and watered and put up in the barn. She knew Ira did not approve of this casual style, so she told Carl he would have to leave and find some other place to park, and that he couldn't expect to come again. It obviously was not an easy thing for her to do, or she would not have remembered it, but if it needed doing, she would do it. I'm sure she never considered leaving the job for Ira to do.

It was not easy for either one of them - Carl and Dalma - but she had spotted and dealt with a situation that had been Carl's usual pattern: Coming without invitation, taking it for granted he was welcome - as well as his horse - interrupting the normal flow, and spending the time "visiting". Carl was probably the best visitor one could find, but obviously others did not rate it as highly as he did. He took it for granted. They were more impressed with working as opposed to sponging; more accepting of responsibility and thoughtfulness of others than of visiting. Carl told me of the episode much later and never had been able to understand why he had been treated that way. He said he had never bothered them again. A detail that interests me, is that Carl's behavior reminds me of the "exploitative" behavior he never forgave the Danes for using in their relation to our parents. The shoe was on the other foot. It is always difficult to see ourselves, except in a favorable light. It is always "I saint, you sinner."

I was not sure Ira was not hostile when he invited me to take a horseback ride with him and I had to ride behind him. A buckle on the back flap of the saddle chewed into my rear end and caused a hole as big as a quarter. It hurt so bad I could hardly sit or walk for a week or more after the ride, but Ira seemed to think of it as a huge joke. He would swat his thigh when he saw me, and laugh loudly. There were lots of things that went on in the world that my life with my own parents never taught me. It sometimes took visits away from home to make me appreciate my own parents. But relations between Ira and Dalma were ever easy and comfortable. Each one respected the other - his or her basic judgement and capacity as well as loyalty, commitment and caring. Ira was never involved with alcohol, to my knowledge, and that must not have been the easiest thing to accomplish in the Girard community as it was in those days.

Quite frankly, despite my exasperation with Ira, I never saw him as a hostile person, or bent on cutting anyone down. This was quite different from Peter M, who never to my knowledge hit anyone. I don't think I ever felt a distaste for vacationing at Ira's home, even with its grindstone, while I dreaded even short visits at Mame's home if Peter M were around. Even as a child I felt the difference.

After Ira died of a heart attack enroute home from Sidney, Dalma moved into Mother's little quarters - a three room lean-to attached to the back of Mame's house. Dalma continued living there until after I returned to Sidney in 1971. Then Paul, her oldest son, also having returned to Sidney, bought a little house and the two of them lived there together until Paul died in 1980 while on a trip to Southern California. Paul is buried in California, where his three sons and their families have lived for many years - in the Riverside area. Dalma died shortly before her 94th birthday in 1981 - following a stroke, and is buried along side of Ira and Baby Albin and Grandma Maren Josephsen.

During the years since I returned to Sidney in 1971, I saw a lot of Dalma. I went to visit her often and noted how old she was, and yet how young. The only rigidity she seemed to show was in relation to her attendance at her religious meetings twice a week. She was always ready to be of help to me or anybody else who needed her sewing expertise. She fashioned a dress pattern a la my specifications, cut and sewed it; I still wear it with satisfaction and warm memories. Not infrequently, I run across something else she has made for me: a pieced "throw" to put over me if I take a nap; a long narrow braided runner rug I use in my kitchen, a pillow cover made out of Len's old neckties, on and on.

When the preachers in her church, commonly two women, were in service in this area, she would take care of them for a month or more at a time, never for pay. Every week when her kids, grandkids, and great grandkids came to town to shop and do necessary errands, she always served a big noon meal she had cooked for them, and served it on her kitchen table that could be extended to seat eight to twelve people. While the grown-ups were doing their errands in town, before or after the noon meal, she was baby-sitting two or three of their littlest ones.

Her role, she learned early, was to work, and work she did, but I never knew her to complain of feeling tired. I know everyone else got pleasure from the products of her working; I imagine she enjoyed it too; she was such an expert at it. I hope she did. She is a pleasant memory. I miss her even right now, for she was the one who had always kept track of all the birth dates in our family, up until shortly before her death.

Dalma's first living child, Effie, was born May 5, 1912. When she was starting school, Dalma and Ira sent her to stay with Mother, Dad and me in town. I believe because they thought the town school was better suited, at least for such a little girl, than the one in their area. I was aware of tension and friction right from the very start of Effie's being with us. Effie was uncooperative and balked at obeying Mother. I was 8 years her senior and had just started high school. I watched Mother get more and more frustrated. She wasn't used to having a defiant child, and she certainly didn't want to spank Dalma's kid. I had no such qualms and entered the fray, giving Effie a good spanking and telling her she better behave. I can't remember if her behavior improved. I've thought of it often and wondered if Effie had not learned, through living with Dalma and Ira, that Grandma didn't rank very high. I knew both of her parents would have expected obedience to their orders. But when the orders came from Grandma, there was no need to acquiesce, is the way I figured it out. Ira always called Mother the old lady - and Dalma felt hostile to her. They gave little encouragement to any warm feelings Effie might have developed had she not been imprinted from early days on, was the way I interpreted it then and still do.

Dad never got any flack. It was Mother who was responsible for Carl not learning to work, according to Dalma, even though Dad was no worker and much of the tension and nagging by Mother arose out of her trying to shame him into working. But for this, Mother earned Dalma's lifelong hostility because she was a nagger. It's a rather confusing world. It seems probable to me that Mother was bad no matter what she did because she failed to give Dalma the love she - Dalma - knew she deserved. She was just as worthy as Niels was - maybe more - and she never was able to compete and win over him.

An ironic twist is that after Dad died and each of us was to receive his or her inheritance, each one got the same sum - $200, I seem to recall. But from some of us Dad had stipulated there be a deduction determined by the information he had put down in his little book. My deduction was something like $50 - $75 to pay for the tonsillectomy I had had while going to the University of Oregon; and Dalma and Ira had a deduction for "stallion services" in the dim, distant past. I remember both Dr. Zimmerman who operated on me, and Hercules, the stallion.

Effie became completely immersed in Dalma's religion and for many years was one of the lay preachers, scattered all over the United States - and internationally. About retirement age, she married Howard Savey, also a lay preacher in that No Name Religion, but working in another geographic area. Neither one continued as preacher thereafter. They retired to Plentywood, MT, which was Howard's family home, and continued living there. They never had any children. I maintained a running contact with Effie, sending her my interesting or unusual canceled stamps, since she was a serious stamp collector. I also sent her all the items coming out in the *SIDNEY HERALD* that pertained to the Albins - and there were usually many; she had kept a scrapbook of family doings. She died quite suddenly in August, 1989, the time of our family's Centennial reunion, and her husband equally suddenly one week later, after a trip to get medical treatment at the hands of a nonorthodox medical practitioner using "chelating" in his treatment.

Paul, Dalma's oldest son, was my favorite. I knew him as a child, and then again many years later, when I moved to Southern California and he lived in Riverside. He had married Alice Hazelrig and they had three sons, Stanley, Allan and Philip. I met all of them while I lived in Chino and San Diego. He and Alice were divorced, and then he married again, and that marriage went on the rocks, but there were no children from his second marriage. Being involved with Dalma's religion as he was, he could never accept himself as divorced and into another marriage. He had great guilt, but at the same time he could not tolerate living with his first wife. Paul worked many years for Riverside County, CA, in the checking-end of house construction while Alice, his wife, had a real-estate office. Having had Dalma for his mother it wasn't surprising his marriage was burdensome, because he certainly was badly (unrealistically) trained as to what to expect from a wife. Some mothers produce unrealistic expectations in their sons.

Paul was as innovative in the construction business as Dalma had been in their home. After his second divorce and the onset of heart symptoms, Paul returned to Sidney, and purchased a little house near the Sidney Senior High School for himself and Dalma. He was always a restless person, and seemed to be happiest when he was busiest, so he made a lot of modifications in their home. Then I helped out by asking him to help put a kind of root cellar in my basement so I could keep my "vast stores" of garden produce from my 15x20 plot in my back yard. I'm still using it quite happily. I hate to have anything spoil or go to waste, so he definitely added to my peace of mind.

Paul and Dalma spent several years together - both of them busy, and despite his pattern of restlessness, they seemed to get along together quite well. Dalma was getting too old to be any place by herself, and Paul's heart problem was forever present.

Once Paul was talking to me about the time he spent living with Mother and Dad and attending Sidney High School. He wondered what in the world his grandfather was doing and saying just before meals, as they sat down to the table. Dad would put his right hand to his forehead and rub his fingers back and forth in front of his eyes. I said it sounded like Dad was saying Grace, but if he could tell me what he heard him say, I could say for sure. After he had told me - and he felt he must have heard it hundreds of times, I asked him to write it down for me - so he wrote, and I still have his report: "E Yeasuno golito gu, espiso su ento lie gu tol leeta - die gu til aere an os to kom; suffera ma eesu nown." What Dad was saying was the Danish table prayer that every Dane knows well: "I Jesu Navn gaar vi til Bord; at spise, drikke paa dit Ord; Dig Gud til aere, os til gavn, Saa faar vi Mad I Jesu Navn." The literal translation is: "In Jesus Name go we to the table, to eat and drink according to Thy word; Thou, God, to be honored, us to be benefitted; Thus receive we food in Jesus name." Paul, apparently had never heard of or experienced saying Grace, and his familiarity with the Danish language was nil, so no wonder he had a bad time comprehending. And Dad would not have believed that one of his grandsons, the son of his daughter born in Denmark, would find his behavior and language incomprehensible.

In 1979 I asked Paul if he would drive me to Portland, Oregon, so that I could attend the 50th Anniversary commemoration of my graduation from Medical School. I felt sufficiently at home with him so I could ask favors of him. He, Jan and I made the trip in his little Japanese car, without incident. Had he not done this I would not have been able to attend. I really appreciated his doing this for me. Then he went to California and didn't return. He died, and that left Dalma alone again.

Mother took care of a lot of sick people during the flu epidemic of 1918-19, and did not get the disease herself, but many in Sidney did get it and there was a high mortality. None of Mother's patients died, for which she was very grateful. Ira and Dalma both had the flu and Mother took care of them in their home at Girard. Dalma was pregnant, but carried her twins to term, and seemingly there were no untoward complications or sequelae.

The twins, David and Donald, born on Abe Lincoln's Birthday, Feb. 12, 1919, right after the big flu epidemic, were different in appearance and behavior right from the start. Dave had brown eyes like his father, and reddish brown hair, while Don was a blond, blued eyed boy. Their interests and patterns were different, and they remained that way throughout their lives. Both married and had several children. Dave married Ethel Myron, and they bought the family farm at Girard. They had six children - three sets of two children - but no twins: two girls, Kay and Judy; two boys, Bob and Richard; and then two more daughters, Shirley and Janet. All of them have remained in the Sidney area. In 1990, Shirley's marriage - with one child - ended in divorce, and Janet's - with two children - ended when her husband died of burn injuries.

Dave, one of Dalma's twins, who runs the family ranch, has been active in various civic projects, including the Congregational Church. Although Dave was probably Dalma's favorite son, I feel sure she would never admit to that. But Dave resembled Ira in looks - brown eyes and red-tinged dark brown hair - in interests and business competence. Dave, along with Ira Jr. and Ira Sr. were the only ones in their family who did not accept and join in with Dalma's religion. Ira would take her wherever she wanted to go, and without a hassle - but he would NOT participate in her religion. He'd wait elsewhere until she was finished with whatever it was she wanted to do, and then pick her up and take her home. For years he was involved with his Masonic affiliation, and Dalma did not participate in that.

Dave has been an outstanding success as a dryland farmer. Seldom a month goes by that a mention of someone in the Albin family does not appear in the Sidney papers. Third and fourth generation Albins are always doing something worthy of note. Dave has been a prominent member of the Richland County Fair Board, and has held this post for years. Now his oldest son Bob is following in his footsteps. His wife is a Buxbaum and they have 4 kids. Dave's grandkids invariably come up with prizes for their livestock.

I actually have little knowledge of many of the Albins. Somehow, somewhere we seem to have lost one another. After I returned to Sidney in 1971, I picked up involvement with Dalma and nourished it, but I did not become part of her family, with a mutual sense of closeness. Perhaps it still is as it was in the early days where they were Albins and we were Andersons, and ne'er the twain shall meet. My fallow years in the 70's and 80's may also have contributed to this state of affairs, since it was a period in which I made few moves toward anybody - which would surely reinforce any feelings of distance which they might have had prior to my return to Sidney.

Kay, Dave's oldest child, married a farmer, Harold Carda, and they have three daughters and a son; all are intelligent, competent, attractive and responsible people.

Judy, Dave's second child is the only one who has had twins. One of them also has bright red hair, and surely suggests that there are some active genes traveling from Ira to Dave to Judy to her son. I am sorry I have so little awareness of what her family is like. We never see one another or talk on the phone. Maybe I can do better in the future. Dave's youngest son, Richard, I scarcely know other than that he is married and has one child. I recall that years ago when family members used to gather weekly at Dalma's table for dinner, it was Richard who seemed invariably to be able to quiet a squalling baby; and I have also heard he and our local surgeon, Dr. Edward Bergin, are friends. To me, these are good recommendations.

I have even less knowledge of Dalma's other twin, Don Albin's life. The fact that we left Sidney for Oregon in 1921 when he was only two may partly account for my failure. He left the Sidney area and went to Minnesota, where he married Margaret Sorg. This name stimulates my curiosity, and makes me wonder if she might be a Dane, because in the Danish language, Sorg means Sorrow. They had 5 children, Mary, Dale, Linda, Martha and Nyla. The oldest girl, I have heard, was retarded. Don was into trucking as well as farming, and eventually moved from Minnesota to Colorado, where he still lives. I have never met any of this family.

Ira Jr. or June, as he was called, Dalma's youngest son, was one of the two youngsters who came with his parents to Portland, to help celebrate my graduation in Medicine. He seemed to be a very unhappy child on that trip, and both he and his younger sister Rose did a lot of crying and made it almost impossible for Dalma to do anything other than attend to them. Many years later I met him again, here in Sidney. He had been in the Service, had been a prisoner of War, and I understood he had been badly treated. To me he seemed somewhat of a dreamer, but I have no firm impression, for our contact was minimal. He married a local girl named Burneal Nellermoe, who had taught school in the Girard area.

They had 7 children, Delores, Gary, Durwin, Cecil, Jay, Rita and Harvey. June had many problems, both physical and psychological, related to a chronic infection of his brain, which necessitated many periods in a VA hospital. They moved from this area to Colorado, where the VA gave him unlimited care for several years, clearly by reason of his POW status. He died in Colorado in a traffic accident. Dalma always attributed his problems to the war experience. I have no personal knowledge.

Rose, the youngest of six live births for Dalma, took her Dad Ira's behavior for granted, and I have never known her to be even minimally critical of him. She did not immediately shift to an acceptance of her Mother's religion, but eventually she did. She married Pat Waldo, from another Montana pioneer family, and they moved first to the Glendive, MT. area, and then to Miles City, MT., where she still resides. She and Pat had six children, Connie, Ginger, Kolleen, Cole, Timothy and Tana.

Then Pat died quite unexpectedly, and Rose was left to raise and support their children. Among other things she did to accomplish this was to turn their home into a rooming and boarding house for selected high-school students in Miles City. It was Dalma who came to her assistance in making the alterations in her house necessary to accomplish this. Rose not only kept the students fed - and well - but she helped steer them straight too, which is sometimes a thankless task, but she did it warmly and generously. She had by this time moved into the orbit of her Mother's religion, and this became for her a veritable passion.

When her youngest child, Tana, was only three or four years old, she was killed in a traffic accident on snow covered roads in which her mother Rose was the driver. It was her stated belief that God had decided that the child's father, Pat, needed Tana with him in heaven, so He arranged the accident in which Tana was killed. It seemed to me this solution spared her both from guilt and from sorrow.

A few years ago, after her own children were gone and married, Rose remarried to a widower, who was also a member of their religious sect, Ralph Caler. The two of them have had endless opportunity to feel good about their good fortune in being Friends of Jesus. They are active in proselytizing, which never seemed to be Dalma's pattern. People don't always follow the same patterns even if their pathways are similar. Her second husband also died quite unexpectedly in 1991.

Dalma was never one to admit to or to make the most of any disability. I am aware she had a period of rather continuous vertigo or dizziness which required bed rest, but I doubt she sought medical help for it and never mentioned it later. Her single encounter with surgery was a hysterectomy for removal of a large uterine fibroid. I never heard her mention it before or after surgery. She verbalized no complaints aside from Mother and Carl.

Dalma got her status from her endless contributions to all of us through her tackling anything that needed doing, and carrying it through to completion. But there no doubt was a hurt which she felt, that made her resent her parents, especially Mother, enduringly. She seemed less able to show overt affection than any of her sisters. None of us really can get very far away from our roots and our early experiences.

Lillian - Montana Made

Mother's and Dad's fourth child, and the first one to be born in America, was Lillian Annette. Lil was born in the log house by the river, August 25, 1890. They had, obviously, dropped the pattern of giving their children four names. This may have signified they felt they might now give their children more than merely names, or that now that Grandfather

Lil & Laurits Jensen Family. Back Row: Ernie, Ralph, daugher-in-law Evelyn, Roy, Peter and Bill. Front Row: Walter, Lil, Larits, Thor.

Niels Josephsen was gone, so was his advice. The name Lil, as she finally came to be called, after going through years of being Lillie, derived from nobody I ever heard of, but her middle name was for Annette Meadors. I suspect she helped Mother in the birth process of Lil, even though this is only my speculation.

Lil was not only the first American product in our family, but she was the first white child born in this area.

When Lil was just a baby she suffered a bad accident when Niels overturned a scalding hot pot of coffee on her. There was no medical assistance available, but Mother immediately used the basic common sense she had in health matters: she broke a whole lot of eggs and poured the whites all over her burned areas, put clean flour-sack towels over her, and for weeks carried her as little as possible and then only on pillows. Amazingly, infection was no problem, and she healed without any appreciable scarring. Mother characteristically attributed this to God's protective hand, to common sense care and everybody's love. It is nice to have an ample supply of all three ingredients. When I was a premed student at the University of Oregon I learned in a research project that eggs tend to have bacteria in them, right in the shell, without external contamination, so it was a wonder Mother's homespun treatment worked as well as it did.

I can't remember much about her in our home and family until I was four or five years and she was almost twenty. She was about to be married to Thorvald Jensen, one of the Danish immigrant settlers who had come to file on homesteads, i.e. register a legal claim to the land. I have heard she taught school one year. I also find Thorvald on various pictures taken of gatherings of Danes in the MonDak area. I had no concerns about Lil ending up an old maid, as I had about Dalma. On June 1st, 1910, the double wedding took place in our big new home, that had seen only one real celebration, namely Mother's and Dad's Silver Wedding Anniversary on August 17, 1909. The double wedding of Lil and Dalma was truly a gala affair, and everybody was there. I was flabbergasted by the profusion of gifts - tables loaded with them. The following morning, after a big snowstorm, Lil and Thorvald headed for their new home northeast of the Brorson church, and surrounded by new Danish settlers on every side. This area was, indeed, appropriately called Dane Flats.

After all her years as a United States citizen because she was born here, Lil suddenly lost her United States Citizenship when she married and became merely the wife of a Danish immigrant. She learned she lost her U.S. citizenship by marrying a man not yet naturalized. She was the one who had come running to Mother when the load of relatives from Denmark was about to arrive from Glendive in 1899, asking her how to say, in Danish, "Come out and play with us." Mother always maintained she had never given any thought to how far they had slipped from the Danish patterns and familiar expressions until Lil asked her the question about playing. Lil never did become a real Dane, but she was glad to have her citizenship rights restored to her after a few years.

Lil, tall, lanky and blond, was neither as organized nor as competent in so many fields as was her constant competitor, Dalma. But she understood clearly the difference between what was important and what was unimportant. She had a pretty good ability for leaving well enough alone, i.e. she was not a hard core, dyed in the wool perfectionist. She was also a hard worker. She had a rather short fuse, sounding off easily, probably from getting a sense of helplessness quite frequently. I was used to quiet, calm, and orderliness, and this was hard to come by at Lil's house. One good reason was that she kept on having babies - one son after another. The oldest was born a couple weeks before she had been married a year, and they just kept coming, and times were very hard, which provided plenty of opportunities to feel helpless.

Dad needed to be free of the load of making decisions regarding the farm; Mother no longer had her family of nearly grown girls to help her get the work done, and Lil and Thorvald needed some steady income, so it was arranged that shifts in living arrangements would be made. Lil's family would join us, live on our farm and manage it. Eventually we made another shift from living on the second floor at the farm to living in town. Christine and I went to the town school instead of having to attend the school right near our farm, where the teacher who roomed and boarded at our house had had me pull her corset strings tight in order to conceal her pregnancy.

The Titanic sank in April, 1912, and I recall very clearly that we were living upstairs in the big house at the time, and how for days nobody could think or talk about anything but the Titanic. Peter, Lil's sick baby would have been a year old on May 18, 1912, so my memories appear to be correct. We left the farm while Thorvald was responsible for it, and that would have been the winter of 1912-13. We returned to the farm about 1914 and Lil and Thorvald went back to their own homestead. Mostly, nobody bothered to explain to me what was going on or why anything was being done. Kids probably would not understand even if they were told, is a common assumption, but explaining might save unnecessary confusion.

Lil's seven sons came in rapid succession. In order of their birth, they were Peter Russell, Roy Bertie, Ralph Soren, William, Ernest Marenus, Walter Joseph, and Thorvald Jens. Her seventh son arrived after the death of her husband, Thorvald, from Cancer of the stomach, in 1922. Peter, the oldest, was 11 when the seventh boy was born. Mother and I had left Sidney for Eugene in 1921, and we were not even aware of any problem with Thorvald's health, so his death was a major shock to both Mother and me.

Rather shortly after Thorvald's death, Lil married Thorvald's younger brother, Laurits, who had served in World War I in Europe, and had been a frequent part of Lil's family after his discharge in 1919. I remember writing to Laurits while he was in the service, as I did to a few other soldiers, who, I was told, needed to hear from the folks at home. Beyond doubt, Laurits was a wonderful choice for a second husband for Lil. He completely accepted Lil's seven sons, and he accepted the job of being their new but full time father. To this day, the seven sons feel they were essentially Laurits's children, and most of them can scarcely recall life with their own father. For all practical purposes, Laurits was the only father they knew. Laurits WAS the father of Lil's eighth and last child - a girl - named Anna, who was the light of their lives - after nothing but boys.

After the birth of this special baby, Anna, Lil had an ectopic pregnancy which had ruptured and necessitated emergency surgical removal of her fallopian tubes and hysterectomy to save her life. This precluded the possibility of a repeat performance of another ectopic pregnancy. This surgery was acceptable because, by any measure, eight children is surely enough, and they had their daughter, and Laurits had his own child. Then came the unexpected and tragic death of little Anna from lung abscess, and they were left without the possibility of trying to replace her. I recall writing a letter of condolence to Lil, and I am ashamed to think about what I wrote. I cannot remember the words, but I remember the sanctimonious tone of my letter, admonishing her to accept God's will and assuring her everything was for the best. How could I sit there and be so smugly wise and untouched when Lil's heart was broken! I was then in a very religious period of my life. I was in Eugene, being a part of a revival-high, which had been set in motion by a follower of Amiee Semple MacPherson. I wrote the way I was thinking and believing, but I saw it later as quite insensitive and bordering on insolence. I never had a response from her, and I should not have expected one. It was not unlike the juvenile insolence of Adam in the Garden of Eden.

It is never easy to see oneself as he or she is behaving in present tense. Sometimes we see what our past behavior was, but even that is problematic. I have wondered if it had any relation to some hostility I harbored toward Lil because of a remark she made years before, namely: That if something happened (some bad thing), the first impulse she would have would be to spank me. I didn't think I deserved that, and I have no idea what led to it. My best guess would be that the feeling arose during that period in 1911 when Lil and Thorvald lived on our farm and in our big house. Their oldest child Peter was just a few months old, and he was sick. He cried a lot and Lil had to give him enemas frequently. At such times his little body would respond by suddenly forcing the enema out, and the fluid would fly out across the room. I often watched in amazement. Of course I may have done something else, but I was not aware of it. I do recall a couple times I stood on the gate between the barns and the house, and swung back and forth, and this resulted in Lil scolding me. Maybe I was noisy and I wakened her sick baby. But to my knowledge, no big thing had been going on between us. But the fact that I can remember it all these years must have meant the air between us was charged. It could also relate to the prevalent pattern of downgrading me because I was Mamma's pet.

When one considered that electricity and indoor plumbing - running water - were not a part of my life until I was in high-school, it begins to dawn on us how full of labor living was. One of the early labor-saving devises was the windmill - not electricity - that enabled people to stop pumping water and letting the wind do the work. I still recall the incredulous shout of Jan once when we visited Auntie Lil in Sidney, and used their chemical toilet: "Auntie Lil has no flushing toilet!"

Life just kept getting more difficult for Lil's family and necessitated their disposing of their farm and moving to Antelope, Montana, in 1926. Finally they moved back again to the Girard area where they had secured a steady job carrying the mail for Uncle Sam over a fifty-two mile round trip route out of Sidney. This meant they were always under pressure six days of every week, in the heat of summer and the cold of winter, to deliver the mail. Mostly, they made it by car, but often the weather or roads were too bad and they had to do it with horses and wagon. We never heard of the "windchill factor" in those days, but they surely experienced it, for if there has been one thing Montana has in plenty supply, it is wind.

Lil's oldest child, Peter, born in 1911, was always shy and retiring, but he finished high-school in Sidney, and married Marcella Trenk, a member of the Sioux tribe. She was related to Princess Ekalaka, also of the Sioux tribe, and to William Russell, brother of Montana's famous artist, Charles Russell. Peter worked for many years for Exxon Oil Co., and was retired in 1981. Peter and Marcella had two sons, Charles Russell (Fritz), and William James (Willie Jim). They lived in the Billings area, and had a summer home in Cooke City adjacent to Yellowstone Park. Their older son is light complexioned like his father, Peter, but heavy set like his mother, Marcella. Willie Jim is tall and lanky like his father, and dark like his mother. Willie Jim and his wife, Louisa, an R.N., have two daughters, the first is quite dark complexioned, and the second is a "decided" blond.

Roy, Lil's second son, was no special health problem as Peter had been. He turned out to be the living-spitting-image of my Dad, his grandfather. Their pictures show them to be true look-alikes. He had an accident when he was a young man, breaking his leg, which required hospitalization in the Sidney Hospital. Fortunately, he made a good recovery. While in the hospital his nurse was Evelyn Erickson, a member of the Olaf Erickson family. They fell in love, and married. After a brief time in Eastern Montana, they moved to the Bay area in California, where Roy was employed mostly in the dispatching end of the trucking industry. They had no children, but they adopted two sons while they still lived in Montana, Roy Jr. and Lars Olaf, who are a valid part of their family. Both Roy and Evelyn had a strong interest in political affairs and community development. They were definitely civic-minded citizens. Roy was the first of Lil's family of boys to die, in 1984.

Lil passed on to her family her own very strong interest in politics, and it was always on the Democrat ticket. Dad would definitely have been her adversary, but it is doubtful if he could have been more verbal or more persuasive with her than he had been with Niels. As far as I know, all her sons are all died-in-the-wool Democrats. Perhaps it is the legacy of F.D.R. to people surviving the Great Depression Era.

Ralph, the third of Lil's boys, is a tall fellow who strongly resembles the Josephsen side of our family. Times were hard and toys were essentially non existent. I can still recall Lil's boys playing day after day close beside their house, for shade, with stones they had gathered from their land. The stones no doubt were the product of the Glacial Age, and their relative sizes were important. These little stones made fence lines, others were cows or calves, or horses, and other slightly larger stones were buildings. The boys all played together in the dirt, and seemingly had a good time. They certainly did not seem to need to be a bother to anybody. They entertained themselves. Their sense of unity has been a strong feature in that family, and shows in the fact that they have for quite some time had Jensen reunions every two years in the area where one of the "boys" lives. Not only does the Jensen clan come for a two or three day get-together, but fringe relatives come too. There often are as many as fifty to seventy people who attend these family gatherings. It is a wonderful way of keeping up to date on what is going on, and it helps cement the close feelings that exist even at the inter generations level. The in-laws become real people instead of mere names, and the solidarity is reinforced at every reunion. In 1989, the Montana Centennial year, the Jensen relatives were hosted by Walt and Mary Jensen here in Sidney and included and featured one of the days as "Anderson Days" to honor our family's centennial year in Montana.

Walt & Mary Jensen

Ralph was listed in the Who's Who Among College Students. Prior to his years in Service he married Lorena Young, from neighboring Fairview, and they had two children, Jenasy and Leon. Ralph was in the service during World War II, and then embarked on a long military career, until his retirement in the mid 1960's with the rank of Lt. Col. He visited us while we lived in Washington, D.C. I have a picture of Ralph, Jan and me taken during this visit; it is still up on my huge bulletin board of pictures, and I frequently stop by to see him.

Ralph's family has had a series of major problems for many years. Jenasy, their daughter, had given birth to twin boys, Reed and Rayburn Rothrock, in New Orleans, where she and her young neurologist husband lived. Shortly after that her mother Lorena was killed in a traffic accident. Then followed the breakup of Leon's marriage and shortly thereafter his disappearance from the face of the earth. Despite years of intensive searching, no trace of him has ever been found. Ralph remarried, to an acquaintance of Lorena's, and this marriage was a distressing fiasco which after a few years was terminated. Then Jenasy's marriage to Russell Rothrock went on the rocks, and after many years she remarried to John Dailey. He is a bush pilot in Alaska, who also graduated in medicine, but had never practiced. They continue to live and work in Alaska, and because they had no children of their own they arranged for a surrogate mother to bear John's child, a strapping son who is now more than a year old. Things seem to be moving along for them. In fact, I hear they have adopted a second child.

Ralph has married again, this time to Lorraine White, and they live in Florida, which has been home to him for more years than Montana was home. During the years since he was discharged from the service, Ralph has done a lot of college teaching. In between times he has spent his time building one house after another for Jenasy and her family in the various areas of Alaska as the family has moved.

I have always found Ralph to be interesting, intelligent and very much alive. I wish I might see and visit with him oftener than I do, but he seems to have achieved a degree of calm after many years of emotional turmoil. I hoped to see him in 1989 at the Jensen-Anderson reunion.

William or Bill, was Lil's fourth child. I scarcely remember him from the time before I left Sidney in 1921, except that he looked like his father, Thorvald. He was too young to get my attention, and he had too many brothers to be a serious contender for my affection. Then I heard he was getting married to a girl from North Dakota, Nellie Fullerton. They had two daughters, Willetta (Billy Anne) and Linda Sue. They lived in Washington State not far from Spokane.

I don't know the whys or wherefores, but Nellie decided to terminate her marriage to Bill and marry his younger brother, Thor. He had been in the service, and had had a hard time readjusting to civilian life after he was discharged. It was a serious blow to Bill, but he eventually accepted it as an accomplished fact and remarried. His second marriage ended when his wife died of cancer. He married a third time to June Welch, and this marriage continues to the present time. They do a lot of traveling but maintain their home at Nine Mile Falls, Washington, where he was employed by Washington Power Company until his retirement in 1981.

For several years Bill and his wife have been involved in a most interesting project which they finished in 1989. It was the gathering of data for a monumental family portrait of the Jensen family. The material has been put together into a book of 386 pages with thousands of pictures. It's title is "*MY HERITAGE BOOK - ROOTS, BRANCHES AND TWIGS.*" It is a wonderful historical document. Of course it includes the Anderson family, through Lil's role. They traveled to Denmark to gather a great deal of information, and throughout the United States. They gave a copy to the MonDak Heritage Center here in Sidney, and I have my own copy.

While Bill was here he came to visit me. I was aware that something was sparking an emotional reaction in him that I did not understand. Later, I asked his brother Walt what it might mean and he suggested that I remind him of his mother, Lil. When I was a child everyone would tell me that I looked like Lil - but I had not heard this since I left Sidney in 1921. Now comes Bill, whose eyes fill with tears as he talks with me, because I remind him of his mother! Bill no longer looks like his dad. He is not spare as Thorvald was, and his beard is dark, tinged with gray.

Lil and I probably did resemble one another a lot. I was not quite six when she married and left home. We were the ones most like Mother. Our build was about the same - we were the "big girls" of our family. Our hair was tawny blond, and we were both emotionally responsive and people-oriented. Lil had a habit of emitting a short, mirthless laugh whenever she would say something she wasn't sure would be accepted. And now, eighty years after we separated, Bill weeps because I remind him of his mother! He was perceptive enough to detect it. I'm sure nobody had tipped him off. There must be something important about genes.

Ernest, Lil's fifth son, was scarcely one of the facts of life when I left Sidney in 1921, so I didn't know him at all until

I lived in Salem, Oregon. He he lived in Portland and worked for the Southern Pacific Railway in the 1960's. By that time he was married to Jean Boles and they had one child, Richard, - Rich - who was in high-school. We visited them occasionally and I was very aware that I knew Richard as little as I had known his father, because the moment he returned home from school, he beat it right upstairs to his room and that was the last I would see him until next visit. Then I left Oregon for California in 1964, and I began hearing from Rich, now married, and gradually producing a family of 3 children, Kathy, Eric, and Denny. Rick works for NASA, lives in Port Orchard, Washington, and they all seem to be dynamic, achieving people. They never forget to make contact with me at Christmas time.

Ernie retired from his job with the railroad in 1978 and they moved from Portland to Toledo, Oregon where they have a fascinating home atop a mountain. Twice I have tried visiting them, but never found them at home. They are quite isolated, but their place is beautiful. I peeked through their windows and would have taken a look had the doors not been locked. Sister Jo's family in Eugene always invite them for family gatherings, so they are included as family members on an on-going basis, and then someone relays pertinent information to me. That information has never included anything about how Ernie spends his time. They came to Sidney for the Jensen-Anderson Reunion in 1989.

Walter was the last of Lil's boys born before I left Sidney. He, too, was too little for me to have any memories of him then. I know he finished high-school, and that he had chronic trouble with his back as a result of an accident. He is the one, who with his wife Mary Micheletto Jensen, together with their daughter Mary Annette, are the chief, caring relatives still remaining here in Sidney, and who in one way or another help me over and through whatever problems I manage to come up with. I am ever grateful for their dependable around-the-clock concern for Jan and me.

Mary's Mitcheletto's parents came from Italy and settled here in Sidney in 1916. Their family was large, and they maintain a close relationship with one another from points all over the United States. Walt and Mary tried making a living at various occupations here in Sidney and in Eugene, Oregon. He worked in restaurants, was a meat cutter, and he ran a dairy and delivered milk. Perhaps he did many other things, but my main association with him was that he had a close and trusting relationship with his mother, Lil. I never was quite sure whether it was Walt or Mary, his wife, who ranked so high with Lil, but it was for sure both of them were tops.

Using this as a guide, when I arrived in Sidney I had my will made out and named Walt executor. There have been long stretches of time during the past few years when I wouldn't have given a dime for my chances of being around for even a few months, and the will might well have been put into effect, but here I still am. I have had no sense of imminent termination for over a year now, and this added time has given me an opportunity to get acquainted with Walt and his family. The first thing I'd like to say is that Lil was right, and it has been a real pleasure to just be around and know all of this family better.

Walt has been manager of the Farmers' Union Insurance Company here in Sidney for many years, and Mary, his wife, has been his partner in the office. They have a big, comfortable home just outside of Sidney, to the southwest, and every year they have a garden to beat all gardens - both vegetable and floral. Mary succeeds in keeping their landscape bright with color, and their home has sprouted a big bay window filled with house plants galore. Walt has a variety of health problems - always has had - which severely limit him and require his use of oxygen on a regular basis, while Mary has prodded him to give up his cigarette habit and do himself a service. Surgery on his bladder for tumors has been a frequent necessity.

Walt tended to be the quiet one, but his overall reticence belied his easy familiarity with an endless procession of subjects and areas, where I found that he not only had familiarity, but solid opinions. Mary is highly verbal and a top notch cook, as well as seamstress. Her skills are endless. I have yet to come up with a problem calling for a practical solution that they have not helped me with. They are forever bringing Jan and me CARE packages - from their garden, from their flower garden, from their oven or their freezer, a wool blanket mended for me, a tax statement that needed my attention, or a hundred and one other caring services. I receive attention from them day by day - it's enough to reconcile one to getting old and more or less useless. Mary is involved in many community service projects, one of which takes a lot of her time: she is a Docent at Sidney's MonDak Heritage Center, helping to keep it an asset to Sidney. She works frequently at our "Good Cents Store" which accepts all manner of clothes and white elephants, sells them for peanuts and donates the proceeds to the hospital for special needs not provided for in the hospital budget.

One of the debts I have to them - chiefly to Mary - is my involvement with writing again, after the elapse of so many years. She said my story needed to be written. When I began trying to do something about her suggestion, I got nowhere. I couldn't remember anything about anything, was what it amounted to. I slowly became aware that my memory was improving. I persisted in writing, and my awareness shifted to problems in identifying what I had said and what I had only recalled from my memory store houses. I wrote everything I could remember, in longhand, in huge notebooks, and discovered I had still another problem: my handwriting had deteriorated to the point of almost complete illegibility.

I've now been at writing for many months. The basic content as determined by my chapter titles covers most of the areas I want to talk about. It has proven to be a constant stimulus to my memory; it has also been an interesting occupation for me, because I have never before sat down to write about me and what has preoccupied me most. Perhaps best of all, it has acted as a sort of experience in Free Association - just letting my mind wander anywhere it wanted - and this has been as self revealing as Freud maintained it would be. I have known for a long time that I am not different from others, or unique, so I can even hope that my frank recording will stimulate some honest self scrutiny in others. But Mary Micheletto Jensen must get whatever credit derives from her vision and prodding, along with my own efforts.

Walt and Mary have three kids - now grown and having their own families - Carlo, John and Mary Annette, who was the apple of her grandmother Lil's eye. John has long been involved in a military career. In fact, he has been in the Military for 20 years, and has achieved the rank of full Colonel. His assignments have been stimulating and interesting, and he has been able to carry to completion a variety of projects. He enjoys both teaching and writing. Perhaps being discrete is one of his prime qualities. He married while in Service, and he and his wife, Cathy McDairmid now have their own child, Joseph, and an adopted daughter, Christina, who, I am told, is a solid part of a solid family. I also get the impression that whereas things and ideas are fascinating to John, people are even more interesting. Walt, his father, has said of him, "He understands people."

Carlo, the oldest of Walt's progeny, is quite a different person from John, and I don't feel I know him very well, even though for a time after I returned he and his family lived here in Sidney. Considering my physical and mental state - my fallow years - this failure of mine is not surprising. His wife, Paula Strom, returned to college and has stuck at it for all these many years, first at Eastern Montana College in Billings, and then in Helena at Carroll College, where she got her Bachelor's degree. Psychology fascinates her. Carlo is general manager of large Shopping Malls in Helena and Missoula in Montana, and now in Arizona, and apparently he is a success at it. He has excellent competence in a variety of areas, all of which are challenged in the Mall job, so it is quite possible he may find the work holds his interests and he will continue in it indefinitely. Walt and Mary describe him as "a typical Yuppie".

Carlo and Paula have three children: Mike, Matthew and Heather - in or having finished college. Each one is a distinct individual. This last summer when Matt was in Sidney he came calling on me and we had a real good session, though it is not hard to imagine that a visit with an 85 year old woman is not too exciting for a teenager. Mike graduated from the University of Montana with a perfect grade point average. He married and has a job in Washington state.

Mary Annette, named for her adoring grandmother, as well as for her mother Mary, has been a veritable godsend to me. During the years since I have been recovering, I have been more aware of my many infirmities than I had been before: my feet, my eyes, my ears, my heart, my hands, all seemed to demand help, and in trying to get this help it has necessitated my contacts with many physicians. This in turn meant that I became involved with Medicare, and that was a nightmare of paperwork and the need to remember all sorts of things I couldn't possibly remember. In vocalizing my predicament, Mary Annette offered to lead and guide me and take me under her wing as long as necessary. Her offer was like manna from heaven; she was precisely what I needed. During these many months I have placed myself in her expert care, and so far the burden on her has not been too great, and my problems seem solvable. I know I could not have done it without her help.

She is also copying my MY DAY: MY SAY columns from the Sidney Herald, and nobody knows what may eventuate from that, but at least we are in the process of doing something about making them available. We are also getting acquainted, and that is worthwhile as far as I am concerned. Mary Annette and her husband, Alan Seigfreid, have taken over from Walt and Mary the Jensen Agency with its Farmers' Insurance, and its Real Estate business. Besides that, the two of them have their own interests and little businesses. Mary Annette has a thriving used paperback book store; Alan keeps busy outside working hours through his interest in and service on the Board of Directors of the MonDak Heritage Center and all that it represents, as well as refereeing sports events. They both have worked in the Junior Chamber of Commerce program, and are involved in a variety of civic activities, which include participation along with their two children in numerous endeavors.

Only yesterday, as I turned on radio station KGCX for the local news, someone was announcing that Mary Annette was working with the Sidney Librarian to set up a new project. It was an educational toy section, which included not only collecting such toys, but assessing the specific levels and suitabilities of each item, cataloging them, and working out a system for loaning and educating parents regarding purchases and use. It is a constant surprise discovering how much we owe to our children for making us learn so many things that assist us in the business of living. The same may be said for the contributions of patients to my education: invaluable.

Mary Annette and Alan have two fine children, Amanda and Erik, both in grade school, who provide never-ending challenges in understanding and management. I expect both of them to visit me, come Halloween. I am grateful that I still have some contact with children. I wouldn't claim this keeps me young, but it does give me important links with the world around me. I am painfully aware of my hearing handicap when I want to communicate with children.

Alan, from "back east," seems content to be a part of the local scene, and this is good, both for him and for Sidney. I gather that he is fitting in well. They have built a home about a quarter of a mile west of Walt and Mary's home, on what was formerly the Micheletto property, and are raising their family away from the "hustle and bustle" of congested life in the heart of Sidney. Alan is addicted to music, and enjoys playing piano. I have wished when he has visited here that sharing our piano and organ with him were possible. Who knows? Maybe some fine day. And it was Mary Annette who made the diagnosis of my Carpal Tunnel Syndrome, when my doctor thought I had Vitamin B 12 Deficiency! She used the standard AMA handbook, and took the time to ask the necessary questions.

In September 1990 Walt died from Emphysema and a tired heart from having smoked too many cigarettes for too many years. Had he quit smoking a year after he started instead of a year before he died, we probably wouldn't be attending his funeral now. His family and friends packed the church - St. Matthew's - and Father Shinnick, with a light touch, alternately chatted, reminisced, reminded and led us past the present somber moment to an awareness of how much so many people have to be grateful for because of Walt - and Mary's - impact. It would have been nice if Walt could have known of John's promotion to full Colonel. The notice came a few days after the funeral. Walt's physician made a positive diagnosis of an important genetic factor in his development of emphysema: "AAT deficiency-related emphysema, an inherited lack of a protected protein, alpha 1-antitrypsin deficiency.

Walt's death has highlighted a number of bits and pieces of life that I think need to be pulled together. Perhaps they can't be integrated into one coherent statement, but I shall try. The first is Dad's oft repeated statement that "One can soon enough die without going to a doctor," which is a good starting point. His life was a living-out of this frame of reference. He lived to be almost 79, and he smoked a pipe, using the puff, puff, puff technique - never inhaling - for 50 years. I was a passive observer of Walt's illness for several years prior to his death. He was in and out of the hospital for shorter and longer periods throughout this time, and was kept busy keeping appointments with doctors and with labs, daily or weekly, for a very long time. The cost in dollars was astronomical. He would have had a hard time paying for these services had he not had assistance through Medicare and other health insurance. He never lacked for medical attention. I did not try to keep abreast of his many symptoms in addition to lung symptoms, such as numerous fractures, and terminal fungus pneumonia, diagnoses or treatment, because all concerned seemed satisfied that the best possible care was being given.

Despite my having no official role, I am still an interested and concerned person on the sidelines, and I felt rather continuously that I was glad I did not have to have the job of monitoring all these facets 365 days of the year: the patient as a whole, the lab tests, the constantly shifting and changing symptomatology and findings, that resulted from his physical pathology and the medications he took to alleviate his symptoms. Most of the time he was taking 15-20 kinds of medicine a day, and often even more. Lab tests were required almost constantly in order to be on top of what was going on. I could not help having the image in my mind of his doctor trying to keep a couple dozen balls in the air at the same time. I didn't see how anybody could really know what was going on. It would have been a complete impossibility for me, and I obviously was projecting.

I was taught in medical school, an old and perhaps outdated point of view which said the doctor should try to do his patient good, but at least he should do no harm. As Dad lived by his facetious slogan, I have tried to live by mine.

Thorvald, - Thor - the 7th of Lil's seven sons, was born after his father, Thorvald, died from cancer of the stomach in 1922. He was in the Service in the Navy in World War II, stationed in the Aleutian Islands, and honorably discharged. He married a pretty young girl named Maria Machay not long after discharge, but I think the marriage was terminated by annulment. Then he married Nellie, the wife of his brother Bill, and there was considerable family tension over this for many years. Thor and Nellie have never had a family of their own, but they have had ongoing contact with Willetta (Billy Anne) and Linda Sue, the children of Nellie and Bill, Thor's older brother, and their families. The scars have been healing, though slowly.

Thor and Nellie have lived for many years in Washington State, in Kennewick, where he was an electrical worker. After his retirement, they established themselves in a trailer court which Thor built with his own hands, and Nellie acts as business manager. They live not too far from my sister Christine and her family in Pasco, Washington, and maintain ongoing contact with them. Not long ago they came through Sidney and stopped briefly to visit me enroute to visiting Nellie's daughter Linda Sue in Minnesota.

As I survey Lil's life, many features seem quite prominent: She was one who was always willing to accommodate others, and this was tied to her great need to be liked. Through many years she had accumulated hundreds and hundreds of salt and pepper shakers, all as gifts from people who liked her and wanted her to know it. The shakers were all unique, but she knew who had given her each set. She enjoyed looking at them and thinking of the one who had given it to her. These gifts were a match to her own giving - in a different way! While she - along with Laurits - was driving the mail route all those many many years, she was a veritable purchase and delivery system. All anybody had to do to get her to shop for them while she was on her noon hour break in Sidney, was to leave a note for her in their mailbox, giving instructions as to what and where, and leave the purchase price with the note in the box. It meant lots and lots of extra effort on Lil's part, but she did it daily and willingly. She never charged for her services, and it was almost inevitable that she accumulated a lot of grateful friends.

Dalma had her abiding interest in her Religion to fill the last half of her life. Lil had her equally strong interest in politics, with all its ramifications. She was as ardent a Democrat and Union booster as Dad was a Teddy Roosevelt Progressive, and then Republican. She was never reticent about voicing her strong beliefs, and I believe that in her second marriage she shared her feelings and beliefs with Laurits. They may not have agreed about everything, but they certainly were primarily in harmony. Then Laurits died in 1962, after almost forty years together. They had retired and spent every winter in Apache Junction, Arizona. After his death Lil continued to spend her winters there and her summers in Sidney.

In 1965 I was living in Chino, California and working at the women's prison nearby. I had a letter from Lil saying she wanted to come and spend Thanksgiving, with us. This was wonderful because it was only her second visit to me in all the years we had lived here and there. The first visit was while I lived in Salt Lake City. I also knew that she had had surgery - for breast cancer - quite recently, and I was anxious to see her and know how she was doing. She came to Chino from Apache Junction by bus, the day before Thanksgiving. I was shocked when I saw her, for she was obviously sick. I was sure the bus trip to Chino had been too hard on her, and I hoped a good night's sleep would make things better. She was unable to eat her supper; she was too tired. So we retired early. I didn't hear her in the night, and in the morning I quietly got the Thanksgiving turkey in the oven and other things ready. Lil slept late and when I saw her it was obvious to me that her problem was greater than a need for a good night's sleep! I asked about her surgery and she told me her surgeon was an osteopath; that he was a very nice person. Then she showed me her breast, and it was obvious there were metastatic nodules even in the scar itself. We did not talk about them. Things were even worse than I had feared.

Before noon, she had decided that she better get back to Apache Junction or Mesa, where the hospital was. I turned off the oven, left the turkey in the oven and got ready to be on our way. She lay down in the back seat of the car the entire trip, and before nightfall we were in Mesa. I got her admitted to the hospital, called the people she wanted me to call, and headed for home, several hours away, because I had to be on duty at the prison the next morning. She said she was among friends who would provide all the help she needed. It was the last time I saw her alive.

After a transfusion she was able to be out of the hospital for a brief time, but had to return, and died in January 1966. Jan and I went to Apache Junction for the memorial service for her. The place was crowded with people and with flowers. Everyone had warm and appreciative things to say about her. I felt terribly unhappy about her choice of surgeons to help her in her time of need, but I feel sure she felt happy with his reassuring "bedside manner" and no doubt also wanted to "waste" as little of her money as possible. The result, in my opinion, was that she died months and perhaps even years before her time. Obviously, Lil and I were alike in our need to waste nothing - to be saving. Could it be that we are foolishly careful?

She was the first of my siblings to be born here in Sidney and the first to die. The two of us never communicated very well, and I have wondered exactly why she came to see me when she did. The people in Arizona seemed very meaningful to her - more closely attuned to her than I ever was. Perhaps she was aware of her subtle rejection of me and wanted us to talk before she died, for she surely knew her time was fleeting. Maybe she actually missed having a family member around to give moral support in her crisis situation; or maybe she saw me not as family but as an M.D., and someone who could confirm or deny her suspicions that all was not well with her surgery for breast cancer. I shall never know, but I often wish we had been better friends, and that we had acted not out of duty but out of affectionate concern, because both of us were caring people. I'm convinced that in one situation after another I failed to meet her needs.

Perhaps a story from her first visit to me might be acceptable; at least it adds a light note to the sad story of her death. On her first visit to me, she and Laurits came and stayed for a brief visit with us in Salt Lake City. Jan was beginning to be somewhat better; Len had his job with radio station KSL, and I saw patients in my office at home. I shifted some of them around so I could help Lil and Laurits enjoy their visit as I gave them a brief tour of the sights of the city. One of the interesting spots to visit, I thought, was ZCMI (Zion's Cooperative Mercantile Institution). It was an original, a truly authentic store - carrying almost anything one might want, and was owned and operated by the Mormon Church. When we got to one of the furniture floors, I became aware that one of the clerks seemed unusually interested in them. Finally, he asked if they weren't Laurits and Lil Jensen from Sidney, Montana. After a bit of checking, they were able to place the man. He had been an itinerant salesman selling woolen goods out in the boondocks of Montana, and each year that he had been on such a trip he had sold them black, woolen underwear - long legs, long sleeves, the works! They would surely have recognized one another had they met in Timbuktu!

The political pressures that impinged on me as a child and young adult came primarily from my family: Dad with his Teddy Roosevelt slants, Niels with his Communism and Socialism bias, and Lil with her Democratic Party orientation came much later. Each affiliation was fervid but non acceptable to the others: these political biases provided what filled their daily lives; they accepted them essentially as their religion, their deep beliefs, and found a sense of security in them. Where did I stand? Perhaps had I had three feet I would have had a foot in each one, but I guess I became increasingly Dad-oriented, and am content to leave it that way.

There is another pattern Mother had which seems to me to come through more clearly in Lil's family than in her other children's lives: this is her attitude toward education. Dad certainly did not disparage education; he was for it rather than against it, but Mother was a kind of crusader for it. She tried to make it possible for her children not only to go to school, but to get some education or training over and beyond the required 8th grade. I've heard Mame declare she had some special educational advantages. Mother got Niels enrolled in the Montana State College in Bozeman. She enrolled Carl in high school, under the auspices of the Danish Lutheran Church in Kenmare, N.D., when we had no high school in Sidney. She arranged for Dalma to get special training to be a seamstress; she sent Christine to high school in the first high school class available in Sidney, and she sent me off to college and medical school because she thought she heard me say I wanted to be a doctor. Not all of her efforts bore fruit. We didn't follow through for one reason or another, but she never gave up. She kept coming back to try once more to get us involved in education. I was the first one to finish high school, and the first one to graduate from college.

Lil's family of boys seems to have incorporated an interest in getting an education even without it being forced on them or handed to them. Of course high school was more available when Lil's kids were ready for it than it had been while Mother was raising her family, but I believe all of Lil's boys finished high school, and the majority had one, two or more years of college. Ralph completed college. They apparently went to school beyond high school level whenever they could. They might go one year here and a few years later go back for another year there, but they kept at it and the next generation says clearly it is important to stick it out and to finish - even graduate, and then more. Their wives get college degrees after they are married, and the next generation takes going to college for granted. This may, of course, be just the modern trend, but I think the trend is more noticeable in Lil's family than in the families of Lil's siblings. Lil may have nothing to do with it - or Mother - but then again, it just might have had an impact. Mother would be happy to know that so many of her grandkids, great grandkids, and great-great grandkids were headed for learning more and more. Two of Jo's grandchildren, Marvin's daughter Virginia, and Bernie's daughter Chris, got their college degrees from the University of Oregon, and Christine's daughter Nell also graduated from college in Washington and spent her life as a professional educator. The other grandchildren were high school graduates.

Niels, the "brain" of the family, and Lil were the only ones of us to be accepted to teach in the MonDak area's schools, even briefly. I felt pleased when I was invited to become an honorary member of Delta Kappa Gamma, an international Society of Women Educators, because I consider it a very special designation. Whereas I have long accepted myself as an educator, I have thought of my primary role as being "one who shares."

Lil certainly had none of the hostility toward Mother that Dalma had, and she was not partial to Dad as Mame was. She had had her problems finding her special place in the family because she seemingly had no special gift to offer, as did Dalma. She apparently placed a greater value on small evidences of acceptance than did Dalma. This continued to show through in her salt and pepper shaker collection. She loved to be liked and appreciated, and was free to display it. She thrived on it, and was willing to spend great effort on meriting it. Laurits was a far more outgoing person than Thorvald had been and I suspect her second marriage was far more happy than her first one. It also occurs to me that Lil was far more Mother's girl in her self-image than her sisters were; her appreciation for evidences of affection remind me of Mother. They were both openly glad to let people know they were aware of and appreciated gestures of affection.

This year, 1991, on the occasion of the Jensen family reunion to be held in Billings, there will be the dedication of an official "Library Fund" at Sidney's MonDak Heritage Center, set up by Ralph and his brothers, honoring Lil and ensuring ongoing support of education relating to our local heritage.

Josephine - Durable and Beloved

The fifth child in our family was Josephine Laureen, or Jo, as everyone finally called her, but for the real old timers her name was always Josie. To the best of my knowledge, she was born in the log house by the river, but was still little more than a baby when the family moved to the reconstructed log house by the stage road. Jo was born December 12, 1892, and was the only one of all eight of us who was not born after the 20th of the month. This makes me wonder if labor had not been induced, because Mother had an otherwise perfect record of having her babies some time between the 20th and the 28th of the month. For Jo's birth, Mother had the help of a doctor, so I suspect there must have been some complication or this would not have occurred. She was named for Mother's only sister, Josephine, Mrs. Ole Olsen, who came from Denmark to Sidney with the large contingent of Mother's relatives in 1899.

Josie & Jim on their Wedding Day

I have consistently felt closer to Jo than to any of my other sisters. It is not easy to account for this. I can't recall any special favors she supplied me. It could be that Jo had less antipathy for me from the very beginning than the older sisters had, and we therefore had a good start. Jo probably wasn't biased against me because she hadn't concluded it was time for Mother to stop having babies; she hadn't made mental notes during the pregnancy that Mother was lying around and babying herself too much; and she wasn't in competition with me, as was Christine, for the position of being the baby of the family. It can be annoying to be burdened with too many siblings. Another basis for my warm feeling for Jo might have been that except for Jo I never lived geographically close to any of my siblings as I was nearing adulthood, and therefore had little opportunity to develop meaningful relationships with the others.

Jo had no special areas of greatness, but she was ever solid, stable, and competent in so many areas, and she was also concerned, caring and quiet - not explosive like Lil or even Christine. I also especially liked her husband, Jim Hendrickson, who had come from Wisconsin with his parents, the Peter Hendricksons, and three siblings to settle in the Brorson area, looking for free land after the irrigation project became established. Jim later had his own homestead in the Three Buttes area near Lambert.

I can just barely recall - with the help of a stereoptican picture Niels took - how on winter evenings we would all congregate in the sitting room in the big farm house to do our thing: eat apples or popcorn, play dominoes or Flinch, talk, do fancywork, or read. In the picture, I sat on Jim's lap with my head on his shoulder. I can also recall how fascinated I was with the progress of Jim's and Jo's love affair. I would invariably look until I found where they were. I was always interested in what they were doing, and then would report to the assembled family members in the sitting room what I had seen. Had Jo been Lil she would have known what to do with me, but Jo stood me with remarkable patience. They were married when Jo was nineteen, and I was seven. I really liked Jim's light red, bristly hair, as well as his decidedly Roman nose. Jo had a nice straight nose, like Dad's, and they seemed to me to be a good pair.

Jo always seemed so organized. She'd get everything arranged in her mind according to its order of importance, and then she'd get done whatever needed doing - no delay, no big to-do, and first thing one knew, the job was done - and done well: clean house, clean clothes, some sewing, a letter written, a meal prepared, a few moments of relaxation with a friend in a game of cribbage, a kid disciplined. Again and again when I have visited her home in Oregon I would get up of a morning to find her out in her garden picking a flower or two, and I'd wonder if it wasn't time to start preparing for the dozen or more guests she was expecting for dinner - only to discover she had already set everything in motion and food was in the oven, and would be ready to eat when we got home after church.

She seemed a lot like Dalma, only less rigid, and more able to take a little time out to be amused, or sociable, or just lazy. She wasn't so afraid of guilt that she denied herself some things that seemingly were not essentials, but at the same time she used good grease that helped things run smoothly. Probably she was emotionally closer to Dalma than to any of her sisters. I always felt privileged that I seemed to be included in her inner circle ever since I outgrew my kid sister image. She was also like Dalma in that both of them had dark brown hair, like Dad, while the rest of us were blond to tawny blond. We were all blue eyed.

She lived in Eugene during my highly-charged religious-fervor period. She never attempted to sway me one way or another - either by approval or frown. She let me be wherever I was, and I always felt comfortable with her. She was also the one who, when there were guests and everyone would be enjoying the conversation and contributing his bit, and then someone would say it was high time to do the dishes, Jo's response would be, "Oh, let's dread it a while longer, first."

She was rarely the leader. That role would not fit her; but she was always there and ready to help the leader, with her perceptive assessments of the situation. She never needed reminding, or prodding. One could count on her to know what was going on and to stand ready to pitch in as needed. This was clearly true in the area of family finance. On rare occasions she would make some comment indicating she wished Jim were more aggressive in work situations than he was, because they were ALWAYS hard up, despite Jim's being a steady worker. Because Jim wasn't about to change, she did what she could to help out through getting a variety of jobs she could handle while still being full time mother and home maker. She sewed for people, and she sewed and mended for cleaning firms that needed help - and that did not insist that employees had to stay right at the shop to do the job. She was always interested in politics, and for years was clerk at the local precinct headquarters whenever there was an election.

There wasn't a big tinted and framed picture of Jo hanging on our walls like there was of Mother, Dad, Mame, Dalma and Lil. I guess they decided by the time Jo was a teenager that the pictures took up too much wall space, so the rest of us never had such pictures either. I can't recall Jo getting all steamed up over anything, or taking sides, or getting her feelings hurt. She was easy to live with. I also liked her dark hair - like Dad's. I also liked the fact she always put her hair up on kid curlers at night, as she was growing up, so she would look pretty in the morning. When I was young I had my hair in rags on special occasions, so I could have ringlets, but I was never impressed that they made me beautiful. While I note her apparent equanimity, she was like Dad in having a lot of stomach distress, which could have meant the presence of tension.

Jim's family, the Peter Hendricksens, had moved to Dane Flats from Wisconsin, and farmed there. We were friendly with them but never developed any close relations. They had four children, all grown up but unmarried when they came to Sidney, and they fit into the Danish community very well. There was Jennie, the oldest, who married a Christiansen, a Danish farmer, and Henry, who married Esther Damskov, then Jim and then Emma, the youngest, who was a very successful country school teacher for years, and finally, when she was an "old maid," married Chris Rasmussen, another Danish immigrant farmer. Through the years Emma had helped hundreds of her grade school students find their way to maturity, and I was privileged to attend a get-together after I returned to Sidney in 1971, honoring her for her long and constructive impact on our Sidney - Brorson community. Jim's parents never learned to speak English.

Jim had no burning passion for learning or for achievement or status, but he was intelligent, personable, was a steady worker, had a fine tenor voice and loved to sing - in the church choir or elsewhere - and he was well-liked by everybody. He filed on a claim in the Three Buttes area west of Sidney, not far from Lambert, and after he and Jo were married they set up housekeeping on this farm. This proved to be a sour investment of their lives because the soil was not very productive and drought plagued them, so life was truly marginal. They had three children, Marvin, Bernice and Hazel born at Three Buttes, and they managed to barely eke out a living with the help of Jo having been appointed Three Buttes Post Mistress and having the Post Office in their living room. Then in 1921, Mother, Dad and I left for Eugene, Oregon, for me to enter the University of Oregon.

I recall an experience from the days in Three Buttes: I had been away at the University of Oregon two full years and was back in Sidney for a very welcome vacation. I even got to visit Jo and Jim at Three Buttes! We went somewhere in their open car the evening I was there and we came back the many miles over the prairie road to their home in a fierce electrical storm. The thunder crackled and rolled constantly and the lightning seemed to split the sky prior to each thunder crack. I hadn't seen anything like it since I left Sidney for Oregon. It was simply beautiful beyond words, and I expressed my delight and awe at what was happening. Jo told me not too politely to "Shut up!" She wanted to hear no more about how beautiful it was; she only hoped we could get home safely. When we got there they showed me the marks of a very recent electrical storm that had struck their lightning rod on the house roof, had followed down their screened porch and grounded in the soil at the base. They had almost lost both their home and their lives in that storm because they were sleeping on the porch. No wonder Jo wanted me to hush up!

I truly have not seen such beauty as Nature passed out since that night. It was a spectacular to beat all spectaculars. This year - 1991 - our world and our weather pattern has made another turn, for which I am grateful. We have left drought behind, and water tables gradually are rising. Seldom a day goes by without some precipitation. Along with this we have electrical storms, but mostly there is "sheet lightning," where the heavens are aglow with glimmering and shimmering sheets of light. Chain lightning, the kind that splits the heavens asunder, occasionally may be seen, but not with the intensity they did in the days gone by. We have also had a couple tornados in the area - a new item except for the one in 1922 which killed Aunt Josie; and this past week we had a vicious hail storm such as I have seen only once or twice before but many years ago. The stable thing about the whole procession of events is the fact of change, and another is the evidence of the power of Nature. It gets to be old hat, and people forget to take it into account.

Montana Dust-bowl days cinched it for them; they knew they could not survive in Three Buttes, so they left the dust behind them and moved to Eugene, where I attended the University of Oregon. It was wonderful having them there, and everything began to be better for them. It is now 65 years since they put their roots down in Eugene, and it would be an impossibility for them to entertain any idea of moving from there. They are even more sold on Oregon than Dad was on the

MonDak. They had two more children born in Eugene: Jim Jr., and John, making five in all. Their family includes four generations, and Jo, now 99, (1991) has had to be moved to a nursing home for care. Her husband, Jim, who worked mostly for the LN Miller Prune Drying Company, died years ago while we lived in Salem. There were times during my years of medical practice when I would feel weighed down with the problems of patients whose marriages were a mess, and I would wonder if there were ANY good marriages extant, and then I would think of Jo and Jim, and this would give me a lift. At least I knew there could be good marriages. Both of them, Jo and Jim, were easy to live with, or so it always seemed to me.

Marvin, Jim and Jo's oldest child, married his cousin, Viola Hendrickson, the daughter of Esther (Damskov) and Henry, Jim's older brother. The young couple survived the opposition to their marrying, and they, in turn had four children - who also had children. I could not really have a competent opinion about the wisdom or lack of it in marrying a cousin. I know that whereas Henry, Viola's father, was a very stable person, both physically and emotionally, Esther, his wife, was a very high strung, unstable, but attractive and likeable person of excellent intellect but with endless physical ailments which were usually treated by having another extraction - surgery. Whether Viola inherited some unstable gene, I cannot say, but she became an alcoholic early in life, and was hospitalized often for neurologic aspects of her disability. She died before all of her children had reached their teens, and I don't think it is an exaggeration to say all of them suffered from the instability brought on by Viola's problem. There has been brilliance in the midst of social and emotional instability, and one of Marvin's and Viola's grandsons - Sparky - was involved with drugs and suicided by gunshot. As far as I know, only Marvin's oldest daughter Virginia has graduated from college despite living in Eugene, the home of the University of Oregon. She was a social worker. Marvin and Viola had three more children: Stephen, Kim and Deborah. I have not been close enough to them to know them except by name, other than that Stephen's occupation was servicing exotic cars.

For many years Marvin worked for the City of Eugene in the planning end of the Water and Sewer Department. Several years after Viola's death, Marvin remarried - to Ruby Salstrom, and they lived in Marvin's retirement home by the Pacific Ocean at beautiful Yachats - pronounced Yahots, an Indian name. They developed a flourishing commercial business, making a variety of items such as wind chimes, candles, and innovative ways of using local driftwood and stones. These helped maintain their contacts with the world and gave pleasure to a lot of people who liked their products. I have one of their wind chimes which sings with the breezes, a beautiful candle, a driftwood harbor detail about 8 inches tall with miniature poles roped together and sea gulls atop, and another spooky arrangement of stones - with eyes peering out from a frightened huddle. I love them, partly for their grace and artistry, and partly because they keep reminding me of times long gone.

When I came to Eugene we were members of Emmaus, the tiny little Danish Lutheran Church "at the end of the line", and Jim and Jo joined it too. But when we left Eugene for Portland in 1925, they shifted to the much larger Danish Lutheran country church, Bethesda, and most of their family have remained members of that church. Jim worked mostly for L.N. Miller Co., a prune-raising and drying establishment; he bought a piece of land right in his boss's prune orchard, built a house there, and raised his family. Their 5th child, John, was born on Marvin's 21st birthday, which certainly tells a story of Jo's long child-bearing years.

It was with Jo, Jim and their three oldest kids that we all saw the Pacific Ocean for the first time. We left Eugene late in the day, headed for Florence, Oregon, which was the closest town on the coast to Eugene. A light rain was coming down, but rain never stopped anyone in Oregon from doing what he planned to do. We soon found that the going was very slow because of the extensive road-building that was going on. Mile after mile we slogged along, seldom meeting anyone and for many miles the rain came down harder and harder. Our car lights were none too helpful and driving was difficult as well as hazardous. There didn't seem to be many places one could turn off - or turn around and go back home. Darkness had set in.

Finally Jim spotted a trail turning off to the right, and just beyond was a big dark building with no lights. It was the first place we had seen where there might be shelter from the rain. It looked like a big barn, built on the side of the mountain, on tall wooden stilts. We were glad to get shelter any place we could find it, and the car was safely off the road. We brought our blankets in with us and looked - or felt - for some place flat enough to spread them out so we could lie down and go to sleep. We found no flat surfaces but we thought we'd better do the best we could with what we found. At least it was dry. Sleeping on a hillside was no easy trick, but we got snatches of sleep.

When daylight came we got up to look around us and get our bearings. What we saw everywhere was stacks and stacks of boxes labeled "explosives". Obviously, this was what the road-building crew was using to clear out whatever interference was encountered. We were glad no lightning bolts had set the storehouse we slept in ablaze.

Eventually the road stopped entirely. We left the car and moved on toward the ocean in a small boat available for a pittance, and followed along toward our goal of seeing the Pacific Ocean down a little "river" also headed for the sea. It was a momentous moment when we could finally see the Pacific Ocean. We made it to Florence, made physical contact with the ocean as best we could, and then headed for home. I shall never forget the trip. Having money to pay my share of the expenses never occurred to me. I didn't have any money; Jim and Jo didn't have any money. I never wondered how much the gas cost. We had no hotel or motel bill, and we brought food enough from home to last until we got back. I'm sure I was like any other child who takes everything that comes to him for granted.

Bernice, Jo and Jim's oldest daughter, born in Montana prior to their shift to Oregon, finished high school in Eugene and married Lat Dawe. They had 3 children, Christine, Kenny and Nancy. At quite an early age Lat took his retirement from his job with the railroad, where he had worked many years. It seemed to be getting beyond his ability to deal with things he had done easily for years. He was in the early stages of Alzheimers Disease. In the 70's, I visited them in Eugene following a Hendrickson family reunion at beautiful Yachats, by the sea, and was saddened at Lat's precipitous downhill descent. He remained at home, Bernie caring for him, and died perhaps a year later. It was the first time I had seen a patient with an Alzheimer's Disease diagnosis, but I suspect I had seen many of them in mental hospitals before the diagnosis became familiar.

When Kenny was born he looked for all the world like a little old man - wizened and scrawny. If I had known then what I learned later I would have asked a lot of questions. Eventually he lost his wrinkles and fleshed out. He developed a propensity for hang-gliding. I believe he survived that without mishap. I believe Kenny is working in the business of aircraft maintenance.

I also visited 2 of Bernie's children, Nancy in Eugene and Christine in Portland, along with Marvin's oldest daughter, Virginia, and his youngest, Debbie. Bernie's daughter Christine's marriage had broken up and she later remarried. She had one child by her first and two by her second husband. Nancy seemingly had a solid marriage and a nice family of three children. Bernie still lives right by a Lake just outside Eugene.

Hazel, Jo's third child, married soon after finishing high school. Her husband, Stewart McLaughlin, was an accountant. They had four sons and a daughter: Mark, Eric, Kirk, Austin and Amy, and all were brought up in their great big house atop Laurel Hill, back of Hendricks Park in Eugene - back of the University of Oregon. Figuring out directions in Eugene never seemed within my grasp but it was helpful when I remembered to remember what was written in one of the University of Oregon Yearbooks. It said that if one ever got his directions confused, it would be helpful if one pictured himself with the University of Oregon statue, The Pioneer, right near Willamette Street and adjacent to what was then the campus library. From that point on it would be simple, "because the Pioneer was facing due South."

Every Easter Hazel has hosted a Hendrickson family get-together at her big home atop the hill, and one year I was able to attend. It was a truly pleasant occasion which left happy memories. Their oldest son, Mark, was an avid mountain climber, and in 1967 he and some of his friends who were also mountain climbers, attempted to scale Mt. McKinley in Alaska. A storm engulfed them and none of them was ever found. Hazel said she was glad he died doing exactly what he wanted to do, but I find it hard to be glad. She's probably more right than I am, but I think of it as a misfortune that snuffed out a promising life. The incident was highly publicized throughout the United States.

Hazel's other children, Erik, Kirk, Austin and Amy have had less spectacular lives. The boys remained in Eugene, often living with Hazel and Stewart while he was still living, or with Hazel after Stewart died of emphysema. The boys are now on their own, and Hazel for the first time since her marriage isn't taking care of somebody. She has always worked and participated in supporting the family. Her field is bookkeeping and office management, primarily in motels. She is now retired, and from what I hear, she is doing very well, is stable, independent and contented. She has had lots of trouble with her hands - from arthritis deformans - necessitating many surgical interventions, but is mostly able to care for herself in her large home. I also understand that the old piano I was raised with, a Williams and Sons Epworth upright, which I gave her when I was having so much trouble finding a place to live in Seattle, is still with her. When her kids come home they still bang away on it. Hazel's only daughter, Amy is married and lives in Canada with her two children. I really know nothing more about her than that.

Jo's fourth child, James or Jim, Jr. was the first to be born in Oregon. A year later, Mother, Dad and I moved from Eugene to Portland for me to attend Medical School. But we had a car by then, and not infrequently made the trip between Eugene and Portland and kept in touch. I felt especially close to Jim Jr. In Oregon I did not have so many other nieces and nephews to compete with him for my attention and affection as in Sidney. Besides that, he was forever doing something to endear himself to me. When he was just a baby he ate ripe olives with gusto, and had to be watched lest he get up on the table and empty the olive dish. The summer he was just past one year they visited us in Portland, and we made an outing to a park whose name I can't recall, but in my mind it is associated with roses. We entered the park and looked out across a big expanse of beautiful green lawn. Jim Jr., walking between us like a big boy, pulled loose his hands, toddled forward, and tried to turn a somersault on the lawn. I'm sure he thought it was too good a chance to have fun to turn it down. Jim Jr. served in World War II, much of it in Europe, and we were happy to have him come back, without loss of limb or life. He married Delores Petersen, also one of my favorite people, and they have a small acreage in the Eugene-Junction City area which they "farm," raising Christmas trees. They raised their family of four children there: Cathy, Carol, Jim III and Danny.

Jim II follows the trade of shingling roofs. He learned that being a top notch shingler involved much more than putting shingles on right. It also involved sizing up people, and it entailed being a competent business man. He found out that having a business of one's own entails far more than a narrow kind of mechanical competence. Unless he was all of these things, in addition to being a competent shingler, he would have to work for someone else. I really don't know what he finally did, but he was quite right, that unless one masters all these details he had better draw wages. In 1989 Jim II and his brother John, who assists him, were selected to do a special shingling job in Honolulu.

True to their tradition from babyhood, family living has been their highest pursuit, and they are a pleasure to be around. All 4 of Jim, Jr. and Delores' children, Cathy, Carol, Jim III and Danny, are married and are raising their own families. Cathy's husband, Tom Maines, is a skilled brick layer, and they have 3 children. Carol and her husband, Captain Richard Snider, recently in Germany for an extended tour of duty, did not have any children, but they adopted two boys, Curtis Mitchell, and Joel, a Korean boy. These boys certainly offer a tremendous challenge to both parents and family. Carol's letters from Germany gave me a peek into the changing factors which impinge on their lives. Prior to Germany, they lived in Great Falls, Montana, where Rich was stationed at nearby Malstrom Air Force Base, and several times I visited them there. They have now opted out of the military and have returned to Oregon.

Jim II's son, James Hendrickson III, knew what he wanted to be when he was just a little boy: He was going to be a fireman. But different from most boys who are going to be firemen, Jim really did make it. Now he is well past halfway to retirement, and apparently is just as much in love with being a fireman as he thought he would be. His wife Joan brought two children from her previous marriage, and they, Jim and Joan, also have a son. Jim II's youngest child, Danny, married only recently. By and large he has lived away from the Eugene area and close contact with his family. I scarcely know him at all.

Jo's 5th, and youngest child, John, is exactly twenty-one years younger than her first child, Marvin. For some years he worked for Eugene and it's airport, but eventually moved to working with his brother, Jim II, shingling, which he still does. They also live in the Junction City area. He and his wife, Toni, have three sons, Jeff, John and Paul. As far as I know only Jeff has established his own family and he has 3 children. John used to play with Jan when he was little, even though Jan was 18 years older. Invariably he would want to play "lady", which meant that he wanted to be dressed up in women's clothes, the more ornate the better, and then prance around the house. I faintly recall having been told that he has been involved in theater productions, but I'm not sure. He surely enjoyed the make-believe world. With the passage of time, it has been too easy to lose touch with my family.

Jo's age and infirmities - she will soon be ninety-eight - have partially accounted for this regrettable eventuation - losing touch - and my own "fallow years" properly taking the rest of the blame. Once something is lost, it is hard to retrieve.

Now it is 1991, and my dear Joey is ninety-seven and has been in a nursing home several years. When I last saw her she was in her own apartment in a Senior's complex, still managing to do most things for herself, with the help of one full noon meal each day. She entertained overnight guests frequently, and could prepare two meals a day for herself, provided she put everything away in the refrigerator herself, so she would know exactly where it was placed. She, like Mother, has become essentially blind and deaf. Now someone of the family visits her every day in the nursing home, and Jo has great difficulty keeping Reality-contact. This causes her confusion and often anxiety, because the "straightening out" effort is short lasting, and she is left with her problems in getting the past and present to fit together.

Mother did not experience a protracted period of such confusion, but she died when she was 93, and Jo's stay here has been considerably longer. If I'm not mistaken, Mother, Jo and I have some of the same genetic determiners. All three of us have had increasing blindness due to macular degeneration, and each of us has had increasing hearing impairment. Mother never used hearing aids but both Jo and I use them. Years ago when I told the opthamologist I thought I had a genetically determined visual impairment, he pooh poohed the idea, saying I'd never go blind; that I had one pretty good eye and the other one was just worn out. I didn't like his dismissing what I had to say so easily. Besides, I knew that eyes don't "wear out." Over-usage is not their lot. But it is hard for me to recall when he was ready to listen to any of my offerings. So I essentially scratched him, despite the fact his office provided me with the best glasses - lenses AND frames - that I have ever had. I really don't like doctors who not only won't take the time to listen to me, but who regularly devalue what I have to say.

Like with Niels, there are so many warm and pleasant memories of all our years that fill my mind as I think about Jo and Jim I, e.g., visiting them at their homestead at Three Buttes in the Fall, and joining with their neighbors in setting the mountain-like piles of dried Russian Thistles - tumble weeds - afire. The dried round balls two to three feet in diameter, tumbling endlessly, blown by the wind and scattering their seeds until they would finally become lodged in the fences around everybody's property, and pile up 6-8 feet high in the fence corners. These piles of tumble weeds would be moved away from the fence posts, and then we would set them afire, and watch carefully lest the fire spread to burn any surrounding grass, which was dry as tinder. It was a necessary activity, for the tumbleweeds had already done too much seeding of more weeds for next year, but it was also a pretty sight to look across the hills and see dotted, here and there, other pyres of fire in neighbors' fields lighting up the night sky. I never knew of such a fire getting out of control.

I also remember how Jo, in Three Buttes, exercised discipline when she felt Marvin warranted it. He was probably two and a half or three by that time. She would send him to the closet in her bedroom - which was dark. He would scream at the top of his lungs for a few minutes, and then the noise would taper off, and in 3-4 minutes more he would emerge from the closet smiling and happy, and announce that he was good now. And that was the way it was. Marvin was the first of Jo's kids to die. It was while he was on a vacation trip with Ruby, his second wife, to her family in Nebraska. No problems, no pain, no distress, no waiting, - he just died, quietly, abruptly and unexpectedly. I believe it was in the middle of a game of cribbage. Almost every Fall they made this trek to

Nebraska, and would come by Sidney and visit us. We have missed them very much.

Jim, Jo's husband had a Roman nose and light, bright red hair, of the wiry variety. None of his kids has inherited these traits. Perhaps some grandchild will. When things were really at a low ebb for me here in Sidney a few years ago, Jim II and Delores drove here from Eugene to size things up and see if there was any way to be helpful. I have nothing but a vague memory of their being here, except that when they were ready to go, I gave them a lot of my books, since they liked reading, and I somehow thought I'd like them to have them. When I began to be better they were among the first to note it. My letter writing had improved.

After I really began to be better, I would frequently look for a book I thought I needed, and could not find it. I had completely forgotten I had given so many to Jim II and Delores. I thought it was my sight that wasn't good enough to spot the book on my shelves, or perhaps I had loaned them to someone. Then came a day I was looking for Sir William Osler's Letters, edited by Harvey Cushing, and given me by Dr. Chittenden, Uncle Ah. They were published in two huge volumes I knew I should be able to spot, and I couldn't imagine loaning them out. Then, for the first time, I remembered Jim and Delores getting my books. So I wrote them, and sure enough, back came my two volume set of Osler's Letters, and I was happy to touch and hold them again. Those books bring a lot of pleasant associations to my mind.

After Mother died in 1955, Jo seemed to take over Mother's function of being the hub of our family. She kept in touch with everybody, and everybody kept in touch with her. Everyone in the family would stop to see Jo if at all possible when they went on trips to the west coast.

It was hard for Jo to give up driving her own car, but after having a minor accident she agreed it was necessary to stop driving. Last year when I unexpectedly hit the curb in turning a corner, of course I thought of Jo and wondered how long it would be before I gave up driving.

Actually, one of the treasures of life - of the fact of being alive - is memory, which enables us to relive. It would be hard, indeed, to improve on life. It's got everything else beat.

What was so special about Jo? Nothing - but everything. It was always a good feeling to know she was there. I love her.

Carl - The P Diamond Cowboy

Mother's and Dad's sixth child was a son, CARL CHRISTOPHER, born July 21st, 1895, in the old log house in Sidney. He was their second son, and came ten years after their first son, Niels. Carl was named for Mother's brother Charlie - or Carl. He was a quiet, generally non-assertive child, and as far as I have heard gave no particular trouble to anybody except Dalma, who voiced her complaints about him to me: He wasn't properly disciplined by Mother, who never really taught him to work. It is not surprising that this would be galling to her, for working endlessly was what she lived by. Also, whatever his shortcomings were in this area, my sisters were expected to make up for his lacks, the worst of which was that he would invariably fall asleep in the kitchen after supper, and could not be aroused to go to bed, but had to be carried to bed - and Dalma seemed to be the official carrier.

Carl, 1919

He was a tall, gangling, towheaded boy and there seemed to be little that was demanded of him as compared with the girls. As far back as I can remember, Father was not a worker either; he didn't do household tasks, or even barnyard tasks, and he was not the disciplinarian. That job was left to Mother, and Carl followed Dad's lead. Whereas his lack of industriousness may have irked some of my sisters, they never, to my knowledge, were annoyed with Dad for identical "sins," but forgave him everything and all his various habits. I guess this was partly because they didn't ever have to carry him to bed. As they saw it, Carl never HAD to do anything if he didn't want to. He didn't like to eat most vegetables, so he wasn't MADE to. Oh, he liked potatoes, peas, corn, carrots and perhaps a few others, but Mother did not raise or cook the whole gamut of vegetables she might well have. Nor did Dalma try to raise him or teach Mother. She let people make their own mistakes without benefit of her criticism. But she cherished the daily annoyances of Carl having to be carried to bed for a lifetime.

There was one thing that Carl did love, and that was horses. I recall Mother telling of an episode when he was well along in his teens, when she asked him to help her milk the cows. He didn't do it, and told her he was raised on a horse - not under a cow. This must not have bothered Mother too much because she not only accepted it, but she occasionally told someone about it - and with a smile that said it was OK to be the horseman of the family, rather than the milk maid. To my knowledge, milking was not expected of any of the girls, either, but I feel sure all of us could milk a cow.

As long as I can remember, Carl hated the Danes, because they disrupted our family life by merely being there. They also, it seemed to him, took from our parents, and therefore from him and from all of us, time, money, material goods, effort, and concern, and they gave nothing in return. He resented this because he saw these things as rightfully his - and ours. He saw the Danes as exploitative, and so he left them strictly alone. Of course he never would have anything to do with their church. It is doubtful he ever set foot inside of either Danish church in Sidney. I don't recall him going to the Old Stone Church, either. Any Dane was suspect. The Danish language was of no slightest interest to him, and he had as little to do with Mother's Danish-speaking relatives as he could.

To be sure, both Mother and Dad opened their hearts, their home and their wares to the ever-growing flock of Danes that came to live in the Sidney area, but they did it gladly and willingly, and none meant to take advantage of them. Dad, especially, saw the influx of Danes as a great benefit to his beloved Sidney and to the MonDak. My parents had no regrets or self pity, as Carl did, even if "the Danes" might sometimes neglect to show appreciation for what Mother and Dad did for them. It was not my parents' battle; it was strictly Carl's. It was not easy for Carl to find anything to criticize about Dad, because he loved Dad very much.

There was a little vignette which should not be forgotten: In 1902, when Christine was four years of age, and Carl was six, Mother, Dad, and Christine made their trip to Denmark, their first since they left their homeland in 1889, and the trip lasted a couple months. I have memories of Mother telling about how Carl stood by the gate and watched them leave in the buggy, crying and waving, until they were out of sight. She carried the picture of her little boy with her in her mind's eye, throughout her entire trip, and it made her sad. Carl, to my awareness, has never mentioned this separation, but surely, it was a glaring instance of someone else getting preferential treatment, while he was left out in the cold. It was the prototype of his later complaint and it was always the Danes. It always seemed to be the Danes that interrupted his life, there is no doubt, and he could never find it within himself to forgive them or make the necessary adaptations. For him, life was good - except for the Danes.

Carl was a bright lad but because there were no schools here beyond eighth grade, Mother arranged for Carl to go to high school under the auspices of the Danish Lutheran Church in Kenmare, North Dakota. But he was bored with it and with its emphasis on religion, as well as it's emphasis on the Danish language, so he managed to drop out and come back home. All his life he loved to read, and he devoured everything available. The old time *SATURDAY EVENING POST* was probably his main standby, but there were also the *CHRISTIAN HERALD*, the newspapers which came daily - because Dad walked the two miles to the post office and back to get them - and occasionally a book. He read whatever he got his hands on. He was knowledgeable about many things but was not the brilliant mind Niels was. Niels was also handy with his hands while Carl was like Dad in that he wouldn't, or couldn't, do anything with his hands. His lack of dexterity never concerned him one bit, and he never would have allowed himself to compete with Niels. He just disdained handiwork; in other words, like Dad, he definitely was NOT a fixer or a builder.

Instead, he seemed to have a knack for getting hurt. Often it was while he was on horseback. He might not see or realize they were approaching some hazard, and would run into it; or he would underestimate a distance or a space, and find out, too late, that he was headed for trouble. This brought him bad scars on his face, broken collar bones and forearms. I don't know how his life on horseback started, but by my time it was well established. Mother was the chief "horseman" in our family in the early years, but she always rode sidesaddle. To put food on the table they had purchased cows on time, and mother milked them, twenty at first, and more later. Mother carried out dairy production, including, milk, butter and cheese, even long after we moved to the new house in 1908, but I can never recall Carl taking any part in any of it. He left cows strictly alone.

One of the things he especially enjoyed, and was very good at, was visiting. Visiting with him alone was always pleasurable, but he shone like a star if he was entertaining a number of people. His tales weren't always too precisely accurate, but everyone seemed to enjoy them. He also loved to play cards, as well as gamble, and passage of time in such circumstances meant nothing to him. He definitely had no intentions of letting someone else's clock run his life. A couple years before he died he stopped going to the Moose Lodge to play cards. He felt he had lost his confidence in his own car driving, and in his abilities at cards. After I returned to Sidney in 1971, Jan and I went to his house every day and he and I would play a couple games of cribbage against Jan and his wife, Martha. It was, invariably, a pleasant episode. Unlike Niels, Carl had no great need to win, so there was never an atmosphere of tension, just pleasant togetherness .

My earliest memory of Carl was that he walked and he talked in his sleep. This worried my parents somewhat. He slept in the bunkhouse with the hired men, and the folks were afraid he might fall down the stairs. He never did, and to my knowledge, they never did anything about it, such as having a railing built around the stair well. The last few years before we left the farm for good and moved to town in 1917, I rode a horse to school in town. The horse, named Kinky, was small, pony sized, and a pretty bay. Once she bucked me off. Carl often met me as I led her to the big cement tank in the barn yard for a drink of water. Once, without any preliminaries he said to me, "You ride like a sack of sand." This was about the closest to a zero grade in living as he could give me. I was scarcely suitable to be counted. It hurt my feelings, but his opinion had never been very important to me, so suicide never occurred to me. But I did remember it.

From that time on, we hardly talked at all. Neither one of us mattered to the other one very much. Then came World War I. He had said they'd never get him into the Service, and first thing I knew, he had enlisted, of his own free will, and nobody forced him. Our sister Christine, who age-wise came between Carl and me, had been keeping house for Niels and Carl on the Prairie Elk, about 100 miles west of Sidney. Mother, Dad and I had visited them a couple of time - which was no inconsequential undertaking. It took most of the day to drive there. We had become acquainted with Harry Brockway, another homesteader in their Prairie Elk area, whom Christine had become enamored of, and he also enlisted. He and Carl went off to the Service together. Harry was assigned to the Quartermaster Corps, and Carl to the Aviation Service. The induction station gave them various tests and assigned them to the department they thought they would best fit into.

Carl's being in the Service changed everything, and brought about the beginning of Carl and me getting acquainted, because all the agencies, including the Red Cross, stressed how important it was to keep writing the boys. By the time the war was over I had developed a feeling of closeness, and fondness for him, that lasted as long as he lived. I even lost my hurt feelings because he had said I rode like a sack of sand.

Horsemanship was his profession, not his hobby. He took great pride in his knowledge of horses - how to mount, how to sit, how to hold the reins, what to do with one's hands, his posture on the horse, even how to behave around horses, what to feed them and when. I used to get into arguments with him concerning his lack of a protectionist mind-set toward them, especially in winters where the snow was deep and food for them was unavailable through their own efforts. He would say this was Montana Winters; they would have to make it on their own, because he certainly could not fend for them. Sometimes they didn't make it, and I would weep over it, but not Carl. This was just the way life was: some made it and some didn't.

Of course he was involved with the rounding up and branding of the horses every year. They carried Dad's brand - our brand - the P Diamond brand - on the right shoulder. The brand on the adult horse measured four to five inches in height. Carl loved that brand, perhaps almost as much as he loved Dad - and that was a lot. He saw to it that the brand was properly registered in his name after Dad died, and he never forgot to attend to reregistering it. Eventually it was transferred to Lee, Oscar's son, Mame's grandson, Dad's great grandson, who also loves horses, and when Mary, Carl's daughter, was recently here, we talked about checking up on it again, for it really is an enduring part of our family.

Carl probably knew the eastern Montana area better than almost anyone. He had ridden over it looking for and rounding up strayed horses for years and years. He knew the lay of the land; he recognized every landmark; he knew where every little stream drained and into what. Every coulee had its significant aspects to him, as did the ridges. His familiarity did not extend beyond the Yellowstone River to the east. The badlands across the river were unfamiliar territory. It seemed to me he knew not only the names of the tiniest streams, but he knew how they got their names. Many of the names dated back to the time when the great herds of Texas cattle grazed during the warm months on our wide open prairies, and then, as cold weather came, were herded back to Texas. A couple of times, Carl and I talked about writing all this information down to preserve it, but we never got around to it.

Carl and Harry Brockway did not see one another from a couple weeks after their enlistment in 1917 until the war was over and they came back to Sidney within days of one another. Carl had been sent first to Texas, and then shipped overseas to England and then to France. Harry never left the States. His assignment did not involve being a pilot, but servicing planes. Shortly after they came home, Christine and Harry were married and Carl and I were best man and bride's maid at the wedding.

Prior to Carl's return, Dad had been worried that he might not return home, or after he got here he might leave again - for South America. To forestall such an eventuation, Dad bought a big ranch not far from Richey - in the Lane area - and made Carl the manager of it. It was called the P Diamond. It was to be a place where he could have all the horses he wanted and keep a steady flow going to market. This plan fell flat for there was a crash in the horse market because everything was mechanized. He spent many years trying to keep from bankrupting both Dad and himself, and what horses were good for was chiefly for dog food. It was a sad time. Horses never did come back. Machines, gas, oil, and electricity did everything, and horses were a thing of the past. To Carl it was like losing both an arm and a leg.

But through his being in the Service we came to trust and to enjoy one another. He visited us in Eugene and in Portland, sometimes staying with us the whole winter. When he came to see us the first time, in Eugene, where I was a freshman at the University of Oregon, I was about as low as a snake's belly. I missed Sidney. I missed knowing everybody, and having my warm feelings reciprocated. Over night things had changed from my being a somebody to being a nobody. I squalled daily. "Nobody at the University of Oregon cares about me. They wouldn't know whether I was alive or dead." I would gladly have dumped going to college for a chance to go back home to Sidney. Mother did her best to comfort and encourage me. Carl was aware of my misery and set out to remedy it. He said he was amazed at me. Didn't I know who I was! It didn't make any difference if others did not know, but I should know that I was Peter Anderson's daughter, and that ought to be enough! He might as well have saved his breath, for to me that meant nothing special. Surely, he knew I was Mother's child - not Dad's! But we looked at our parents with different eyes, and his pep talk didn't help a bit.

On that same visit to us in Oregon, a group of my church friends and I went out in the woods one Sunday to gather wild orchids. I invited Carl to join us. He figured as how it sounded more boring than interesting, but he finally came along on his first-in-a-lifetime flower picking expedition. It wasn't long before he, too, was captivated by the orchids' beauty and the lush green everywhere, and he gathered the delicate flowers with the rest of us. Not only that, but he picked enough to fill a box he sent to a girl in Montana, because he felt sure she had never seen anything like it. Obviously, he had his tender and gentle side too.

We had all sorts of deep discussions about mostly anything. Once I asked him if he could tell me why he was so fond of Dad. He said it was because of a conversation he had had with Dad when he was quite young, in which Dad had set him straight on Sex and relationships with women, and he had been grateful for that talk all his life. Father told him one should be very careful to not get sexually entangled because it would ruin one's life, and one could no longer be free. Dad had apparently spelled it out in sufficient detail so it all came alive and was meaningful to him. In later days he walked out of his first marriage, when he came home to find his wife in a compromising situation. He didn't wait to argue or pick up any pieces; he just took his hat, coat and departed; no ifs, ands, or buts. He never looked back. He just marched on.

For several years prior to World War I, he and Niels lived together on the Figure Eight in the Prairie Elk country, and ran horses. The close contact with Niels resulted mostly in hostility and not in love. Niels, with his strong need to be accepted as the teacher, and Carl, with his strong need to be his own boss and his own man, did not mix well. After he was discharged from the Service, Dad, with the help of the P Diamond ranch, did manage to keep him in the United States and reasonably close to home. But their business venture in horses went sour and was as non-lucrative as farming in the dust bowl would have been.

I think it was on my second vacation trip home to Sidney from Eugene when I made a trip out to the P Diamond to visit Carl. The ranch house was frame and I seem to recall it had three rooms. It was unbearably hot and muggy, but we used our time to do some good visiting. I noticed it was beginning to get dark early and then the range cattle began coming home on a high lope, bellering at the top of their lungs. Next thing I knew it was hailing big hailstones - about walnut size - in sheets. The windows were open and had no screens, so the high wind blew them through the window, bounced them across the floor and they stacked up against the opposite wall in a sizeable heap. No wonder the cattle bellered - they hurt! The storm lasted perhaps fifteen or twenty minutes. We swept the hailstones out the door and were glad we weren't grain farmers who would have lost their crops.

In the morning there were still drifts of hailstones piled up here and there but we headed for town anyway and found such roads as existed were pretty well cut off and we had to find our own way through the gulleys to better roads. But we made it to Sidney without mishap - by car, which gave us no trouble. Carl was constantly in and out of the car, splashing through the mud and hailstone drifts, but we always knew where we were because we kept Chimney Peak, across the river to the east, as our dependable marker or north star. It was the last hail storm I saw until recently - in 1991 - when there was a repeat performance right here in Sidney. One doesn't soon forget such events.

Quite unbelievably, it was Carl who got me into Psychiatry: I had finished my internship in Portland in 1930 and needed a job. The fact that I had graduated in 1929, and completed my internship just as the great Depression caused by the New York Stock Market Crash was getting its tentacles into everybody, did not really register on me. I had always thought of our family as economically marginal, so the Depression just meant more of the same - a continuum. After seeking help in finding a job through the Medical Bureau in Chicago, a medical placement agency advertising in the Journal of American Medical Association, I still was without a job. Finally, about mid-December, 1930, they located two jobs where women doctors were acceptable. One job was in a psychiatric hospital in Binghamton, New York, and the other was in a tuberculosis hospital in Texas. Each one paid about the same - something like $2000 a year plus maintenance. I had gone home to Sidney to stay with Mother and Dad until I could be placed in a job. One is not able to afford many of life's necessities when one has been earning $15.00 a month and maintenance, as I had done for the year of my internship at Multnomah County Hospital in Portland, one of the University of Oregon Medical School's affiliate hospitals.

I had to make up my mind: Would it be the job in New York, or the one in Texas? I told Carl about my quandary, including the fact that I had what I regarded as a top-notch background in Tuberculosis at the University of Oregon Medical School. I had the world renowned Mattson Brothers and Dr. Bissalion as my Professors, but in Psychiatry I felt I knew scarcely anything. Carl listened to my tale, and then said, "Why, of course you'll go to New York. I sold a load of horses in Oneonta, in the Finger Lakes region, only a year ago. It's a beautiful country, and you'd love it!" Binghamton was only a short drive from both Oneonta and the Finger Lakes, and with his positive approach, I accepted his appraisal. So I got into Psychiatry on a load of P Diamond horses. There was no agonizing or weighing. The decision was made at that moment, and I was on my way. I had no way of knowing what a wonderful choice it was, or how I never would regret it. It was just a relief to have something as important as a job, settled. It was not the last time he came to my rescue with a decision, or a positive opinion. It is easy to get lost weighing the pros and cons of anything. He weighed the factors he knew and understood, and left out the other factors, such as would I like Psychiatry, and was this a field with a good future outlook.

It was much later, while I lived in Philadelphia, that he came to stay with me one winter. He had gotten a job as an attendant in a nearby Veteran's Mental Hospital at Coatesville, probably the only real job he ever had. He didn't like the job one bit, but he stuck it out for several months, until Spring.

One Sunday we were talking, and I told him how lucky I was to be in a profession I really liked. I told him how I often felt guilty because I had received so much more than my siblings had. He wanted to know what I was talking about. I told him of our parents sending me to high school, to college, and medical school, and I was the only one of us eight kids who had even gone to high-school. He wanted to know if I had ever kept track of what I had earned during those years, as well as what my school costs had been. I said I had always kept a record of my expenses as well as my earnings, but I had never added any of it up. I just kept track. He suggested we get out the records and do a little adding and subtracting.

As a matter of fact, I had kept track of the teeniest expenditure - even for an eraser or an occasional candy bar. The only thing I had left out was my clothes and my room and board with my parents during those eight years. Everything else was there, even car fare. My earnings had been from all the ways I managed to earn money - picking prunes, picking hops, working in the cannery, working in the assessor's office, typing manuscripts, typing books, teaching in the Physiology Lab - well, just everything. I was flabbergasted to discover that I had earned and contributed considerably more than my expenses had been.

Carl thought my room, board, and clothes expenses could be canceled out because of the pleasure I had given both Mother and Dad in living with them all those years. He said it with such conviction that for the first time I lost my guilt over having received so much more than my siblings. His matter of fact approach was far more effective than a therapy session for assuagement of guilt could have been. He had a way of dealing with the important things. Just as I hadn't kept track of board and room, neither had I kept track of the procession of packages I had sent home to the various family members - during the Depression years following 1929 - from the time I got my first paycheck in January 1931 to my losing my job due to tuberculosis in August 1932. It wasn't always easy to give him something he could chew on when we talked about his various problems. He probably found it harder to entertain new concepts about himself and his patterns of living than it was for me, but we kept working at it. I think I could have helped him more had his questions come fifty years later.

was for me, but we kept working at it. I think I could have helped him more had his questions come fifty years later.

Eventually he married Martha Eriksen, a divorcee with 3 children, whom he was greatly enamored of. Evelyn, the oldest, was 17, Keith was 9, and Ted was 4. Martha had had good cause to terminate her marriage, and Carl had bowed out from his first marriage. Thank goodness there were no children with that venture. Anybody in his right mind ought to be aware of the great difficulties commonly involved in being a step parent or a step child. Unlike Niels, Carl had never been fond of children. He really had no idea how to accept his new role, no matter how much he valued their mother. I am sure life was very hard for all of them. He still had occasion to come visiting me, and as per usual, we talked about a thousand things. It was during the first couple years of their marriage that he talked about his many troubles.

Carl & Martha, cc 1955

To him, Martha was still a very fine person, but "She is a very strange person." When I asked what he meant by that, he said, "She is different from me." It was just that simple, and I ought to understand how she was strange. It IS simple, and it is universal: Anyone different from me is strange! We take our assumptions, our beliefs, our opinions, our values, our ways, our patterns, for granted! Although he didn't know it, he had joined the human race. Nothing about our ways and our values are strange! No sir. We're the normal ones! We're the base line. We are the measuring stick. We are the norm. Others should make the adjustments to our ways of feeling, thinking, believing, and doing! It would never occur to him to challenge anything he believed. He wouldn't have held his beliefs if they had been wrong! The fact that someone did not accept his point of view made that person suspect - strange. But he wasn't

Even as a psychiatrist it is easy to slip into the error of assuming that our opinions are clearly the correct ones.

Martha has also had her chance to tell me how hard it was living with a husband who lived by the slogan totally unlike her own, i.e. "never do today what you can put off till tomorrow", or who thought nothing of imposing on people - e.g., stopping in unexpectedly just at eating time - even with several in the entourage - and much, much more.

Then Martha became pregnant, and their only child, Mary, was born in 1947. Martha was 43. She had great importance to Carl and to all in our family right from the beginning, for she was the first, the last and the only descendent of Peter and Bertha born with the Anderson name. Things began happening when she was still a baby that made her almost not survive. She had acute spinal meningitis - but with the expert and devoted help of Sidney's Dr. Hyde, and the nursing care of the Abelines, who turned their home into a hospital for her, she made it, and seemingly, without complications or sequelae. There was also a train derailment between Sidney and Richey, where they were living, which was a near catastrophe for Carl and Martha as well as for Mary, but somehow, they survived. Carl threw himself over Mary as they saw what was happening, and this no doubt was what saved her, but the scars of their injuries remained in Carl and Martha throughout their lives.

Carl's physical disabilities were oft times overwhelming, chiefly related to gastric ulcer, which perforated and he developed extensive peritonitis. This led to wound-healing problems, with herniation of abdominal contents at least on two occasions, and extensive hospitalizations. He accepted his many problems without conflict or whining. He took life as it came. I don't know what he - or they - or we - would have done without the V.A. Hospital in Miles City, Montana. The professional competence was tops, their demonstrated caring was reassuring, and it was close enough to Sidney to make it possible to keep in touch. The whole family had nothing other than appreciation for the help the V.A. provided over a long period of time. I never read of the criticisms the Miles City Hospital has had in recent years, but I registered a silent vote of confidence in the place. Staffs change, I know, but when our family knew the hospital, it merited our vote of thanks.

Carl's daughter, Mary, was not an easy child to raise. She was bright, but she was also willful and regarded herself as competent to decide. Abiding by the rules was not in her lexicon. She took after her father's and not her mother's patterns and values. They enrolled her in the Catholic elementary school in Sidney through the eighth grade. Then she was sent to a Catholic boarding high school in Richardton, North Dakota, and graduated from there. Carl accepted her enrollment there, even though he was not a Catholic, and was, instead, an ardent Mason. It appeared to be for Mary's good, and that sufficed for him. Martha was the staunch believer in her Catholic religion, and provided a solidity that was stabilizing without being oppressive. Things between Carl and Martha began improving, according to Martha, when she ceased trying to make Carl over to fit her measurements. It's a strange world.

Mary adopted many of Carl's values, such as love of knowledge, independence, good horsemanship, and probably many others. One value I recall her telling me about was, "If you put it off, lots of times it is not necessary to do it at all." Another one I have often heard him express - partially facetiously, to be sure, but still in the background of his thinking was "If I've done anything I am sorry for, I am glad of it!" It is difficult to know what to do with someone who is a stranger to regret. Mary started college but could not settle down. Instead, she married Doug Wagner from nearby Savage, who was in the Service and stationed at Camp Pendleton in Southern California. Doug was a Navy man and they lived in Fallbrook, CA, right near the Base, while at the same time Jan and I lived in San Diego and worked for the State of California at the California Institution for Women located near Chino.

Doug and Mary had two babies less than a year apart, David and Elizabeth. Then Doug was killed instantly as he was bicycling home from work, when a motorcycle ridden by his supervisor ran into him. Mary's youngest was just a year old. When Mary called to tell us the sad news, we headed at once for Fallbrook and stayed with her that night. The blow to Mary was too devastating, and it seemed to me I couldn't possibly provide the support she needed. It is possible all she wanted of me was to be there, but that seemed to me totally inadequate, so I returned to San Diego, and she prepared to bring Doug's body back home to Sidney and Savage. I'm sure

I was not sufficiently attuned to them so I had no feeling I could be of help.

After the funeral in Savage, Montana, Mary returned to Fallbrook, California, caring for her two babies, and then decided she would return to Sidney where she would be close to both her parents and to Doug's family. During that same time I had shifted gears and had decided that I would pull up stakes in San Diego and go back to Sidney too, and the five of us, Mary and her two and me with my Jan - arrived here almost simultaneously.

Mary had a new house built here in Sidney, but her restlessness continued, and she moved back again to California. There she met and married another Service man, Chuck Davis, and they were transferred to Rhode Island, and remained there long enough for Mary to have two more babies, Charlie and Tom Davis. Chuck retired from the service and they moved to Joplin, Missouri. Chuck was on the road driving a truck most of the time, and the marriage came to a screeching halt with divorce. Mary remained in Joplin and finally was ready to reenroll in college. She got her degree in Business Administration this past year, and is half planning to reenroll to get her Master's degree. She holds a job, manages her home with the help of her wonderful daughter Elizabeth, now making tentative plans for college at Loyola in Chicago, Illinois. (Later: Elizabeth has completed her 1st year with flying colors).

Mary's Children & Carl - Elizabeth, Tom, David, Carl & Charlie

In 1983 Mary's son, David, was walking home from some activity, and was run down - and killed instantly - by a car. It was almost a repetition of the accident that killed his father in California. I suspect that her loss of David played a part in her subsequently being engrossed in college work, which demanded her full involvement, and provided unlimited interesting stimuli to keep her from giving in to her sense of bereavement.

Not too many weeks ago, when Mary, along with her brother, Keith Eriksen, came to Sidney for a few days to visit Martha, Mary and I spent a whole afternoon visiting. She was keenly and happily aware of my general improvements from my "fallow years", since she was here in Sidney last year. We did some wonderful communicating, and many details were most gratifying. She has become aware of the importance of having roots, and she wants to do something that may help her own kids establish some. She spent some time looking through the Jensen Family Book by her cousin Bill Jensen, and this reinforced her feeling of the importance of family. I told her of my project of making a record of my life, and she hoped some day she might read it.

For some unknown reason I began telling her about my living through some changes in the field of Medicine, and am still doing it. I told her that when I was in medical school and studied anatomy and neurology, there was a part of the brain near the base of the skull that characteristically had long ascending nerve fibers surrounded by endless tiny filaments as they entered the brain. These filaments were called "Supportive Stroma", and were seen as devices to give support, by their very presence, to the long spindly ascending nerve tracts. They seemed to have no other function than to keep things from rattling around - like excelsior around some item to be shipped through the mail. A few years ago I became aware that things had changed in Medicine, because now the "Supportive Stroma" had a new name: it was now called THE ASCENDING RETICULAR ACTIVATING SUBSTANCE, or system, and as far as I have been able to comprehend, it is now seen as the place where previous experiences and "recordings" make connections through the filaments, with incoming impulses, and put their input into them and thus modify the end product so that nothing can be registered in the cortex of the brain without some modification brought to it by the sum total of past experience. Nothing we perceive or experience can be prime or pure. It is definitely touched by what has happened before. If this is not the correct interpretation or is an incomplete version, I am sorry, for I'd like to be reasonably accurate.

It is as close to what I have found to be true clinically as I can get. Everything that happens and is registered as a perception is biased by previous experience. Prejudice is one of the facts of life. It cannot be eliminated, and from what I understand, it is the product of the Ascending Reticular Activating System, that graduated from being supportive stroma to being the most fascinating aspect of brain activity. Then I told her of other changes that had come about: Recently after many fallow years during which I had not attended a single lecture, I had then gone to a lecture held at our Middle School, and which was primarily for teachers. My good friend, Georgia Petersen, a retired teacher and one of the regular members of our Study Group, had asked me to come with her to the lecture. The presentation was to be "Attention Deficit Disorder in Children", and the lecturer was Dr. Ned Tranel, a clinical psychologist, whom I had met many years ago when we were both involved in examining a particular case.

I had no idea he would startle me out of my boots, but that is precisely what happened. As though it were old hat, he proceeded to tell the audience of teachers about the formation of the brain prior to birth. He talked of cells that migrated from the umbilical area to the preprogrammed destination, and thus made - constructed - the brain that we know. In all my life I had never heard of this! Had I been asleep? Was the man just talking about something he didn't really know about? If it was known, why had I never heard about it? Cells MIGRATING, and forming the brain! But it must be true or he would not stand there and talk so blandly about it - as though it were common knowledge. I wanted to stop the man and go over it again - but after all, I wasn't a teacher, and I didn't feel entitled to butt in. Then Mary, after listening to me relate what I had heard, said, "He's talking about laying down history." At a point like this it feels good just to be alive - and receptive! Mary's visit was a pure delight. She heard what I had been saying, and she carried it farther than I had gone, and put it into simple terms. Never will I forget it. To me, ideas are marvelous things. They bring about in me the most delectable "high" I can conceive of.

As I see it, not only is prejudice normal, but is necessary if one would have growth and development. I see autism as the result of not being able to make use of previous incoming impulses, so no connection is made and every impulse reaching the cortex is as though it is the first one. It is not reinforced, or modified or biased. It stands alone, and therefore the autistic child is both vapid and immature and in essence hopeless. For any of us to develop and grow we have to be able to hold on to what has gone on before. Even each cell has its long and incalculable heritage.

Since that date in 1988 when Mary came to see me, a new development has emerged. Mary, who has her Business degree and her own Word Processor, has taken on the job of putting what I write into her Processor. We manage to keep teamwork going, and whatever emerges from our activities will be the resultant of our joint efforts. It has been a genuine pleasure to have first hand experience in how modern technology can assist in performing a task.

Elizabeth, Mary's daughter, has been enrolled at Loyola and expects eventually to get her degree in Law. Mary still wants roots, but it could possibly be that they will be elsewhere than in Montana.

Carl fractured his hip in 1980 and in the process of getting care he was shunted from one hospital to another - Sidney - Miles City - Helena, and back to Miles City, where he died. Considering the closeness of our relationship for many years, I seem now, in retrospect, to have been extremely bland. Carl died in 1980 at the age of 85. I must have been well into my fallow years when this occurred, for I literally cannot recall much of it, neither the sequence of events, nor his funeral, nor much that happened afterward - for perhaps five or six years - and then I gradually began to emerge from the fog in 1986.

And what about Martha during all those years? Obviously, no matter how strange Carl had found her to be, she never violated any of his strong or important values or beliefs. Together, they loved Mary, went places, danced happily, worked, played cards, and visited with themselves or with their many friends. She had her beliefs but no longer tried to pressure - or shame - or frighten - him into accepting hers. She may have tried to change his attitudes toward his step children, but his patterns did not stem from strong beliefs he had since childhood, nor did they have an important place in his scale of values, because he had never had to face such situations. Therefore, Martha violated no essential code he held. As time wore on, Martha's three children were increasingly out from under foot, and therefore less in the limelight, and Martha began to learn that no matter how desirable a change might be, there was no gain to be had from trying to change Carl. Whatever bitterness she had, she did not let it curdle their total relationship. There were many good things they had out of their togetherness and she managed to find life not unbearable and in many ways quite good.

For the past 23 years, Martha and I have been going out to a local restaurant for dinner every Sunday. Martha never objects to my taking Jan along, and fortunately, Jan is devoted to Martha. Neither one of us goes out from home very much, and this break is good for both of us. Also, fortunately, neither Martha nor I has any need to change the other person, so we are free to interact without pressuring. During all my fallow years, when I guess I was pretty much of a mess, feeling little and remembering little, Martha never embarrassed me with any comments concerning my state, nor did she put on me any feeling of defensiveness. We ate together, exchanged chit chat, and started a new week. Neither one hosted the other; we carried our own freight, and remained, day by day, friends. She is solid as a rock. Carl picked a very good wife - even though she is strange - as every one is strange, in his or her own way. I'd vote for her any time. The bond between Martha and her children is close. Scarcely a week goes by but one or more of them calls her on the phone - from California, from Kansas, or from Missouri. Additionally, Mary and the boys, her half brothers, have a very comfortable relationship. Carl and Martha must have done something right to be so blessed.

Throughout many years Carl was a Mason and felt a real involvement with Masonic beliefs that he had never felt for any other philosophy. It seemed fitting that he was buried with Masonic rituals in the family plot, right next to Mother and Dad, Niels and Johanna, Len - and a place for Jan and me. It is a beautiful spot - in the heart of the MonDak.

Martha died in 1993, after several years of ill health. She is buried next to Carl in the Anderson plot.

Lots of people don't even like to think about cemeteries, and certainly would never form an attachment to one. Some are nicely kept and even attractive. Our cemetery was part of me from the beginning, because it was carved out of our - Dad's - homestead. It is bordered on two sides by country roads - one of them paved. The western little hills come right down to the fence, seeming to hold it as though the cemetery itself is in the palm of an encircling hand. One looks eastward across the big ditch toward our old farm and the lush fields, and the Yellowstone river 23 miles farther east, edged by trees. Beyond that, we see the bluish badlands that form the backdrop for our MonDak valley.

Everything is clean and green and orderly and "manicured." There is an occasional tree and a single little hillock on which Pella church was built - and remained for a couple years until it was moved to town. It is quiet and orderly, verdant and peaceful. It invites one to spend time. There is no hum of farm machinery, no airplanes buzzing overhead, and essentially no traffic. There are so many people I know there that it is a friendly place.

Dad used to enjoy going to cemeteries in Oregon, and would come home feeling he had achieved some grasp of the history of the area by looking at the grave markers. Cemeteries certainly are not repelling places to me. I get no eerie feeling when I visit one. The only cemetery I can recall visiting, and getting a feeling of wanting to sit down and rest for awhile, was in Winnipeg, Canada in 1920. It was not only big and well kept, but it felt like a park. It had lots of seats and pathways and even a few little tables. Lots of nannies came there with their babies in their buggies, ambled about for a while and then settled down to chat with other women and their charges whom they had seen many times previously, as they gave the babies a stroll and some fresh air. I thought it was an excellent idea. Perhaps it is a common custom, but if so, I have never seen it elsewhere.

Christine - Prize Winning True Survivor

The seventh child in our family, and the one just older than me, was CHRISTINA ISABEL, who was born on February 21, 1898. All the kids except Jo had birthdays in the 20's in different months, and half of us had our birthday on the 21st of some month: Mame on May 21st, Carl on July 21st, Christina on February 21st and mine on June 21st. Christina was named for Mother, Bertha Christina Dorothea, but I never figured out who the Isabel was for. Perhaps it was related to 1898 and Spain. Anyway, her name evolved from Christina, to Stina, and finally to Christine. Eventually, for the younger generation at least, her name was shortened to Chris.

Harry & Christine with their children, Dan & Nell

She was more than six years my senior, and this may have contributed to our lack of a sense of togetherness. But it wouldn't take much imagination to suspect that after over six years of preferential treatment by reason of being the baby, she could hardly have sponsored a welcoming party for me. The baby boy, Christian, who was born dead between Christine and me in 1900 also provided time as well as circumstance calculated to reinforce her assumptions of specialness in her world, perhaps in perpetuity. I think it would have been natural if that had been her assumption..

I was sure she was the prettiest one in our family; her features were chiseled and finer than some of us had; her hair was blond and kind of curly; she was slenderly built, and at the 1st Dawson County Fair which was held in Sidney, she got the prize for being the prettiest baby. In addition to my thinking of her as the prettiest, I also thought of her as liking the boys too much. She repeatedly got a mild crush on one or another of our hired men, who were almost a part of our family. By that time irrigation was in full force, and big farming was the normal pattern of the residents of the valley. Dad did little of the actual work on the farm, but relied, instead, on his hired men to get the job done. Every morning he walked the 2 miles to Sidney to get the mail at the post office, which included the daily paper from some Western or midwestern metropolis - so we always got a daily paper.

Christine was not so far beyond me in age that we did not play together at all. Our favorite together-activity was playing paper dolls. We cut out these likenesses of people of every age and in every imaginable occupation and activity from the catalogs and reenacted their various lives as we placed them in cardboard boxes to represent rooms in houses. I can even recall using Russian thistles - tumble weeds, - in their lush, green stage, to substitute for the cardboard boxes. There was another big-top weed, whose name I never heard, which was lacy and had tiny pink flowers, and grew between the old log house and the new big frame house, that we enjoyed using when playing with our paper dolls. We liked the boxes best, because we could also have cut-out furniture, wagons and sleds from the catalogs to make our play more realistic. We didn't have to imagine there was a sledding party; it was actually there in catalog cut-outs. But I don't recall any other game we played together.

When we left the log house in 1908, we also left behind the trees that had accumulated and grown there: two cottonwoods, an ash, I believe it was called, and most important, the wild plum patch. Our family was always on the lookout for berries or larger fruit to make jelly, and Mother had once discarded the culls from such a find, only to have them sprout and grow the following year, and eventually provided not only a wild plum crop of fruit every year, but a place to play house for any kids who stopped in to visit. We couldn't be seen from the outside, and it had several rooms and paths leading from one room to another. We played house there with one being the mother, another the father, until everyone had a role - so we needed all the rooms the plum patch provided.

I'm sure Christine was young enough, four, to make the ocean voyage to Denmark with Mother and Dad for free, or they no doubt would have left her at home. But she managed, according to Mother, to captivate the people they visited in Denmark, again and again. Once it involved her expressed disdain for their dark bread, which was regularly served, but which our family had graduated from. She called it "dirty bread" and therefore would not eat it. She was not old enough to have retained much of the entire trip; I have never heard her mention anything about it, but it must have offered many opportunities to have confirmed her belief in her own specialness.

It was a very important trip for Mother and Dad, for it cemented their attachment to America, and liberated them from their strong ties to Denmark. They found Denmark much smaller than they had remembered it: "Why, one could almost jump across it." It was also "too cold and too damp," and "People there had no chance to get ahead." They were so glad to get back to Sidney, where people had both a present and a future. In Liverpool they bought a dollar's worth of oranges to take back home to the family in Sidney, and were incredulous when the shopkeeper filled one bag full of oranges after the next - and all of it for a dollar! They got a hundred oranges - a penny a piece. By the time they had been on board over night, the smell of ripe (and overripe) oranges filled their cabin space. By the second day they had to begin throwing them overboard, and the last of them went the same way by the time they reached New York. When the train reached Mondak, close to home, they bought another dollar's worth, so as to bring home a treat, but this time there were only a dozen oranges. Mother claimed she never could stand oranges and never again ate them after her encounter with the penny a piece ones.

None of Mother's or Dad's relatives lived in Denmark any more, so the folks could not visit them, but they did find Mother's old school teacher, who still remembered her. He didn't see or hear well any more, but when she spoke to him he said happily, "Isn't this the voice of a Josephsen?" There were so many incidents that made the trip worth while for them. But from that time on, they no longer belonged to Denmark. Their reunion with little Carl when they got back to Sidney was, indeed, a happy one for all of them. They never again spoke of another trip to Denmark.

When I think of Christine's Denmark trip when she was three or four, I also remember my first trip - this one to Spokane, in 1919, when I was fifteen. Word of Uncle John's death had come by wire the day of Christine's wedding, in June, and since Mother could not go to his funeral she determined to go as soon as she could. I am sure that she took for granted taking me with her. I don't suppose that Mother even for a moment considered taking Christine: she was now married to

Harry Brockway, whom she had met and fallen in love with while she was keeping house for Carl and Niels. Now they were to set up housekeeping of their own on Harry's homestead, also in Prairie Elk country.

Many years later I was flabbergasted to have Christine tell me of her feelings about that trip of Mother's and mine to Spokane. She said Mother had engineered things so that she, Christine, would be left out of the trip, that Mother wouldn't take such a trip until she was "out of the way", safely married. I knew it was an unfair accusation, because it was getting word of Uncle John's death on Christine's wedding day that gave rise to Mother's plan, and Christine's accusations hurt me. Anything that reflected negatively on Mother hurt me - always. There was nothing I could do to help take away Christine's jealous and discriminated-against feeling. It isn't strange that she should have had such feelings, because, in truth, Mother adored me, her present baby - no matter how old I got. Christine had learned early while she was the baby that it was she who was entitled to be taken along on trips. But I had no guilt feelings as a result of my good fortune; I just felt that Christine didn't have a good attitude. Nobody had picked the time for Uncle John's death.

The first high school in Sidney was opened not long after Christine finished eighth grade. Mother, always interested in education, was happy that Christine was to have this opportunity to be enrolled in a high school. Mother sent her to school but it took only a few days before Christine was ready to call it quits. She felt that the other students, the daughters of Sidney's elite families, chiefly the Adams girls as I recall, didn't like her and made fun of her clothes. They were not friendly toward her. This could well have been, for to the Adams girls - there were Georgie, Mabel, Mary and Winifred - we were no doubt peasants and foreigners - Danes - who had no status. Mr. Adams was an important man - he had an important job at the First National Bank, and they were part of "the Minnesota clique." Youngsters can be very cruel - even without trying to or meaning to - often even without knowing what they are doing. But looking at it from this vantage point, it is not surprising that Christine elected to quit school.

Christine seemed to me to be more Mame's daughter than she was Mother's, in many ways. She seemed to have a closer bond with Mame than with Mother. This did not change through the years. I can, however, still remember Christine on occasion sort of mothering me when we would have one of our violent electrical storms. We shared the same bedroom and double bed. When the lightning and thunder would seem as though it just couldn't get worse, and our white roller curtains with their border of pink flowers, couldn't possibly keep out the flashes that came - one after the other - I felt very frightened and would be ready to cry. Then Christine would reassure me and hold my hand in hers, and I could settle down and go to sleep again. She was a great comfort when I needed her. It seems to me I always had a special girlfriend, but Christine never had one that lasted for years, as I had. Maybe she had enough adoring older sisters so that she didn't have the needs I did. We had no close neighbors and I was pretty much alone. Many of my siblings' children, or grandchildren, have been named Christine, but never, even one, Camilla. I guess this reveals our ratings as well as my hurt feelings. But I'd never heard of sibling rivalry until I was a psychiatrist.

After Christine turned thumbs down on high school, she had a number of different jobs: she was a telephone operator for our new local phone company. I liked that job because I got to stay with her at the telephone office sometimes, and one could never tell what interesting situation would arise from some of the calls that came in at night. I always thought of her as a competent operator. She also clerked in the basement of the Yellowstone Mercantile Store. That was less interesting because it did not involve staying over night with her. Then she kept house for Carl and Niels at Prairie Elk. That was always interesting for me if I visited them because they would always do special things for me and whatever girlfriend I brought with me - like Dora Damskov, on one trip there.

My family at Figure Eight would stop any activity they were involved in when we came and we'd have ourselves a ball; once we drove around the country in the topless, beaten up car rather aimlessly - to Paxton, to Prairie Elk, to Weldon - just to be on the go, perhaps a distance of 40-50 miles. We gathered up stray fellows, homesteaders, as we proceeded, invited them to come on their own to Figure Eight for supper, and then after supper we went to a dance, at the nearby - 15 miles away - hall known as Dreamland. There, I tried valiantly to dance, and to return the winks of the young men, though I never really learned how either to dance or to flirt. I attributed my clumsiness to the fact that I did it so seldom that I couldn't possibly be faulted for not being expert. But it was all exciting and so different from life at home.

Harry Brockway, whom Christine married after the war was over, came originally from South Dakota. He was dark haired, well built, handsome, and he had a lovely speaking and singing voice. This enabled him to be the caller at the square dances, and everybody liked the way he did the job. His younger brother Bill, was also part of the scene, but he never rated as Harry did. Part of the attraction of the outings to Figure Eight was, no doubt, that in my home, dancing was ABSOLUTELY forbidden; Dancing was "the work of the devil!" It led to trouble and straight to HELL.

From my earliest memories, I was a big girl, and long before my teens I was much bigger than Christine - though six and a half years her junior. Everyone said I was very grown up for my age. Of course I liked to believe it, and I tried to act as grown up as I could - dancing and flirting, and stealing a kiss now and then. I wouldn't have had any idea what I would do if one of the fellows had made a pass at me, but fortunately, I never had to do anything. Whether we were at home on the Figure Eight or at a dance, it was more like a family affair and everybody took care of me. I was never aware of anything irregular. But dancing was inordinately fascinating and I wanted so very much to learn. Christine could dance; Carl could dance - and I couldn't! It was most frustrating.

Right after Christine's and Harry's wedding in June 1919, which took place at our home in town, Christine and Harry moved out to Harry's homestead on the Figure Eight, near Niels' and Carl's place. The poverty was pervasive. They just didn't have one nickel to rub against another, and trying to farm that dry country was a lost cause. Their home was a 2 or 3 room tar paper shack, but they carried on, picking up whatever fun they could find as they moved along. In as short a time as possible they had two children, Nell and Dan, with Christine coming the long 100 miles over very primitive roads to Sidney and home, to have her babies delivered. There is a saying that "whoever hath children gives hostage to fortune." It certainly is true, but there are few of us who have them, along with the pains and heartaches as well as the joys that go along with it, who would choose to forego the experience of parenthood. Children are almost a necessity, if the reservoir of people is to be maintained, as well as a prime source of emotional development and maturation.

There were, of course, no bags of candy or other goodies at Christine's house, with the exception of raisins. The kids would come, with hands cupped, saying "I want some." It took me a little while to catch on that "some" always meant raisins. I remember, also, when little Dan would come and say to his mother, "Do I have to whine and whine and whine to get you to pay some attention to me?" The poverty in no way diminished their love for their children. Things finally got so bad that they no longer could put up with the eternal marginality they were living in. It was too much. So they left it, as Jim and Jo had left Three Buttes in 1923, seeking better climes. They tried Sidney, they tried Fairview. There simply was no work available for either one of them.

While they were in Fairview, Christine developed an arthritic condition that resulted in replacement of both hip joints many years later. Throughout many years she endured much pain and disability, and she has taken daily, literally, handsful of aspirin. The hip replacement alleviated the pain, but made her completely helpless without her cane. She has never used a wheelchair, and this still holds true, now when she will soon be ninety-three.

Harry's parents and their family had moved from South Dakota to Fairview and bought a farm there, but even their farm - under irrigation - had no place for Harry because there were too many other younger sons in the family, and they had prior rights to work with their Dad. So Harry and Christine moved on again, this time to Eugene, where Jo and Jim lived, and they tried to make a living there. They gave up after a couple years, and moved on to the Priest River country in Idaho, where they knew no one, but Harry found a job in the logging industry. It looked as though it might be a steady job, and they were grateful they had found it.

Then Harry sustained a logging accident that cost him his life. He was felling a tree on the side of a mountain when a fellow worker higher up on the mountain also felled one, and the tree slid down the mountain, right toward Harry. He escaped being crushed, but a spicule from the cut tree pierced his leg and gave him gas-bacillus gangrene. Ordinarily it is so rare an occurrence that I have never to this day seen a case of it, so it is purely textbook knowledge of the disease I present.

It is a very rapidly progressing disease, and almost invariably fatal. By the next morning Harry was very ill, his tissues were loaded with the gas the organisms produce, and he was flown to Spokane to a hospital where amputation of his leg at the hip was done.

He got steadily worse, and within a day or so he had died. It was regarded as a highly contagious disease and no one was permitted to touch him for fear of being contaminated or spreading the germs. The tragedy pounced on them out of a clear sky and left them bludgeoned. Their son Dan was in high school in Priest River, and their daughter Nell was in Portland attending Reed College. She came back to Priest River at once to be with Christine, and did not return again to Reed College.

I was living in Philadelphia at the time of Harry's death and was in the midst of my training psychoanalysis with Dr. O. Spurgeon English, who was also head of the Department of Psychiatry at Temple University Medical School in Philadelphia. I am not embarrassed to say that in my session with Spurge that day I wept openly. My memory of the session was that Spurge said he wondered what I felt guilty about! I was incredulous that this was his response. He obviously could not see that I was just hurting, terribly, for my sister Christine. I knew she would be devastated, and I felt so very sorry. In the midst of seeing so many unhappy marriages in the world, I could point to at least two marriages in my own family that I thought of as good ones: Jo and Jim's and Christine and Harry's. Now this was over. I had always thought of Spurge as a very gentle person with compassion, but it seemed to me he failed me when I needed better understanding than he gave me. If there was one thing I did not have in relation to Harry - or even Christine - it was guilt. Spurge's inadequacy to meet my needs reminds me of my own inadequacy with Carl's Mary when Doug was killed, and with Lil when her baby daughter died.

Sometime prior to Harry's death I had visited them in Priest River, Idaho, accepting their generous hospitality. I'll never forget the dinner Christine purveyed from their own larder. They had ump-teen varieties of meat dishes: beef, pork, fish Harry had caught, venison he had killed, chicken, and even bear meat he had killed. It was like something I had never heard of, but they were happy to have me come and shared with me the best they had. It was a real feast.

While I was there, I saw what a fine young woman Nell had become, and I wanted her to have a chance to go to a really good college that I thought was worthy of Nell. I was always hearing about the superiority of Reed College when I was in Medical School in Portland and my good friend, Dr. Jessie Laird Brodie, a couple years ahead of me in Medical School, had graduated from that school. So I told Nell I'd send her to Reed if she demonstrated to me that she was able to find a job and be completely on her own and responsible for herself for a year prior to enrolling at Reed.

I was in pretty close contact with Nell, and though she definitely made the grade at Reed, I soon began to see that I had made a poor choice of College for her. It wasn't that Nell didn't like Reed, or that Reed failed her. It was just that they were not meant for each other. I had meant well, but as in the old slogan, "Meant well, did little, failed much." With Nell's almost exclusive background in rural living, and poverty, and never having lived around people going to college or living in some degree of affluence, and with little or no experience with money, sophistication, or with people with an academic orientation, it was inevitable she would feel unsure of herself at a place like Reed, where students are supposed to feel sure of themselves.

Nell had kept her part of our bargain; she had been on her own and fully supported herself for a year - which no doubt was a better record than most of the other students had. She hadn't been foolish or stupid about anything she did, but the Reed experience just wasn't fair to her. I was aware of so much less in this situation than I should have been aware of. Nell trusted my judgement - which was not all that good, and she made good in her studies, but it was an experience in unhappiness that she did not have coming to her. She never complained or berated me, but I wished I had not done this to a lovely young woman. She wasn't planning on quitting, but when her father, Harry Brockway, died, it provided the perfect reason for withdrawing.

I wish I could say that our experience with Reed College had probably been more helpful to me than to Nell. I could have learned that it might be a good idea if, from time to time, I stopped to doubt the wisdom of my own judgments, and that I better find out more about a situation before I jump to conclusions. But I really doubt I benefitted all that much. I continued to make impulsive judgments: meant well and failed a lot.

It took a long time for Christine to put together a life for herself again after Harry died, but she succeeded in doing just that. She got a job in Hanford at the atomic energy plant; Her daughter Nell went back to college, to a smaller State College in Washington, and one that was not overwhelming in its self concept, and implied expectations. She became a teacher. Then she married a young man, C.F. (Buck) Whetsler, whom she had dated in high school in Priest River. The years passed and when her three children were no longer little she began teaching in the Pasco school system and continued in this until her retirement only a few years ago. They lived for several years in Clarkston, Washington, and then moved to Pasco, where they have lived for many years. Buck was in charge of the Water, Sewer and Parks division of the City Government for years. He, too is retired.

Meanwhile there were big changes in Christine's family too. Buck Whetsler, Nell's husband had joined the Marines and was stationed in Quantico, Virginia. Dan Brockway, Christine's only son, had joined the Navy and was stationed near New York City and was being trained to be a Frogman, and Nell was pregnant with her first baby.

Then I had a letter from Christine saying she was coming east to be able to be closer to Dan, stationed at New York City, and she wondered if she couldn't make our home her headquarters and she could help us with Jan. I was too grateful for words. I knew how hard it had been for her to struggle out of her slough of despond after Harry was killed in the logging accident. I saw this as an opportunity to kill two birds with one stone - both of us would be helped by Christine's coming.

Shortly thereafter she arrived in Washington, and it was Labor Day weekend. Dan, her son, came from New York to visit her. He looked fine and she was relieved he liked what he was doing and learning. After two happy, talk-filled days, Dan left by train to return to his base near New York City. Just outside Philadelphia the train was derailed, and a great many passengers were injured, was the word Christine received over the phone. They said Dan was hurt, but that the confusion was so great they would ask her not to come to see him until the next day.

The next morning bright and early Christine and Len, my husband, set off for Philadelphia. That was Len's home and we felt he could no doubt be of real help to her there, because he knew his way around. When they got there and went to the hospital, Dan was already dead. It was difficult to get a coherent or reliable picture from anybody, but one of the Gray Ladies said she had seen him and that he had died several hours before Christine got there.

One tragic loss followed right on top another. It was almost unbelievable. She returned to Priest River to bury Dan beside Harry. And then she came back to us in Washington. But there was no way she could help; she was too shattered. She could scarcely manage to care for herself, much less Jan. Then Nell came to us to be able to be closer to Buck, in Quantico, Virginia, and her coming was extremely helpful to Christine. Nell took her along to Quantico, and became her mother's magnificent support. Eventually they returned to Washington State, the War was over, and Buck, Nell's husband, returned home to Washington too. The healing process was, understandably slow, but it did come about.

Nell and Buck and their family have a lovely home in Pasco, and Christine lives nearby in an apartment for senior citizens where she has lived on the 6th floor these many many years. She tends her home, prepares her own meals, and is at home with her neighbors. Nell has been goodness itself to her mother, and I would say she has always been as protective of Christine as I used to be with my mother. There have been still more changes.

Nell and Buck's three children, Dan, Kay, and Chrissy, were attractive children and grew up to be very different from one another. Dan enlisted in the Navy after high school and served during the Korean War, until he became ill and was returned to the states to die of Hodgkins Disease. The government used all the new drugs on him to no avail and felt he would be best served by being at home. He had a large physical frame and was simply skin and bone when I saw him. Nell took care of him most of the time, except for short periods when he would be hospitalized. It was a very hard period for all of them. Dan died and was relieved of his great misery. Now both Christine and Nell had lost a son, Dan.

Kay, Nell's second child was a most attractive young girl, but I never felt I knew her, nor indeed, did I ever have a real conversation with her. I can remember very plainly, however, my distinct annoyance with her because of her excessive (I thought) preoccupation with her hair. It was during the period when the young women wore their hair in great puffs at the side and top, and there really wasn't much time for anything else after fixing their hair was accomplished. I, who was brought up by Mother, who had a great abhorrence of mirrors and primping or any evidence of vanity, had taken on many of her values which surely showed through in me and my attitudes. I simply couldn't stand Kay's need to have such a "perfect" hairdo. I don't know whether I said as much, but I have no doubt my behavior expressed my disdain.

I was quite surprised not long afterward to learn Kay had been on a trip to Sidney and had had a happy time getting acquainted with her cousin, sister Dalma's granddaughter - Dave Albin's daughter Judy. Whereas I really didn't know Judy well at all, it seemed to me that Judy must have some real solidity to her or Dalma wouldn't like her so much. That made me think maybe I had been too quick to pass judgement on Kay, for if Judy liked her, Kay must have some worthwhile qualities for her to like. So, by reason of my accepting attitude toward Dalma's assessment, I was willing to drop my negative feelings toward Kay!

I saw Kay once after that. She was married and lived in Portland. She was still attractive, and I forget what her hairdo was like. She had two children and the oldest, an attractive boy, was quite hyperkinetic. I believe Kay was working away from home a good deal. From time to time I'd hear some little snatch about her from Nell, and it always had something to do with Kay's job, what a success she was in it, and her involvement in it. Then quite recently I had word that Kay's second child, her daughter Dana who was in high school, had suicided by gunshot. It was a terrible shock to everyone. Nobody had anticipated it. Nobody seemed to know what lay back of it all. It was a great mystery, and a very great shock. I understand that her brother, the one who had been hyperkinetic, wouldn't talk about Dana's death at all, and it was particularly hard on Nell, her grandmother, and on Christine, Dana's great grandmother. At least Nell sought professional help in this family tragedy. Nell has said to me on one occasion she felt Kay, the mother of Dana, needed to do a lot of talking before she could begin to heal, and that she was probably keeping too much inside herself.

Michaela Turner

I am sure I have no right or even competence to have any opinion - because I haven't seen or talked with any of them. Because of my professional status, perhaps I should not say anything, but stray thoughts have wandered through my mind and I share them here with you, and hope they can be used constructively by anyone who may use them at all.

Kay was probably expressing her felt need for perfection in some important area, when she was preoccupied with her hair. Dealing day by day with her hyperkinetic son surely must have been a frustrating and rather thankless job over many years. So she buried herself in her job and in a career in merchandising which was far more rewarding than domesticity had been. It was her life, and it was a successful life. She was good at it. This, her preoccupation, almost inevitably could have caused her to deprive her daughter, Dana, of opportunity for closeness and communication and a sense of meaningfulness to one another. This may have left Dana with a sense of futility and isolation which led her to toy with the idea of ending her loneliness and her search for her mother. And so she suicided. I could be way off, but it is not an uncommon scenario. It always seems to me it is too bad that those who suicide, and who expect what follows will be surcease of pain and stress, don't understand that there can be no surcease without awareness or consciousness. What's the advantage of having no further pain if one is incapable of anything - even awareness of oblivion? It takes life to have awareness. Life is a most wonderful thing just because its many attributes are available in no other state.

I hope someday Nell will talk to me about new insights her therapist has helped her find. I am sorry someone didn't spot Dana's misery in time to get some competent help. Suicide can come to any family, and it involves many people - just as an alcoholic family involves everybody. But it is always sad; it is always regrettable, and in my opinion it is always futile. The goal they seek can never materialize, because it is only in being alive that there can be awareness.

I'm glad Christine has Nell, who will never leave or forsake her. Anyone who has had the troubles Christine has had, and has come out of it all with the serenity and freedom from self pity that she seemingly has, is fortunate to have a daughter like Nell, who genuinely appreciates her. It's another segment of my family I love and am emotionally involved with.

Christine always took her place on a par with the rest of my competent sisters. She is an immaculate housekeeper, an excellent cook, and a top quality seamstress, sewing everything for her kids, grandkids and great grandchildren. In her 90's, she still lives by herself and manages her daily affairs. I'm ready to bet she still plays cribbage with anyone who enjoys cribbage, and until a very few years ago she drove her own car. She has maintained her independence and her interest in the world around her. I'll cast my vote for her.

Christine died on March 23, 1996 in Pasco Washington. She had lived 98 years.

Christine's great grand-daughter, Michaela Turner, was born on my 90th birthday, June 21, 1994. This picture shows her at eight months old - and just see how involved she is with living and what's going on. I think she's very special.

Camilla - Perennial Pioneer

I, Camilla, the eighth and last child of Peter and Bertha Anderson, was born June 21, 1904, in the same old log house in which the last five of us were born. To be sure, the house had changed its location in those years, from the west bank of the Yellowstone River. It had been moved, log by log, to a spot beside the stage road, away from the river, but still in the locale called Sidney, Montana. The move had been made to facilitate contact with other people. Roads, at best until into the 1900's, were only trails, and almost non existent. The Stage Road led from Glendive, Montana, northwest to Ridgelawn and Fort Buford, which was at the confluence of the Yellowstone with the Missouri River, perhaps 20 miles northeast of us.

There was another event in addition to my birth that marks 1904 as an important date. It also marks the birth of Sidney as a spot on the map. The general area had had a name since 1888 when the federal government authorized a stage stop for mail delivery at Sidney. But it moved from place to place depending on who was willing to take the responsibility entailed. The name Sidney came from a little boy named Sidney Walters, whose family had submitted the name, and it was chosen for the honor. But it wasn't until 1904 when Edgar Kenoyer came riding into the area on his bicycle and leading his horse, that the necessary machinery was set in motion to create a town named Sidney.

Camilla May Anderson
High School Graduation, 1921

Eddie Kenoyer bought a tract of land, platted it, created the boundaries, the streets, the alleys, the parks, the principle sections of the city, and then sold the lots to people interested in buying, and presto, Sidney was born. The building that Mr. Kenoyer had erected for his sales office still stands and functions in the center of town as the Eagle Cafe. Members of the Kenoyer family continued to live here until the 1970's and I had returned to Sidney, retired. Eddie Kenoyer had been a favorite of mine because he never failed to call me by my full name: Camilla May.

Now, 90 years later it is still home to widely scattered members of the Anderson clan. Many of them return here time after time, or they live elsewhere for a period and then return to Sidney, or they never left Sidney to dwell elsewhere. Thus it is home to four generations of members of our family. Some only come home to be buried in their final resting place. At the present time progeny of my oldest sister Marie (Mrs. Little Pete) Anderson, sister Dagmar (or Dalma) Albin, sister Lilian Jensen, and I, Camilla, actually live here. The only building which was on the townsite when Eddie Kenoyer bought the tract was the old stone (sandstone) Methodist church, and that building still stands, but has an ugly stucco coat on its exterior. It functions as a warehouse for Gurney Electric Co. Things do change but they also remain remarkably stable.

Mother was used to being in the family way. It was her tenth pregnancy, and all but her eighth and ninth pregnancies had ended well. The eighth ended in a miscarriage when she was encamped in a sheep-herding project out in the hill country to the west, and the ninth which ended in a full term stillbirth. The tenth pregnancy had been more difficult than the other because she was unable to get about and do her usual homemaking chores throughout much of the pregnancy. She seemed well enough, but couldn't walk. She was going on forty-two, and perhaps she thought she was too old to have any more pregnancies. At any rate, she did not relish the idea of being in the family way again.

No doctors were in attendance nor even midwives, throughout the entire pregnancy and delivery, because no doctors were closer than Glendive, fifty miles to the south. Besides, it was common practice for neighbor to help neighbor in the birthing process, so what was done or not done was the common practice. May Blake, the wife of Rev. Pearl Blake, the minister at the Methodist church in Sidney was picked to be Mother's birthing helper. They were already fast friends or Mother would not have asked for her help, but the ordeal they shared in my birth surely cemented their friendship.

Mother named me Camilla May. She had like the name Camilla and had wanted to name a couple of my older siblings Camilla, but had been overruled. Now, she was pretty sure I would be her last child, because she was past forty-one, so the family gave in and let her have her way about the name Camilla. My middle name, May, was Mother's way of thanking and honoring her neighbor-helper for having piloted her safely through another birthing. I still use my middle initial in my signature, and thereby tip my hat to May Blake every time I sign my name.

You might say I was born a Methodist, because our whole family were faithful members of the Methodist church, and since the turn of the century it was the only religious denomination having a church edifice in the entire lower Yellowstone valley. In addition to God and May Blake delivering me, within a few weeks Mother brought me to the Old Stone Church over which Rev. Pearl Blake presided, and he baptized me and signed his name on the beautiful scroll attesting to my baptism. It became a sort of legal document attesting to the fact of my existence. The actual legal record of my birth was kept in Glendive, the county seat of Dawson County. The scroll was so beautiful that Mother had it framed and I had it hanging on my walls for many decades.

I always like my name, and I liked for it to be pronounced correctly. Seldom a day passes without a mispronunciation of my name. I am called Ca-Meal; Ca-Meal-ya; Camel-a. It is none of these; it is Ca-MILL-a. I am Danish, and it is pronounced the Danish way. I have always been grateful I didn't get nicknamed Millie.

It was a wonder that there were no complications when I was born, because I weighed in at 13 lbs. At per the usual, no anesthetics were used, and the mothers of that age truly lived out the Biblical injunction to bear children in pain. This had been Mother's most difficult pregnancy in that she could scarcely get about. She couldn't do her routine work and she sat or lay down most of the time. For this she was roundly criticized by Mame, my oldest sister of almost 20. Mame married in April, and I was born in June. I was a Mamma's girl from day one, and I resented hearing, years later from sister Mame, about how Mamma babied herself, lying around, and not helping with the work.

I never think about this criticism of Mother without a good bit of irritation with Mame. Good daughters don't criticize their mothers, and besides that, I though my birth weight - 13 lbs. - entitled Mother to be permitted to lie around and not help. It was 1930 before I would have vindication of my irritation. I had just graduated in Medicine, and Mother had asked me to help get her a doctor in Portland, who found a complete prolapse of the uterus. She had never complained to me, and I'm sure she never talked about it even to family members, because one never talked about sexual matters. But Mame should have known that Mamma was no cry baby, and that she never shirked working; she just could not talk about sexual matters! No doubt my huge size had contributed to the prolapse. It's funny how understanding something helps to eliminate moralistic judgment - like walking a day in the other fellow's moccasins.

The fact that I was a very big baby - and then just kept on growing - to the point where I was a very big child, played an important part in determining my self image, my identity. Mother couldn't carry me around, but I often sat on her lap, and there, with my arms around her neck, and with Mother wearing a dark red wool wrapper, I would feel for a big, soft, pink mole or wart on the back of her neck. In no way was I encouraged to remain a baby because everybody in the family was more than accepting of my doing as much for myself - or others - as I could. They had all had their fill of baby tending. There no doubt was still much they had to do for me, but none of them was assigned to be my special caretaker. I can recall a little intimate talk I had with my sister Dalma when I was in my 70's and she told me of what she did when it was her turn to put me to sleep: she pinched my eyelids together so I'd sleep faster!

I had to picture myself before age one year, standing on a chair and holding on to the back of it, looking out at the world as though I had full power to make it do whatever I wished it to. I don't known what happened to that picture, but I can't find it. It reminds me of another baby, a ten month old great grand nephew, the son of Tim Albin, whom I had known slightly when he was a teenager. Tim, the baby, two slightly older sisters of the baby, and Tim's wife came to call on me when I was well into my 80's. I thoroughly enjoyed watching this baby make his sisters do what he wanted them to do. My mind flitted to that picture of me standing on the chair. Each of us looked as though we took for granted we were cock of the walk.

Do you suppose it could be that this is what the Biblical story of the Garden of Eden meant when it said Man was created in the image of God? God had just finished creating everything - out of nothing - and it was ever good! It's really true that Man is the only creation that can make miracles happen out of an idea, or out of a vision of what he wants. One miracle after another! Nothing like it before or since. Man is truly unique. It surely is remarkable what a brain can do. I guess, I'd have to say I really believe Man was created in the image of God - God the Creator; Man the creator! There seems to be no determinable limits to what man's brain can do. It is staggering, and it carries with it the responsibility to do nothing that might damage that wonderful gift. How can anybody in his right mind do drugs - including alcohol, and place at risk this precious aspect of himself.

In 1907, when I was going on four, we moved from the log house to the big new two story house. Everything about the log house and about our life in it is gone from my memory except that I can sort of recall how it looked on the outside, with the wild plum patch between it and the road, and two trees, a small cottonwood and an ash, beside it. I can also recall gathering eggs at the new home, and playing with paper dolls with my sister Christine as we placed them in a big round weed with pink flowers. In the new house, Christine and I had a bedroom of our own on the second floor. My first clear memories of my new home was of people coming early in the morning of Aug. 17, 1908, to help my parents celebrate their silver wedding day. Then there was walking a couple miles to school in 1909, and the event to top all events: the double wedding of my two sisters, Dalma married to Ira Albin, and Lil married to Thorvald Jensen, on June 1, 1910. Everybody, bar none, came for the wedding and then the reception and the big dinner that continued for hours and hours, and ended in a once in a lifetime huge snowstorm during the night.

I don't even recall the incident that I have heard Mother tell about many times. I must have been two and I came in from the yard at the log house and asked for a piece of bread and butter. Mother fixed it for me and added some sugar. I took it and threw it on the floor - and refused to pick it up. Mother finally spanked me, but I did not capitulate. Then she spanked me some more - and some more - and still some more - until she was sick at heart. I don't know how long I stood my ground or how long it took me to decide to mind, but I finally did. I darted over to the bread, picked it up and gave it to

Mother. She went into the bedroom and cried. She said she knew she had to win the battle - but it cost her a great deal. She also said it was the first and the last time we made contact in this fashion. I had learned who was boss and that I had to mind, and I never forgot it.

Some people may not be able to make sense of this story, but I credit it with teaching me a fundamental lesson, namely, that the dependent one must obey! The Ten Commandments had it straight when it said "Thou shalt honor thy father and thy mother THAT THY DAYS MAY BE LONG IN THE LAND." Not having learned to mind external authority has certain predictable consequences: it places too much responsibility on the child even for his own physical safety. It is not unlike the law of gravity bringing about enough security so that one can feel safely tied down to earth. It lessens or eliminates the need for all that arguing, defiance, and the rejection that will follow defiance. It saves time and makes life a pretty good place. Whoever has not learned to mind is a poor leader of people - even a poor boss. Dr. Benjamin Spock, the apostle of permissiveness, did a good job of paving the way for the me-generation and our current youth problems. Giving in to a child - of any age - is no great service to him. Parents have failed in this essential role and are the root of many of our current problems, including being poor role models. The current experimentation with boot camps for young adults having difficulty growing up and taking their place in the world, may turn out to be valuable tool, or a useful arrow along the road. Time will tell.

The biggest penalty is, of course, society's inability to tolerate them and their expressions of independence indefinitely, when they have lost their place in society. They have to be eliminated in one way or another: kicked out of the land, as the Mosaic Commandment says. It is necessary to obey constituted authority - parental figures - or one will not be eligible to remain part of the scene. It's basic; it's factual; it's realistic, and we better learn this. It is no easy job to be a good parent: one who has the guts as well as the strength to say yes or no - and mean it!

Obviously, I'm glad my mother had the necessary wit and strength to do her job. She made my life into a sort of breeze. If she made me into a weakling, I am not aware of it. Everything in its own time - and obedience becomes the dependent one. I didn't have the wit that my mother had, and my daughter Jan therefore has many more problems than necessary. Some of me must have rubbed off on her, and that is all to the good, especially because, unlike many mothers and sexual topics, Jan and I can and do talk about it.

I thought life was moving along pretty comfortably after my two sisters had married in 1910 and moved to their own homesteads out in the hill country west of us. I had moved from the log school to a one room frame building school only ¼ mile from our house. Then Dad decided he would turn over management of the farm to his new son-in-law, Thorvald Jensen, Lil's husband. They would occupy the ground floor and Dad, Mother, Christine and I - all the family that was left at home - would live on the second floor. I probably did not understand the arrangement too well, for I was forever getting into Lil's hair. That was 1911. I was seven. Lil had a baby a few months old, and I was always coming in at the wrong time, making too much noise and awakening her sick baby whose digestive tract needed constant attention. Since I was always doing the best I could I felt unhappy and persecuted by Lil, so I was relieved when Dad decided we'd move to town and I'd go to school there. No more fighting with Lil.

I can remember many details of our family life in the new house prior to our moving to the second floor to live. I remember Dalma having the treadle sewing machine going early and late, sewing clothes for all of us. I remember the light over the dining room table, that pulled up and down, and I remember how fond I was of my sister Jo's boy friend named Jim. I was glad when she eventually married him. There were always lots of hired men, and most of them did not mingle with us as family - but a few special ones did. The hired men had their own quarters in the bunk house, which was the second floor of the back addition to the house proper. We ate together, but we did not mix freely, and I was never permitted to go into the barnyard except briefly to gather eggs, and we did not participate in their lives.

I have always presented myself as a member of a big family: I had 7 siblings; this is factually true, but it is not the entire story. They had become grown and were getting married before I really knew them or had much to do with them. Sister Mame was married before I was born, two more were married before I was 6; another sister married before I was 9, so I scarcely knew them, and the two boys had their own lives, and mostly were gone from home. Niels had a room of his own, but Carl preferred sleeping and spending his free time with the hired men in the bunk house. So only my sister Christine and I might be said to have lived together during my childhood. She never was close to Mother, as I was, so even with her, there was a gulf between us. I always had one reason or another to be critical of her - mostly because she did not love Mother the way I did. She would often do things she knew Mother would not approve of. I was more like an only child.

In many ways Christine was the pet of the whole family, and I always thought of her as more sister Mame's child than Mother's child. This would not have been strange, because each child in turn had been shoved out of the role of the baby of the family, to make room for a new baby. Christine was baby of the family much longer than any of the others, because Mother had had a miscarriage and a still birth before her pregnancy with me. Christine had become the favorite of everybody. She was everybody's baby. Some of them named their babies after Christine. Nobody ever named anybody after me!

I don't think I resented Christine or my siblings' devotion to her. Nobody so much as ever mentioned it - sibling rivalry. It never occurred to me to feel gypped, because I was safely and securely - as well as permanently - my mother's darling baby. That was more than enough to keep me happy. We were surely meant for each other. Before I came, Mother had never had time to baby anybody or to enjoy her babies. She was a natural born worker, and work always came first. She did tend to derogate Dad, because he was no worker, and that was BAD! So I didn't love or appreciate Dad as my siblings did. Working was the right thing to do.

I have no doubt but what I elevated working to the degree that it was an important virtue. I am convinced that it was a factor in my beautiful self image. It was basically responsible for the part of my family that lived in Oregon - sister Jo's family - getting bad vibes from me and my everlasting working at my studies. They saw me as a grind, and had no yen to go to college if that was what it took! And toward the tail end of my work life, one of my staff called me a workaholic! I not only had incorporated the work ethic; I had built it into a virtue - and I'm sure I considered myself pleasing in the sight of God because of it!

I can understand my life even better when I remember what my mother taught me: Never count your own work. If you succeed in what you are trying to do, that is pay enough. I know there is a saying which agrees with my mother's contention: "The reward of a thing well done is to have done it". I suspect this has had a lot to do with the fact that I have experienced so little resentment in life. I learned early in my professional career that a sense of entitlement is the basis of much trouble for people, for frustrated entitlement gives rise to many of the common symptoms that plague humanity and lead to need for psychiatrists. Had I not had a mother who gave so generously of herself, I might well have traveled through life feeling sorry for myself. But I am fortunate in that I felt so little self pity and this made life a good place. Nor did I have much sense of competition, and little if any feelings of guilt. I recognized early that I was incapable as compared with all my sisters, who could and did run circles around me. I always attributed that to the fact that I was so much younger than they were, and eventually I would grow into greater adequacy. So I didn't weep for my shortcomings. The only person I was knowingly in competition with was Esther Combes, my classmate in high school. She finished valedictorian and I was No. two - salutatorian. It made no sense to me: she was only half as big as I was.

I always felt I was not important to very many people, but the ones I was important to were the most important people possible and all that I needed. The only two people I was sure really like and accepted or believed in me, were Mother and my brother Niels, who was 19 years my senior. We were a sort of threesome: Mother, Niels and I. Mother preferred her son to her husband because he was "just terribly bright." Dad was no dullard, but he had the handicap of having changed languages in mid stream, and he had a hard time holding his own in the verbal battles between himself and his oldest son. Niels had the unfortunate habit of making Dad's inability to joust with him truly visible, so that Dad became the beloved underdog and Niels became the intolerable braggart. Dad was never my role model as one thinks of fathers for their children. For me, it was Niels who was my male role model. Dad seemed to close doors for me in the learning process, while Niels opened doors everywhere he went. Niels taught me to be interested in the simplest things around me, as well as the things I could not understand or even perceive. To be with him and to be taught something new - which he was always doing - was pure delight. I never saw Niels's behavior as vanity or intolerable.

Niels set the pattern of the types of people who interested me. He opened the world to me, and I have loved him for it - even to his death. I can recall a session with my first training analyst, Dr. Spurgeon English in Philadelphia. I was supposed to say whatever I thought, so on this particular occasion I told him, "I could never be interested in you because you don't scintillate!" So here is me, with a mother who bids me to work till you drop, and Niels, who gave me a love of the stars in one's eyes. But Niels was also a worker. He always worked with everything he touched, and felt sure he made it better. He was always sure that what he did or made, was better than what one might buy. He had a virtual passion for knowing how anything he was in contact with worked, and his goal was always to make anything he became involved with, work better.

Dad, on the other hand was never interested in how anything worked, but he was always glad when he could see that something growing looked better than when he came to it. He was a gardener by training, and a yard must look better when he left it than when he came to it. I have his favorite flowers growing in my yard: Lobelia, tiger lilly, and geranium. It is strange how people live on in one and determine how we live our lives. It would never have occurred to me to disobey Mother, or to make her give an order twice. I minded upon her first command, and I was never in competition with her authority. That made life good as well as easy. I knew Mother was proud of all her children, but she loved Niels and me the most, but she was also very proud of his intellectual gifts. I remained her beloved baby. She wasn't proud of me as she was of Niels, but she was glad I was a forward child and not a backward one.

Mother's placement of high value on intellectual capacity was very apparent on an occasion when Jan was perhaps three years old and we visited her in Sidney. Jan had to take a great deal of medication because of her digestive impairment, and I can still see Mother clasping her hands in disbelief in front of her and saying, "Just imagine! She not only knows the names of all those medicines, but she knows the Latin name for them!"

I walked early and I talked early. I have heard many times about my first sentence construction: It was Spring and I would have been two in June. I came into the house carrying a posy, went over to Mother, turned my back to her and said, "Put fower in hine." That was where flowers belonged - in buttonholes - which were behind. I was making proper connections.

As I recall, nobody in the family seemed to make a big deal of their feelings, they did not seem to have mood swings, and I have the impression of great stability in my home. If making productions was there I was not aware of it. It was not a worried home. I always accepted being part of the family, present or absent - and each of us counted or was important. Perhaps I was most conscious of the annoyance Niels caused by his knowing so much. But I loved him and was glad he liked me enough to bother with me and share with me. He'd teach me how to read musical notes, draw me a picture, take me with him to Epworth League meetings at the Methodist Church, or rub his whiskered face against mine.

Niels was my first teacher at school because he was Professor Hicks assistant. I liked him as my school teacher, but I did not like the fact that I had to forego calling him Niels, and call him Mr. Anderson. It was in those early weeks at school that I lost my identity as "pioneer" and became merely "a Dane". I don't recall that he did anything to comfort me, or even whether I asked for his help. It was to Mother I went with my tears, and she not only comforted me but she made me believe that being a Dane was just fine, so that I never lost the Dane in my subsequent identity.

I also incorporated into my identity ease of accepting other people and their families. I was permitted to visit girl friends by myself and to stay over night at their homes, as well as having them stay over night at my home. Probably five or six girls were included in this list. I had boy friends too, but staying over night never happened. I remember saving a seat beside me in Sunday School for one boy; later my boyfriend and we rode home from school together, he on his bike and I on my bay mare, Kinky. Finally my current boyfriend took me for a buggy ride in his buggy with a fringe on its top. The first time I remember being on a risky track was during the war -

WW I - when Christine and I, heeding the often repeated message that we must write to the boys in uniform so they didn't get lonely, wrote to several without parental knowledge or consent, and had them address their letters to us to a box number which was not the box number of the family. It was quite exciting, but I was glad when the war was over and the duplicity was gone. It was easier when one did not have secrets from Mother.

This war that was waged to end all wars involved everyone and of all ages. It was our daily fare. It ended Nov. 11, 1918, and for the next months there were endless changes - with homecomings, marriages, unitings and readjustments. Some of the weddings had been postponed for two or three years. Christine married Harry Brockway from Prairie Elk, and my favorite cousin, Bertha Olsen, married Hans Mattson, a Canadian soldier, who took her immediately away to Canada. I was bridesmaid at both those weddings, and I recall reminding myself to be cautious, because there was a saying: "Three times a bridesmaid; never a bride"; and I didn't want that to happen to me. Another big change for me was the move of Rev. Niels Damskov, the pastor of our Pella Danish Evangelical Lutheran Church, and his family to Winnipeg for an important new job. His daughter Ella and I had been bosom pals since they arrived in Sidney about 1909, and I didn't know how I'd stand losing her. After a few months, Mother and I traveled to Winnipeg to visit them, and then I transferred my affections to Ella's cousin Ruth Damskov still in Sidney. All of it was part of the growing process in the area of friendship.

Our area had no high schools until about the time the war started. We were expected to finish the eighth grade, and then school was over. Mother, who was ever interested in a good education, had sent Niels to the Agricultural College in Bozeman, and sent Carl to a high school in Kenmare, North Dakota, where the Danish Lutheran Church sponsored and ran it. She also sent Christine to the first opening of a high school class in Sidney, but each of Mother's attempts failed. Niels ran out of money and went off on a threshing rig; Carl hated both the Danish pressure and the religious emphasis; and Christine felt the other students down-graded her attire, which was too countrified. By 1917 when I had graduated from eighth grade, high school was a going concern in Sidney, and there were enough of the local families who entered their children in high school classes, so that one could safely enter high school without being labeled as stuck up. I remember very well the first Sidney high school student who was killed in World War I. His name was George Ahlquist. I can still visualize him - with his lovely dark red hair.

I was still in grade school when I decided to go to college and to medical school and to become a doctor. Ella Damskov and I had attended the first nurses' graduation Baccalaureate service at the Congregational Church. The service was so beautiful and such an awe inspiring experience that Ella and I sat down on the vacant lot on our way home and talked about it. When I got home I asked Mother who she thought did the most good in the world - a minister or a Christian doctor. She pondered a moment and said she thought a Christian doctor did the most good because he ministered both to the body and to the soul. She interpreted my question as my wanting to do the most good in the world, i.e., be a Christian doctor - rather than merely for a statement of her opinion, and that was the beginning of my life from that point on.

I'm sure she would have denied a misunderstanding on her part, as well as that she might be pushing me. I cannot say she was wrong, but from that moment onward, she never let me forget where I was headed.

There was nothing in my past that would have induced me to want to be a doctor. We had a doctor, Dr. John Beagle, who we rarely if ever went to, because we were always in good health. Dad often said, partially facetiously, "One can soon enough die without going to a doctor". Everything about doctors and medicine was strange and unfamiliar territory to me and my family, but it did embody the things that were most important to Mother, namely, doing the most good, and a good education. So now you know why I became a doctor. Don't think for a moment it was my strong pioneering spirit.

I spent twenty years of my life getting my M.D. degree. The biggest part of that time I functioned as a Christian. Since then I have worked steadily and I hope I have helped a few people in one way or another, but the greatest good, beyond doubt, was done for me - in broadening my knowledge and my perspective, as well as my sense of belonging. It is a good thing it is called "practicing medicine", because everybody in it is different, and it takes a lot of practicing before one can rightly claim to be a good doctor - much less a Christian doctor. I can say with positive assurance that my identity is that I am a doctor - just like I say I am a female, or an American, or a mother. Medicine has moved past my original training in so many ways, but that does not deter me in the least: I am an M.D. and I am grateful that I am. It has more than filled my life, and it has made so much of it more interesting than it could otherwise have been. It was always bigger than I was or even than I had envisioned - and this does not derive either from a sense of great good accomplished, or great financial or status benefits. It has promoted growth in me. In fact, at my ancient age, it still does.

When it came to choosing where I would get my education and training for my M.D. degree I continued to be about as competent and discerning as I had been in choosing to be a doctor, so it was more luck than wit that guided me. Some may think I chose my specialty of psychiatry because of my goal of ministering both to the body and the soul. If you are thinking that, you must be aware that the dictionary equates soul and psyche. I didn't know this at the time I made my choice, and I assure you I chose psychiatry because it seemed to be about the only job available in that year of 1931. I didn't choose wisely, but very well, I would say.

It not only kept the wolf from the door, but it was fascinating from the start, and brought me into psychiatry at a very important time. Sigmund Freud was king and cock of the walk. I avidly pursued understanding of his broad theory of the nature and dynamics of human beings and their behavior, but when I could no longer follow him, it necessitated that I find a new leader or that I stand on my own feet and build my own theoretical formulations. It brought me back to pioneering again. It has been an interesting half century developing my own concepts. When I had given up accomplishing the task I had set out to do, finding a new leader, I found it in my hand.

Without even wanting to, I found there was a link in psychiatry between my past and my new formulations, and nothing was wasted or lost. Anyone who knows me at all knows how important it is to me not to waste. Practicing my specialty was also within the scope of my physical abilities and limitations; it was a sedentary occupation, and that enabled me to survive tuberculosis and to keep on working. In addition, it enabled me to turn the problems within my family into opportunities for pioneering in the field of early brain damage - isolating, enumerating and teaching the symptomatology characteristic of the entire spectrum of developmental disabilities, many of which are still not recognized as organic in origin. It held my interest throughout over half a century.

One of the nice things about living is that I am forever getting surprises. Take yesterday for example. I was paging through a couple of huge scrap books Bev Peterson, my great niece, had brought me a week ago. The scrap books had been compiled by Myrtle Anderson Johns, my oldest niece, during her lifetime, of all the notable events that had impinged on her and her family during a long lifetime. Their variety and scope were almost staggering. So was the skill she had displayed in securing and arranging them in the scrapbooks. There was one which had the N.Y. Times banner on it that caught my attention. It was dated Jan. 3, 1950. The clipping seemed to be front page, was two columns wide and the full length of the paper. It was from the Science Revue section, and concerned a report on an experimental project that had been tried in a V.A. hospital.

The project represented an attempt to verify or reject my behavioral concepts which tied stress to the dynamics of behavior, and the conclusion was that my concepts were valid. No one had ever alerted me to the project or to the existence of the N.Y. Times lengthy report. This was my first knowledge of it, forty-five years later! Of course I was surprised and of course I enjoyed it. I checked the dates and knew that I was in private psychiatric practice in Salt Lake City when the report came out. I also recalled that in 1950 I had recently been expunged from the faculty rolls of the University of Utah School of Medicine by Dr. Hardin Branch, head of the Department of Psychiatry, because I had strayed from the exclusive teaching of the Freudian concepts of behavior to the medical students, and had interjected some of my own ideas. The world continues to be an interesting place in which to live!

Yes, I was a conscientious student. I worked long and hard. I got good grades as well as scholarships to the University of Montana from high school - which I did not accept because Montana had no pre-Med department; and the scholarship to the University of Oregon Medical School which I did accept happily. All the while I was apparently so successful, I believed I would qualify as a hard-working student, but not as a good student. I don't yet know just what was wrong with the way I did things, but I suspect nobody had told me how to do it better and in shorter time. It must have had something to do with my lack in organizing or appraising ability. I am sure it contributed to my being perceived by my relatives in Eugene as a grind. I have even wondered if there might be a genetic flaw determining my lack in assessing, because when I look at my school placements, and even my life goals in which my parents or my family always were determining factors, their conclusions - however well or poorly they turned out - never were based on factors that would generally be considered valid or pertinent.

It happened again and again: the conclusions I came to and the pathways I took seemed illogical or bizarre. Even my goals seemed ill conceived, but I got where I was headed for and life turned out better than I had envisioned, and I wasn't carrying some big load around with me. Actually, what seems ill-fitting might be just the thing we need at that stage of the game; it enables us to get by some unexpected or unrecognized hurdle; we grow as a result and are the stronger, or have greater flexibility than we otherwise might have had, and life's procession of events resulted in "progress." It really is a dangerous thing to think one knows what is right and what is wrong. Looking at it through the lens of the original story of Man, it would be hard to be creative if we had always done the "right" thing. There may be a right way and a wrong way, but it not only is hard to be sure about it, but more often than not it is in the eye of the beholder. Our inadequacies create the proper climate for creativity.

My first year at the University of Oregon in Eugene was an exceedingly rough year. I missed Sidney! I missed knowing everybody and being known by everybody. I'd come home after a day of classes and cry to Mother, saying, "They don't care whether I live or die." Carl, my cowboy brother, visited us and tried to reassure me by saying, "Don't you know who you are? You're the daughter of Peter Anderson!" But his words fell on deaf ears, because Dad wasn't all that important to me. I knew Dad was important to Carl - but not to me. Why was that? Because Dad didn't love me, and only those who loved me were important to me. I later decided that they were the ones who had been able to teach me anything. Years after that, when I was talking to my older sisters and said that Dad didn't love me, they said I was terribly mistaken in that. Couldn't I tell he loved me by his keeping my grade-record all through school? I said that didn't mean he loved me; he was just proud of me, and that wasn't the same thing as loving me. It took me a whole lifetime to get it all together.

Despite my desperate loneliness for Sidney during my first year in Eugene, Dad stopped me from going to the campus library evenings to study, and then walking home afterward with some male student. Dad took away from me the only obvious source of "counting" which is the on-ramp to belonging. It was the not-belonging that made life so miserable and brought me closer to a depression than I have ever been. Mother saved the day by taking me to some revival meetings held at the Eugene Armory, where Dr. Charles Price from Amie Semple McPherson's base in California, brought me on-going joy in discovering God loved me. I learned I had right at my fingertips a source of belonging - not at the University, but at the little church at the end of the street car line on the edge of Eugene. We were members, and there developed an immediate fellowship in association with a group of young church members who also had attended those revival meetings. It provided everything I needed: belonging, being needed, self worth, my parents feeling safe in this new turn of events, and room for growth. I became Sunday School superintendent - and then for eight years - in Eugene and then in Portland, religious activity became the center of my life.

The good things the churches have to offer gets lost in attention to ritual and lack of understanding of behavior and its dynamics. It prepared me to take my place in the world - even to stand and survive being alone in a crowd, and the ability to talk on my feet and to teach. Perceiving, and then sharing, became my rules for living. In one specific situation or context after another, my insight grew, and lecturing, teaching and writing filled my life. If I could see it, so could someone else! It led to my return to being a pioneer: using the ongoing events and points of learning to open up new doors for someone else. It has made life not only a learning experience for me, but also a togethering with people. It takes a thief to catch a thief, they say, and it seems to be true. "I've been there ahead of you" awareness makes for empathy and caring - and thus for teaching and learning for others. Had Dad not spoiled things for me, I probably would not have ever made it to graduating from college and later from medical school. He was never one to step in and usurp Mother's role as disciplinarian!

I was brought up to believe that there was a right way to look at or to believe and a wrong way. My parents did their best to teach me the right way to believe about everything. A failure to believe the right way was dangerous - like asking for trouble. I didn't really see anything about my parents' beliefs that I found fault with. I accepted without question a belief in God, a belief in the Judeo Christian religion as right - particularly the Protestant version of it, and that Martin Luther, the Catholic monk who had unintentionally brought about the great schism creating the Protestant religion, was especially close to the right way to believe. So I was an active church member. Religious convictions, as well as practices, were important to me. One of the important practices was "to do good". This included "doing the most good", which almost took me to Nigeria.

It wasn't surprising that on the campus at Eugene I was regarded as one of "the Christers," and not one of "the rounders." Probably the degree of narcissism would be comparable in both groups, but when one is intent on "doing good" - or in my case "doing the most good", one does not usually assess it as narcissism. Nor should it be surprising that I learned of a national organization called the Student Volunteer Movement, and became one of its members. The slogan of this organization was to the effect that one's call to service was at the point where the world's greatest need intersected with one's capabilities. Clearly, I had to find my place in the cosmos. It was not appropriate that I should go about doing good in a haphazard way, but I must find where I belonged.

When I though of the world's greatest needs, I settled on Nigeria, British West Africa. Neither was this surprising, because it was the only foreign mission field I had ever had personal contact with. One of the missionaries there was Alfred Thompson, and not infrequently he came to Sidney to spend his occasional Sabbatical leave with his sister, Mary (Mrs. Jake) Johnson, out in the Dane Flats area. He was a member of a missionary group sponsored by the Danish Lutheran Church in Denmark. I felt reasonably certain this might qualify as the place where the need was greatest. So I began a correspondence with Alfred Thompson in Nigeria, to ascertain if I was correct.

Before I graduated in 1929 with my M.D. degree, I had received ample assurance that my hunch had been correct, and that they would be happy to have an M.D. as part of their staff. But first I must qualify not only with mission personnel, but I must qualify with British medical authorities by enrolling for a two year training period in the London School of Tropical Medicine. I was off and running, and Alfred Thompson and I maintained a correspondence, because I felt committed and intended to comply.

I was in the middle of my internship in Portland when Rev. Thompson came to Portland to get acquainted with me, and to be of whatever assistance he might be in my making my preparations to go to Africa. By that time we were into 1930. Many things had been happening in my life, chief of which was that I had become enamored with a young doctor, and we hoped eventually to be married, and he certainly did not want me to go to Lagos, Nigeria! I sparred as best I could with Alfred Thompson. I didn't want to renege on a promise, and a big mud hospital had already been built for me and my coming. I wasn't prepared to tell him the whole story of my hopes and plans, so I asked him questions such as, What was the leading cause of death in Nigeria?, and when he said it was starvation, I responded that that fact made my coming there a futile gesture. What was needed was not a qualified doctor, but involvement of the nation in improving water supply, or changing the crops or the machinery in raising crops. They were attacking the problem the wrong way! Our session was an edgy one, and it was the beginning of the end of our relationship. But I did not formally resign for another two years, when my plans for marriage had been dashed, and I had been in a tuberculosis sanitarium for many months.

Tuberculosis let me save face, because it made my bowing out due to my illness and not to my defaulting. People - me included - do remarkable things not to be or to appear guilty. I was involved with the Nigeria plans for perhaps six years. By that time I was completely immersed in Psychiatry and carving my niche in the U.S.A. But it took quite a piece out of my life, and I still had no inkling of the psychologic distortion of my own worth. I epitomized a person who took seriously her ability to determine where the world's greatest need lay, and what were the special competences I had to offer to meet those needs. I learned a few years later that I was definitely not meant for the kind of tropical climate Nigeria offered, and I'd probably have come home in a box shortly after arrival had I gone there.

Len, Jan and I in Washington DC, 1948

There was no point at which I said to myself that I was finished with Religion, or that I didn't believe this or that. But my life had changed and a few of my values and convictions had changed. I saw some values and beliefs as less important than I once had thought. I was no longer hell-bent on spreading the gospel or converting anybody to accept my values or beliefs. I took things as less part of my personal responsibility to achieve, and was better able to let other people have their beliefs.

Factually, by that time I was so involved in so many things that I didn't have the time or the strength of will to go far beyond my own boundaries. I had enough of my own troubles and problems to preclude high involvement in other things. I did not become a disbeliever; I was just too busy to have any "religious drive".

In my first job placement in Psychiatry in Binghamton, N.Y. in 1931, I became a follower of Sigmund Freud - through the persuasive force of his followers, and it took nearly ten years to untangle myself from Freud's theories. I was always looking for a new leader, but none materialized. It was no joy to be alienated from my colleagues who still believed in him.

One of the things I was scarcely aware of was the passage of time. It just flew! And suddenly I found myself almost at the end of my thirties - as well as being a female equipped with an in-built time-clock that said I better hurry if I did not want to miss the boat entirely: I'd miss the opportunity to become a mother unless I got busy and got married! - and quick! So in 1941, when I was past thirty-eight, I married a former patient whom I like very much. I felt I knew him pretty well - I had treated him for about a year for an anxiety neurosis, with remission of all his symptoms and I felt strong enough to be optimistic as to our future. A strong factor in my safe feeling related to the fact that he dearly loved his work. He was a musician - a long time theater organist who had become a displaced person as a result of the coming of sound movies.

But he was beginning a new line of work in music with the electronic Hammond organ, and was getting pleasure from that.

Marriage taught me far more than I expected to learn - the most important of which was that whereas I thought I knew Len, my husband, up one side and down the other, I really didn't know him at all. And this discovery reinforced my growing conviction that what I had been taught as a student of Freud - from its theoretical base, to the way psychotherapy was carried out - just would not hold water. A search for a better leader than Sigmund Freud was necessary if I was to be a competent psychotherapist! Then shortly after we had been married a year, we had a wonderful baby girl - Janet Carol Friendly, who suffered a terrible accident at ten months, from sunstroke complicated by cerebral thrombososis. This taught me more about psychiatry and behavior and the basis of behavior than I probably might have learned in years of formal teaching. I had truly wanted to know what makes people tick, and the stage was set with all the ingredients for teaching me the essentials I had to incorporate. It is over fifty years since I embarked on learning, and there still is scarcely a day in which I don't learn something new and important about behavior, whether psychodynamically or neurologically determined.

Life has called for many adjustments to realities. Many have been painful, but all have involved learning and growing, hopefully, also, in grace, as well as in wisdom. After getting into the field of medicine in 1929 I lived in an entirely new world that did not include attention to religion. I came to think it wasn't important or pertinent. Then some surprising events were thrust on me and I had to be off again - running - learning, and a new religious awareness overtook me and remains strong. I shall share it with you in due time.

Almost everyone experiences events that seem world-shaking. My life has been no exception. Some of the events were short in duration and others took years to complete. Contracting tuberculosis was one of the short ones. It took only a couple of years out of my life, and then I was able to continue on, almost forgetting about it. Writing books was another short project. Once I had them in print they did not possess me on and on. I was finished with them. A succession of jobs came and went. I never set a time limit on how long I would stay in any job, but I tended to stay in any job several years - even up to eight or nine years, and then something would move me - often death - and when it was over, it was over.

A few events have stretched indefinitely and filled my life for decades. Such was my search for understanding the nature of psyche, and finding a theory of psychodynamics which would replace Freud's fallen teachings. My marriage, and my daughter's succession of problems hampering her overall development were also long commitments.

Who were the heros of the people who taught me? The actual people might fade, but their heros lived on. Martin Luther, the German Catholic priest who was the one most responsible for the great schism creating the Protestant revolution was ever an important man who influenced my thinking. He had tried to call attention to what he considered matters needing reforming, namely the belief in the infallibility of the Pope, the selling of indulgences, the elevation of the mother of Jesus to the status of deity and access of the laity to the Bible. Reformation did not take place and schism prevailed. Through parental teachings I also became a Protestant. I'll let you decide if I'm still one!

During my childhood Theodore Roosevelt became President of the United States, and he was the hero and idol of my father - and perhaps even of my mother. We had Teddy Roosevelt's family picture in brilliant color on our dining room walls all through my childhood, and I can recall seeing Dad weep when he died. Although my beloved brother Niels gave me a copy of Karl Marx's Communist Manifesto when I was a child, I grew up feeling more comfortable with Dad's hero than with Niels'. But I have retained an active interest in politics.

My next figure of importance by reason of what I was taught was Sigmund Freud, and whereas I have in a variety of ways discarded him, I am ready to accept the fact that his teachings were not all invalid, and that as a by-product of what he did, there have been positive - as well as negative - results. He brought psychiatry out of hidden places and into the open - into the highways and byways, and into everyday life. Associated with his relatively brief reign there occurred many changes that I consider regrettable. But I may not permit myself the luxury of blaming Freud for all the things in the world that seem to have gone wrong. With his interpretations that emphasized the Pleasure Principle and the strength of the Id - all of it leading to a change in our value system - he had many helpers, and I feel sure he did whatever he did with the best of intentions. It all might have happened without his help. Furthermore, I hardly have the qualifications needed to pass judgement. Everyone thinks his judgements are worthy - or we would not have them!

My opinions are not the last word, but one will never know the correct answer. But we are what we are, and I also have the privilege of expressing my opinion, which is that Freud's influence on our world has been more destructive than constructive. What he helped to do was to change our value system. He really did not change mine appreciably or for long, but his influence reached into the smallest nook and cranny of our world. He affected the value system of our world. So did Karl Marx. Jesus still does.

No matter how little or how much Freud changed my value system, in my earliest experiences in psychiatry I got a conviction that to understand the nature of psyche, and the consequent nature of dynamics of human behavior was essential. I still believe it. My teachers were correct. It was not a trivial gift. But Freud, whom they elevated, let me down, and I spent years looking for another leader. I found none. Instead, I had to lead myself - and the answers I got constitute my contribution to psychiatry and to anyone who understands what I have to say. We are already on the way! So please be patient and hear me out til I have finished. I believe that what I learned is worth waiting for. I also see it as a worthy pioneering effort.

The time came when I repudiated not only the role of Freud in American Psychiatry, but I rejected its next offering, which was psychotropic drugs given on the basis of symptomology. Gone was psychiatry's deep involvement with psychodynamics, and a replacement with what I regarded as unwarranted optimism with regard to the role of drugs for curing sick behavior. Drugs not only were very costly, but they started the revolving door operational pattern of psychiatry: The patient was admitted to the mental hospital, studied and tested, and he was put on drugs. His behavior became more tolerable to onlookers; he was released to the community, and because he had a good bit of resistance to acceptance of the drugs for one reason or another, he would stop taking the drug. This was followed by relapse and return to the hospital, and the revolving door scenario had begun.

The next move in psychiatry was toward freedom - freedom from involuntary commitment and hospitalization, freedom from institutions - which were described as warehouses, and every unfortunate aspect of hospitalization was blown up and derided, with the result that hospitals lost their former role of being asylums, and became places to avoid at all costs. Even the meaning of asylum was lost - namely a safe place - and asylum became synonymous with a sort of hell hole.

With the new freedom-attitude, outpatient status was in and specialized training and professionalism eased out, and counseling became number one. Psychiatrists had no noticeable role except as providers of answers to sticky problems or to take the rap for incompetent handling by novices.

Something not anticipated also happened when the institutions were closed: the nation lost its facilities for training people in the art and science of care for mentally sick patients. Nobody was left to train people - or places to get the training on how to care for mental patients. We had shot ourselves in the foot. And there was no way of calling for help because we had thrown the baby out with the bath water. So mental patients again cluttered welfare rolls, jails, prisons, the streets, and homes as it had been for centuries. There was no one to cover emergencies. The new people in charge had never had years of contact with hospitalized or chronic patients, and would not have known what to do in an emergency. It takes a long period of one to one contact with all manner of patients to provide a sense of ease in handling the problems. Psychiatry had certainly not done the world a service by aiding or abetting the down-grading of in-patient care. The training base was lost; the personnel that had that training were lost - all in the name of progress. One had only to experience the deprofessionalization generated by Maxwell Jones at the Oregon State Hospital when he became Clinical Director. It was a harbinger of sad things to come. Why did it happen to this excellent hospital? And to hundreds of other good hospitals throughout the land?

People who meant well - many of them young psychiatrists - were unhappy with the status quo, and they set about to do good and rid us of those horrible warehouses. It was not unlike the steam roller of the Freudian crusade. It just came two decades later. It is hard to find redeeming features in what happened. But as with everything else, what we see is through our own skewed lenses. Between Freud, who focused on non-hospitalized patients, the development of psychotropic drugs for all manner of symptoms, the near demise of interest in psychodynamics, and the downgrading of hospital care and rise of non-medically trained experts, psychiatry has been on a roller coaster. No one yet knows when or if the succession of changes will continue, or if stability will come through acceptance of the cyclic nature of everything.

I found my niche, which was psychotherapy with non-hospitalized mentally ill patients, plus awareness of an organic neurologic impairment from very early defect or injury, and the modification of treatment approach from insight to training. I never used drugs as my approach to change. There are few basically normal people who would not benefit from my orientation and approach. It embodies no magic, and is not excessively costly, as was psychoanalysis, and was not a matter of selling a patient a bill of goods. I believed in what I was doing.

The pressure for change did not abate, and it was while I was in Oregon that I saw the handwriting on the wall which said it was time to get moving from my Outpatient Clinic at Salem. But where would I go? The problem of drug abuse had intensified, and made treatment of these patients as pressing a problem as caring for aged mentally ill people. Life spans were getting longer, and multi-generational homes were almost non existent, so the hospitals care for more and more old people with mental problems. Nobody has yet invented a way of living long and remaining free of the degenerative evidences of aging. My problem was complicated by the fact that I had no license to practice medicine in Oregon. So I couldn't just quit my job at the State Hospital and go into private practice.

I had made many moves to many states, but I always had my license to practice in the state I went to - but not in Oregon. Why? Because Oregon had a law requiring anyone getting a license to practice Medicine to also have passed certain Basic Science examinations before his license was granted. I had taken my Basic Science exams in Oregon - under the auspices of the National Board of Medical Examiners many years previously, but Oregon did not honor this. I was not about to try to catch up and get ready to pass current exams. I figured it would take at least a year to catch up - and I was too old and too near retirement. I really did not need an Oregon license as long as I remained at the State Hospital and practiced under the aegis of Dr. Dean Brooks, the Superintendent, who took responsibility for my actions and competence. But move away from that situation and I would be on my own.

I thought and I thought, and finally came up with an idea that I saw as being not only within the law but would be a real pioneering innovation, and would keep me busy for as long as I should want to work; I felt well and able to work hard for a long time: I would not practice Psychiatry. I would not see patients. I would be a teacher - and I liked the role of teacher. I'd not be an institution that people would have to leave home and place of business to come to see. Instead, I'd be available all over the state - through setting up teaching meetings lasting several days in length - for seminars for all manner of groups - professional or lay, even parents who were interested in/about behavior and the meaning or problems, symptoms and signs. I would teach about the available resources for helping or dealing with the problems; and what one might expect. I figured I might be asked to meet with enough groups so that the communities would begin to have a broad and competent general outlook, and realistic expectations. Maybe I'd spend a few days in every part of the state at least once a year, and the chances of finding their own solutions would be enhanced. There would be better communication of one group with another, for there would be the nucleus of a common vocabulary and attitude.

The possibilities were staggering. And the cost would be minimal as compared with leaving home, or with not having this resource, and there would be enough to pay me too. My husband had died while we were in Oregon, so our home had been broken, and Jan would be able to participate and be a significant source of essential learning for any group - with her problems due to early brain damage. And her life would be broadened and enriched by participating in such an undertaking. We'd probably live mostly in a mobile home.

I asked the Oregon Board of Education if they were interested in my proposed project, and they were! They asked me to talk with the head of the Department of Psychiatry at the Medical School, to get his blessing. I wrote him, telling him of what was going on and asking for his OK. His answer was a flat NO, with no explanation and with no conference about it. And that was the end of my dream. Nobody other than the

Oregon Board of Higher Education had known anything about it. I had nobody to cry to; nobody to console me. But I was deeply hurt.

I have no doubt the plan and blueprint would have worked. I probably would have been pressured to some extent, but I think I was well enough to have survived, partly because I would have been happy on the job, and partly because Jan and I would have been together all the time, and both of us would have been kept busy growing.

I heard later that the man who turned me and my pioneering plan down was actually in process of requesting a huge grant - in the hundreds of thousands of dollars from the Federal Government - to carry out a state-wide program at the medical school, for non-medical people. It would have had some resemblance to my project, but I would have been a traveling one woman endeavor going to the ends of the state rather than having them come to me, and I would have made it pay for itself. I never heard if he got the grant, or what happened. I never went back to bid him the time of day. It could be that it did not materialize. Nobody has ever mentioned it to me.

I put away all the blueprints, and went about seeing if California might want me. I served five years in Southern California as chief psychiatrist at the women's prison, the California Institute for Women (C.I.W.) before I was retired at age 65 in 1969. It was my first experience and I am grateful I had the opportunity to be there. I submerged the entire event so successfully that I actually forgot about it until I discovered the folder on the story of my dream in my file while writing this book and reread it to refresh my memory.

After my retirement I wrote my fifth book, *SOCIETY PAYS, The High Cost of Minimal Brain Damage in America*, published by Walker Co., in 1971 after I returned to Sidney. The title should have been not Minimal Brain Damage, but Early Brain Damage. It was another pioneering effort in that it ran a red thread through the many aspects of disability due to early brain damage. Almost before it was out, it was out of print, so it would not make too much difference what its title was. The focus was on the categories of disability that are a continuing pain in the neck to taxpayers as well as society, and the fact that evidences of early brain damage abound in all of them. I still believe it is an area to explore thoroughly. There is little hope of cure, no matter how much one spends on doing that job. But there is hope for amelioration of the social problem through prevention if its occurrence. There are a great many ways in which the damage can be prevented, and it would make sense to make all-out efforts to do exactly that.

The move toward caring for developmentally disabled people in group homes rather than in large schools for the retarded has many worthwhile features. My Jan is still a member of that large family. There is much more creature comfort than in the large institutions. They are often located right in one's neighborhood - and that is a real plus. But they cannot alter the basic problems and despite their claim to be less costly to the taxpayers, I am unable to grasp how they come up with that answer, because their enrollment is very small and smallness usually costs more per capita. By and large there is an emphasis on working but little or no realistic expectation of producing self sufficient graduates. Their work is all to the good. It is accepted practice and legitimized by wages and I have heard of no union complaints. But they are, like the old mental hospitals, asylums - safe havens - and I am not nearly as fearful of dying and leaving Jan behind as I would be without them, because there is genuine acceptance of their limitations, and that is saying a lot.

The pressure for change led me to do some new pioneering in my effort to stem the tide of change. In 1973, I think it was, I turned myself into a lobbyist and spent two months in Helena, Montana, lobbying - not for closure of our mental hospital at Warm Springs, but for opening a second hospital in eastern Montana, maybe even in Sidney. That way we in the east part of Montana might have round the clock access to competent mental health care whenever we needed it. And it would be close enough to home so one would be able to get to it with only two or three hours driving time rather than eight to ten hours. There were essentially no train or plane services available.

I wish my efforts at lobbying had paid off, but Governor Tom Judge had read the lay of the land well, and my lobbying efforts came to naught. It would also have helped had I been more familiar with the entire legislative process or carried out an education effort in eastern Montana. But I was a novice just contributing my time for something I believed in. I did have many people from western Montana who told me this was the first time they had ever thought about eastern Montana. The common viewpoint in western Montana is that Montana stops at Billings, which is about 250 miles west of Sidney. A state, like a body, cannot remain healthy if it is not in constant communication with all its members and parts. Eastern Montana, the prairie half of the state, is also part of Montana, whether Helena - or even Billings - knows it or not. It contributes more tax dollars than does the west, but has fewer voters than does the west with its larger cities.

If I should try to assess where I am today, I would say that I have increasing confidence in the trustworthiness of my perceptions and the conclusions they lead me to in the field of behavior. I am delighted when someone claiming to be an expert in this field agrees with me, but I am also able to stand alone without such bolstering. I am glad I have been a pioneer several times, and I hope I remain one as long as I shall live. There is always room for one more pioneer.

That sounds almost too optimistic and rosy. Life is rarely like that. It's more like gray - lighter and darker, than black and white. Life isn't done up in neat little labeled packages, because everything runs off into something different and usually not anticipated. Even people are paradoxes. I recall my brother Niels often saying that people who have been given great gifts, would also have great blemishes. He ought to know!

Most of us try to make life as easy as possible. Often it is easier to continue working tirelessly, because that is simpler and easier than trying to chart and live out another way. Most of us have cliches by which we live, rather than dealing in extenso with one item at a time. Most cliches - and sacred cows - save us a lot of time and energy in trying to come up with something better. The cliche or aphorism : "There is a destiny that shapes our ends, rough-hew them as we may" has stood me well through the years. And you know something? It just might be true. Often we do not dream of the many factors that influence what we do and how things turn out. Judging from my own experience I would say that we have a remarkable mechanism working for us night and day that helps us retain and even use information - even when we are unaware that we have been entering data into the system: Our unbelievable brain! We can't pull things out on command, but remarkable conclusions surface time and again when nature decides to do it.

One of the most abhorrent behaviors and definitely not sanctioned by either of my parents, was pride or vanity. I still spend little time at the mirror. But there are other ways of displaying it - usually secret, and scarcely admitted. In line with this, I had a little plaque on my desk while I worked, and which I transferred to my table near my chair after I retired. It does not blare. It just sits there and speaks its piece: "It's hard to be humble when you're as great as I am". Now that I'm old and on the shelf, life gets really lonely. Then I try to remember that few people are concerned about those who are adequate. People want to be needed. If the image one portrayed is one of adequacy, it follows that being left pretty much alone will be the order of the day. So I can't even generate frustrated entitlement.

Where am I now? Well, in 1969 I retired because I had reached the magic age of retirement and returned to Sidney and have lived here twenty-eight years. It is not incumbent on anyone who has reached the ripe age of ninety to be any particular place. I have soon spent about eight years - 1986 to 1994 - recovering from an undiagnosed illness which stole almost eight years - 1979 to 1986 - from me and that I still have almost no recollections of what happened during that time, But I have used these last eight years to recover the memories of my life, review them and understand them in context with the whole of it. Writing this book has been the tangible result of this eight year effort. It has been far more productive and rewarding than the several hundred hours I spent on the couch of three eminent psychoanalysts who were getting me ready for becoming an analyst in Philadelphia. I have not seen any analyst since the early 1940's. I didn't become an analyst, and this was because I chose not to.

I am grateful I recovered from whatever illness it was I had. I think it was an organic neurologic impairment - perhaps an atypical stroke. The odds were against me that I should have recovered, but I am very grateful that I did, because had I not, I never would have had the fun of reliving my life - and this time around, being able to see what it was all about! I hope you will be glad you met me, and that it may stimulate you to try to understand yourself. If I remember correctly, the good book says "Know thyself." If you take that suggestion seriously you will never regret it.

BOOKS PUBLISHED BY DR. CAMILLA ANDERSON

Emotional Hygiene
Published by Lippincott Co.
Saints, Sinners and Psychiatry
Published by Lippincott Co.
Beyond Freud
Harper and Bros.
Jan, My Brain Damaged Daughter
Durham Press
Society Pays; The High Cost of Minimal Brain Damage in America
Walker Co.

BOOKS TO BE PUBLISHED IN 1996

Camilla, Montana Prairie Pioneer, Volume 2
From Pioneer to Professional M.D.
To be published by P Diamond Enterprises
Due out in August, 1996

Camilla, Montana Prairie Pioneer, Volume 3
Evolution of Identity
To be published by P Diamond Enterprises
Due out in October, 1996

Camilla, Montana Prairie Pioneer, Volume 4
The P Diamond Psychiatrist Retires and Strikes Pay Dirt
To be published by P Diamond Enterprises
Due out in December, 1996

The first leg of my life's journey was from Sidney, MT to Eugene, OR. I earned my M.D. degree from the University of Oregon Medical School, now the School of Health Sciences, in 1929.

ORDER FORM

Please send me _________ copy/copies of the following books by Camilla M. Anderson, M.D.

o *Saints, Sinners and Psychiatry* - $14.95 ______

o *Jan, My Brain Damaged Daughter* - $14.95 ______

o *Camilla, Montana Prairie Pioneer - Volume 1 A Century of Transitions* - $14.95 ______

Total: ______

Missouri residents: $ .96 per book _______
Shipping and Handling $3.00 per book _______

Total Due: _________

Mastercard and Visa accepted.
Card No:____________________ Exp. date:________________
Signature: ____

For volume discounts, please contact P Diamond Enterprises, (417) 782-6885 voice or fax.

P Diamond Publishing
1520 S Kentucky Ave
Joplin MO 64804-0744

Name: ____
Address: ____
City: ____________________State: _________ Zip: _____
Phone: ____